Natural Burial

ALSO AVAILABLE FROM CONTINUUM

Cultural Blending in Korean Death Rites, Chang-Won Park

Death, Ritual, and Belief, Douglas Davies

Theology of Death, Douglas Davies

Natural Burial

Traditional-secular spiritualities and
funeral innovation

DOUGLAS DAVIES
AND
HANNAH RUMBLE

continuum

Continuum International Publishing Group

The Tower Building
11 York Road
London
SE1 7NX

80 Maiden Lane
Suite 704
New York
NY 10038

www.continuumbooks.com

British Library Cataloguing-in-Publication Data
A catalogue record for this book is available from the British Library.

ISBN: HB: 978-1-4411-2296-4
PB: 978-1-4411-5278-7

Library of Congress Cataloging-in-Publication Data
Davies, Douglas James.
Natural burial : traditional-secular spiritualities and funeral innovation /
Douglas Davies and Hannah Rumble.
pages cm
Includes bibliographical references and index.
ISBN 978-1-4411-5278-7 (pbk. : alk. paper) – ISBN 978-1-4411-2296-4 (hardcover : alk.
paper) – ISBN 978-1-4411-6958-7 (ebook pdf : alk. paper) – ISBN 978-1-4411-6509-1
(ebook epub : alk. paper)
1. Natural burial–England–Cambridgeshire. 2. Funeral rites and ceremonies–
England–Cambridgeshire. 3. Barton Glebe (Burial site : Cambridgeshire, England)
4. Church of England. I. Rumble, Hannah. II. Title.

GT3244.C36D38 2012
393'.10947–dc23
2011049754

Typeset by Newgen Imaging Systems Pvt Ltd, Chennai, India
Printed and bound in India

Contents

Preface

This book owes an original debt of gratitude to the Arts and Humanities Research Council and the Economic and Social Science Research Council through their Religion and Society Project which funded a collaborative doctoral award to the University of Durham and The Arbory Trust to engage in research on woodland burial, with a special focus on The Barton Glebe site of the Trust near Cambridge. Douglas Davies, Professor in the Study of Religion and Director of Durham University's Centre for Death and Life Studies, and Dr Matthew Lavis, Diocesan Secretary of Ely Diocese and a representative of the Trust, and also an academic geographer in his own right, were joint supervisors of the underlying research project to which Hannah Rumble was appointed as a doctoral researcher with previous training in anthropology at Durham University.

We are grateful to Dr Lavis, to Arbory Trustees and to Barton Glebe site staff for all their help in our research. Much gratitude is extended to all those users of Barton Glebe who gave their time for interviews. These included funeral directors, clergy and civil celebrants, and most especially bereaved relatives and those who have indicated their desire to be buried in this place. We also gladly acknowledge the support of colleagues working on the Sheffield Project on Natural Burial, who have generously allowed us to use their mapping of natural burial site location and ownership. Other help has come from Mr Ken West, the pioneer of natural burial in Britain, and from Professor Charles Watkins of Nottingham University's School of geography, a notable British expert on trees. Additional research has drawn upon some further sites and upon previous and subsequent conceptual analyses of funerary rites to produce this present volume. Accordingly, we thank owners and managers of a variety of those woodland burial sites who have hosted visits and furnished a variety of information during the preparation of this book.

Thanks are also due both to the Centre for Death and Life Studies and to the Wolfson Institute of Durham University for additional funding that permitted the commissioning of Sarah Thomas, an ethnographic film maker, who made the film *Natural Burial and the Church of England.* This focused on the Barton Glebe site users, and information from it has been incorporated into various parts of this study as well as having been shown at a variety of venues within and beyond the United Kingdom.

Finally, we thank our publishers, and especially Lalle Pursglove, for working with us on this project.

Douglas Davies and Hannah Rumble

1

Funeral forms, lifestyles and death-styles

Introduction

This book is about ecological, green, natural or woodland burial, various names given to a general style of burial that began in Britain in the early 1990s and had grown to over 200 sites across the country by 2011. Each of these names carries its distinctive emphasis as the later chapters will show. Briefly, however, we might suggest that 'ecological' carries a science-like validation, 'green' suggests an element of political activism, 'natural' desires independence from the 'unnatural' interference of commercial ventures but an alliance with the organic world while 'woodland' carries its more specific cultural affinity with British landscape tradition. This very diversity of names does, however, indicate the variety of ideas surrounding death and the affinity that may attract some people more than others. This will become apparent in Chapters 2–4 which provide the empirical basis for this study through the single burial site of Barton Glebe near the village of Comberton, not far from the university city of Cambridge. These chapters report the thoughts of those who have or intend to use the site in due course, using materials obtained from interviews and other fieldwork activity in order to develop theoretical topics from interpretations of what various users of this site have said and done.

Although the naming of this practice differs among those who have used or intend to use such sites, as well as owners or managers of these facilities and advocates of this approach, we will usually speak of 'natural' burial. Though this is largely for reasons of utility and brevity, we are fully aware that the 'natural' will need some considerable explanation and interpretation as our chapters unfold. In Chapter 1 we introduce some of these key themes and will, subsequently, develop them in exploratory ways. Not only will this provide some cultural and historical context for natural burial practices but it will also suggest some theoretical ideas to help explain the emergence of natural burial in Great Britain as the twentieth century passed into the twenty-first.

Key concepts

Individual identity in relation to kin, to place and to changing cultural values underlies many of the issues of this study and can be expanded in a variety of directions. When speaking of individual identity, for example, we find it hard in this study to think in terms of some discrete autonomy of isolated persons, and much more realistic to acknowledge individuals as part of a variety of social networks and webs of personal interest in the world at large and in the perceived future of things. This is not to say that discord or family rupture does not prompt some to exercise the choice that a market economy and consumerist motivation allow and act in stark independence. For whatever reason, however, some people do exercise choice and opt for what is, in effect, a cultural innovation. In the process their family and friends respond and come to experience a form of funeral previously unknown to them, and this causes some of them to rethink their own views and funeral plans.

In this study of a new burial practice, then, we have one example of the process of social change, one allied with changes in aspects of a person's self-identity and social network. Many of those interviewed as part of this project were already elderly or old. Although they had grown up through the two successive eras of the dominance of traditional burial and of cremation – with a pivotal point in the mid-1960s – their option for a newer innovation shows them far from being conditioned by either of these. The old can do new things. At this early stage of innovation we find that the novel idea of natural burial has been encountered and appreciated as much through attending such an event as through newspapers or online media. The snowball effect of one person's attendance at a single funeral that was found appealing should not be under-estimated, especially in an ageing population where funeral attendance is relatively high as peers die. Moreover, many older people are web-literate and utilize their easy access to the rapidly expanding online presence of funeral options, including those of natural burial sites.

Then, as far as kin are concerned, this potential for individual choice and natural burial is unlikely to be met with family opposition not only because of the respect many pay to personal funeral wishes but also because of widespread ecological concern over the very future of the planet. Moreover, in natural burial we find a strong potential for elements of traditional burial to be aligned with increasing doubts over the ecological credentials of cremation. At a symbolic level some deeply interesting issues arise from notions of continuity arising from the process of natural burial where on the one hand graves 'disappear' while, on the other, the very place where graves disappear becomes what is deemed a natural landscape and the site for an imaginative creation of identity. This imagination involves not only the one who is dying or who has preregistered for a grave at Barton Glebe but also subsequent mourners and their engagement with this area. The change from 'space' into 'place', a well-known idiom of transformation in geographical terms, involves the complex interplay of personal identity and its ongoing imaginative reconfiguration with various kin relationships and with wider cultural concerns over core values.

These core values, at least for some people, now also embrace issues of ecology. In recent years shifts in British society over the ways in which the land and its produce need to be conserved have gained high profile, not simply in abstract terms but in the most concrete of daily actions directed at household waste. Having to use different bins, bags and containers for domestic refuse itself fosters an ecological ethic. While energy-efficient vehicles with lower noxious emissions are also relatively popular concerns, these simple acts of waste disposal serve as social refinements of the practice of composting of waste organic material that has been a lively interest for millions of British gardeners across a number of generations. Refuse, as a background fact of life, is far too easily taken for granted, just as it is easily forgotten that millions of urban residents in Britain own gardens and do things with them. Gardening programmes are popular on radio and television, with major chain stores focused on homes and gardens advertising and carrying many related 'home and garden' products. It is in and through many of these very ordinary activities that social values make their impact, and when combined with major international debates on such issues as global warming, they conduce to a positive view of 'nature' and human relationships with it.

At the same time, levels of what would be regarded as traditional beliefs in life after death are relatively low and of many mixed perspectives, providing a viable opportunity for innovative views to develop. Similarly, priests are far from the only people now available and utilized for funeral ceremonies. Funeral directors may well mention the option of having a person conduct the event in 'life-centred' and celebratory ways that reflect the family's values and not those of any particular religion. The British Humanist Association is also lively in this field. On a wider front, choice and options, far from being simple mantras of government over matters of health and education and of television advertisers of health and beauty products, are also realities that provide opportunity for self reflection and some degree of self-realization in terms of one's funeral and post-death identity. So, when the notion of therapeutic landscape emerges later in this book we will be able to see in it the transformation of space to a place where, as imagination plays with traditional and innovative values and practices, images of self may also be transformed. Such images of 'self', along with numerous sociological accounts of 'self' should not, as intimated above, be read as a discourse that takes for granted some radical individualism of autonomous persons. For a great deal of 'individual' life in Britain remains driven by family, work, leisure, friendship and neighbourhood networks, and even though a person may hear of or encounter a cultural innovation such as natural burial and decide on this as their 'choice' of funeral 'option' it is still likely to be because of some networked experience or to have been developed in conversation with others, including family members.

Background

Following this broad introductory outline we now sketch a background of how this study came about. Certainly, this natural burial project would not have emerged without a sustained number of previous studies concerning death and funeral rites conducted by Douglas Davies since the late 1980s.[1] These began with cremation and British crematoria research supported by Nottingham University and published through The Cremation Society of Great Britain,[2] and continued into social surveys on attitudes to death, life and afterlife as part of a major project on religion in Britain funded partly by the Leverhulme Trust and the Church of England.[3] A later project, funded by over 70 local authorities within the United Kingdom, analysed popular attitudes to forms of funeral, pinpointing the issue of reusing old graves as an attempt to increase the use of full cemeteries.[4] That study, of over 1600 individuals interviewed in their own homes, was perhaps the most detailed and extensive account of funeral attitudes conducted in the United Kingdom up until that time. Its findings were presented to a House of Commons Select Committee on burial law reform. Davies, alongside research colleagues, added to these empirical studies a series of books embracing both academic and popular accounts of funerary rites, cremated remains and death, both from anthropological–sociological and theological perspectives.[5]

Those themes led, almost inevitably, to this account of Barton Glebe natural burial site, focusing on those who created and manage Barton Glebe, as well as on bereaved people who have relatives buried there or those who have preregistered for their own grave space. Funeral directors, too, and those who conduct burial rites here have also been interviewed. In retrospect, what may be seen as the first step of this study lay in a visit Davies took to speak to Ken West, then managing the Carlisle Cemetery and in the earliest stage of developing what would become a woodland-style cemetery in which trees would be planted over new graves. He had been responsive to questions about the use of cardboard coffins and the like and his open-minded creativity saw analogous possibilities in using a field-like area at the cemetery to develop an innovative arrangement of burial and memorialization. At that point, in the early 1990s, the idea of graves marked by trees rather than formal rows of headstones seemed innovative and yet bore some association with the use of rose trees to mark cremated remains. Not long after, through personal contacts with Stephen Sykes, then bishop of Ely, Davies was an informal discussant with people considering the establishment of a natural burial site near Cambridge, prompted by one of the diocese's ecologically minded clergy, the Reverend Peter Owen Jones. Some years later, when the site was up and running, another personal contact, Dr Matthew Lavis, then Ely Diocesan Secretary and a Trustee of the site, suggested that it would be of real interest to study the ongoing development of the site, named Barton Glebe, in the light of his observation that a certain supportive attitude towards the site had seemed to develop among its users. Davies responded to this suggestion and their mutual interest led to a successful grant being awarded by the UK Arts and Humanities Research Council's and the Economic and Social Science Research Council's joint Religion and Society Programme. This took the form of a 3-year collaborative doctoral award between Durham University and The Arbory Trust running between 2007 and 2010. Hannah Rumble, joint author of this book with Douglas Davies, was appointed as the key researcher and successfully completed her Doctor of Philosophy degree in 2010, after three years of intensive research activity supervised at Durham University by Douglas Davies, whose background lies in the anthropology and sociology of religion as well as in theology, and at Barton Glebe by Dr Matthew Lavis as representative of the collaborative charity and whose original Durham doctorate lay in Geography. Hannah Rumble's undergraduate and postgraduate Master's degree work lay in Durham University's Department of Anthropology. In terms of this book, the great proportion of fieldwork material and some of the theoretical concepts presented in Chapters 2–4 are derived from Rumble's doctoral thesis which can be consulted for further empirical material, but to allow the chapters to flow more easily in this volume we have not referenced them item by item.[6] These varied academic backgrounds and experiences have all been helpful for interdisciplinary discussions framing this particular project on natural burial. Professor Charles Watkins of Nottingham University's Department of Geography, an authority on trees, was also kind enough to give some advice of an arboreal nature. From these personal background elements, we now move to this study's theoretical preoccupations.

Goal, methods and issues

At its simplest, this study's goal was to ascertain the significance of the Barton Glebe site for its users, with an associated issue being that of understanding the Arbory Trust as an Anglican initiative that established the site. We saw our task as descriptive and interpretative, with anthropological–sociological issues as well as theological considerations being of theoretical interest to us. The social scientific perspective was pursued through questionnaires and interviews held with numerous planners, managers and users of the site, as well as in visits to Barton Glebe and participation in its open-days.[7] Some focus groups were held at Comberton, the village nearest the site. Though it had not be planned at the outset of this project, as we moved into the last of its 3-year period of study the idea arose of making a film in association with the project. After suitable funding had been secured, we recruited Sarah Thomas, also an anthropologist by background and now an ethnographic film maker. The outcome of her work was the film *Earth to Earth: Natural Burial and the Church of England.*[8] This, in itself, then furnished further interview material that is included in this book. Numerous theological issues also emerged from all of these materials and events and we explore those in Chapter 5.

In dealing with these various materials it must be said that we are all too aware of the provisional nature of our analysis and interpretation. Such provisionality is basic in social research not only because of limitation in time and resources for extensive comparative study but also because of the difficult task of engaging with questions of 'meaning' in people's lives, especially when they may only have arrived at some partial rationale within themselves over what is a novel social practice that still lacks the full weight of conventional significance. Here, more than is even necessary in ordinary social research, we have to be careful not to over-systematize ideas that may, in practice, exist only as clusters in people's thoughts. So too when discussing ritual and symbolism and the way personal experiences and thoughts interplay with those of others, all framed by distinctive cultural conventions. Closely aligned with these thoughts and experiences is the very issue of identity in which the rational–emotional meanings of a life cohere in an embodied sense of self and of the worth of that self in society.

In terms of ritual and symbolism it is wise to bear in mind that one debate in anthropology asks whether ritual is or is not 'like' a language? Is it a practice whose code can be cracked to find the meaning or is it better viewed simply as something we do that is an end in and of itself?[9] In reality the answer is probably somewhere between the two. Some people give extensive accounts of what, how and why they are doing what they do, while others simply do what seems appropriate for themselves with reasons being minimally expressed no matter how deeply rooted they may be in personal or family history.

What cannot be ignored is the place of a kind of emotional understanding of the appropriateness of a practice that many of our informants had only encountered fairly recently. The theme of allurement that appears in later chapters gives some expression to that complex sense of the appropriateness and desirability of a practice once it is encountered as a viable cultural option. And that viability is especially important in a society and for a generation in which the very concepts of choice, options and personal worth have become hot political motifs focused both on educational matters of choice of schools and, most relevant for this book, over healthcare. But healthcare is one thing, death is another. One of the most intense debates over choice that has been pursued both in the British Parliament and by the press has focused on choice over death. There is tremendous irony here, however, in that at the time of this research and at the time of writing this book, the much vaunted theme of choice in education and healthcare as well as in commercial advertising for practically anything, stops at the point of doctor-assisted or simply assisted suicide. The state draws the line at the point in helping one of its members to die even if they might wish it in the light of impending disease and the likelihood of a terminal period someone regards as utterly debilitating, beyond their control and therefore undignified. It is fully understandable that palliative care specialists should seek to allay such fears, while the concerns of medical doctors are also very understandable in terms of their daily goal of life preservation. In such a social atmosphere of commercial and political heralding of choice, despite constraint over a key existential fear of the day, the debilitated indignity of dying, some individuals see the issue of choice in funerals as all the more appealing. And not simply the choice between traditional burial and cremation, even with all the choice options over what can be done with cremated remains, but over an option that seems replete with ritual action and symbolic associations that speak to people of their own deeply held life-convictions. Chapter 3 begins to explicitly identify what these life-convictions are that foster pro-choice for natural burial.

Cultural contexts of funerals

This account of choice and natural burial finds its place in a long history of British funeral traditions. For centuries, the British interred their dead in graveyards surrounding their parish churches, with some of high status finding their resting place within such churches and in the Abbeys and Cathedrals of the land. All this was an extension of the earliest Christian practice of relating places of worship with the faithful dead, especially martyrs. The extension of the parish system as a mode of Christianizing Europe brought extensive geographical coverage that enabled the dead to find their proper place in this world in anticipation of their eternal destiny. These processes of change ensured that, with time, new ways became established as custom. But the social world is seldom static, and sometimes undergoes rapid shifts as with the Black Death, the sixteenth-century English Reformation, the Industrial Revolution of the late eighteenth and nineteenth centuries and the twentieth century's two World Wars. Each touched different aspects of human life. As across Europe, the Black Death dramatically reduced the British population and heightened the status of the surviving workforce. The English break with Catholicism forged the Church of England, produced an influential English Bible and generated English language liturgies, including those of marriages and funerals, and with a Holy Communion rite that ousted some key features of the Mass that had related to the dead. All these rites had been experienced by the great majority of the population.

Post-reformation, married clergy, especially in parishes, provided a ritual base for pastoral care of varying degrees of quality. They linked life and death with formal religious ideas through marriage, baptism and funeral rites. Religious services and forms of words at funerals and in association with the Eucharist that once suggested that the living could assist the afterlife destiny of their dead were formally abandoned or transformed; requiem masses and indulgences ceased, though many older attitudes doubtlessly endured in many people's minds over the dead in the parish churchyard. Their destiny in the afterlife becomes less vital while the Church of England drew its new liturgies away from prayers for the dead. In a more firmly Protestant-Scotland burials were even conducted in silence, thus eliminating the possibility of theologically dubious expressions regarding the deceased; God knew their destiny and that alone mattered. For those with local prestige or national status, tombs or grave markers would announce their status to the world while for many of the poor an enduringly unmarked grave was likely.

No sooner was the new regime of the Church of England underway then the late eighteenth-century Industrial Revolution witnessed a dramatic demographic shift as many agricultural workers migrated to industrial towns, leaving their largely unmarked dead behind them. As urbanization intensified so did the need for cities of the dead, with such necropolises rising around many great British towns. By the 1830s the need for the sanitary welfare of the living led to the building of civic cemeteries beyond town centres with their newly built cemetery chapels often as mirror images of each other, standing at the entrance, one for the use of the established Church of England and the other for other denominations. In the planning and form of grave marking, these cemeteries often reflected the status and power of the dead while they lived. Lifestyle and death-style were poignantly mutual. The rise of rich industrialists, along with emergent middle classes, working classes and the distressingly poor was evident from elaborate memorials through to unmarked paupers' graves.

Era of cremation

Even large scale civic cemeteries did not achieve all that might have been desired of them so that between the 1860s and the 1890s Victorian creativity led to the development of cremation, a practice in which European sharing of ideas regarding civic health and sanitary urban planning, along with a degree of religious-ideological freethinking, found opportunity in the engineering skills established through the industrial revolution to produce crematoria. Starting in the 1880s among the upper echelons of English society the practice of cremation was slow to gather popular speed until the First, and then the Second World Wars, inflicted their devastation upon the life of generations of men and of grief upon their female kith and kin. By the mid-1960s cremation was taking over from burial as the dominant form of English funeral but with practically no serious liturgical change to match. New crematoria were being rapidly built and the public at large were adapting to cremation. Cremated remains were, largely, being buried or scattered within crematorium grounds. By the mid-1970s, however, increasing numbers of people were taking the cremated remains of their relatives away from the crematorium not so as to bury them in a family plot elsewhere, as had hitherto been known as a reason for removing them from the place of the cremation, but to bury, place or scatter them in a spot of significance to the deceased and to the remaining kin (Davies and Guest 1999).

While, in retrospect, that shift towards retention and personal or family disposal of remains was significant for many reasons, we draw attention to one in particular at this point because it relates to what we will discuss as a romantic ideal that we think became a significant motivating factor in the choice for natural burial two decades later. When a person's ashes were taken by a family member and buried in their garden, at a shared holiday place or to the location of a hobby or interest, they were being used as a symbol of the deceased person, that is, the ashes participated in what they represented, they 'were' the deceased person in something of an idealized form. And it is this idealized aspect of ashes to which we draw attention for, now distinct from the corpse with its material image of the person who had once lived, the ashes were set free to symbolize whatever the survivors wanted to symbolize about the dead person. The portability of ashes made many things possible that had not been possible before. They could be taken and left in places, or even be surreptitiously placed there, according to the wishes of the living as they conceived of the dead and of their relationships with the dead. The living could project their own ideas of the relationship onto the ashes and, through a private rite, achieve a goal that might well not have been achievable with a corpse in a cemetery or even in a graveyard.

Davies developed the idea of retrospective fulfilment of identity as one interpretation of this private ritual placing of the ashes. In other words, the ashes in their specially chosen place served to enhance something of the life of the deceased by rooting him/her in an environment of personal significance or of mutual significance with the survivor. As is obvious, this action was significant to the living and of their imagined relationship between the deceased and some physical place. Here we see the importance of a particular place and its dynamic role in the identity of the dead and of his/her identity in the ongoing life and in the identity of the living person who conducts the private rite with his remains. Davies contrasted such a retrospective fulfilment of identity with what he called an eschatological fulfilment of identity, a term used to link this developing custom with ashes to a theological and liturgical frame of reference; eschatology being the doctrines surrounding traditional Christian beliefs of death, judgement, Hell and Heaven. He linked the development of ash placement with changes in British attitudes that allowed little or no place for ideas of an afterlife conceived of in terms of a negative judgement and Hell. Research in the closing decades of the twentieth century seemed to indicate that in Britain a large minority of people did not hold beliefs about the afterlife, especially among men. In the absence of such an afterlife destination it seemed to make sense that people would ritualize death in such a way as to maximize the sense they could make of it. And this, it seems to us, paved the way for later developments in natural burial, itself a further maximization of meaning in the face of potentially meaningless death.

Maximizing meaning in mortality

It is this feature of meaning-maximization to which we now wish to draw attention. To place cremated remains in a spot that was 'meaningful' to the deceased, as in a well-loved garden, mountainside or a river where he fished, was to add meaning to a death. Death does not 'mean' the heart attack or the cancer that killed this man or that woman: significance is not left with the cause of death as it appears on the death certificate. The person's death has become the occasion for thinking again about his/her individual life and about his/her relationships with their survivors.

It is important to be clear about this role of meaning, meaningfulness and meaninglessness in relation to death. This was important for our project on natural burial given the work on 'meaning' that Davies had previously developed in terms of the sociology of knowledge and of sociological phenomenology and their notions of plausibility and the universes of meaning that individuals develop within their social worlds. Taking up the widespread idea of human meaning-making he had related it to religious studies by arguing that meaning-making was an integral part of the idea of salvation.[10] He argued that salvation could be interpreted in a sociological rather than in theological terms as a maximization of plausibility within particular social and life contexts. In subsequent studies he developed the concept of superplausibility[11] to describe how one level of meaning overtakes other levels as in processes of religious conversion. Something similar can also be argued over death. For one of the features of human life is that people, and their societies at large, do not like death to be a meaningless event. This, too, was something that Davies had taken up previously when deploying the idiom of 'words against death' to capture the rhetorical goal of liturgies, memorials and many other kinds of cultural markers of death.[12]

When death comes at an appropriate age and after a person has achieved a certain number of culturally acknowledged goals there is little or no impetus to need to find meaning in a death. The life, itself, has been meaningful and now it is, roughly speaking, time to die. So, for example, if a person has formed positive relationships, brought up children, had a successful job or career and a happy retirement and then died after a relatively short illness, people are wont to say that 'he had a good life'. In fact the phrase 'a good death' seems almost rendered redundant in such a case because the 'death' has been subsumed in the person's 'life'.

What many find difficult is when that ideal-type life and death is contradicted in an accident or illness killing a child or a young person or if a parent with a young family to look after dies. Of such things people say 'it is a shame'. Much the same follows acts of murder, and produce expressions such as 'senseless murder' or 'senseless acts of violence' that result in death. Neonatal deaths fall into the same category, especially at a time of relatively low birth rates and when prospective parents often invest enormous psychological energy in their anticipated baby and their anticipated identity as parents. The very existence of scans during pregnancy and even of scan-derived 'photographs' of 'their baby' reinforces the meaningfulness of their pregnancy and the senselessness of a neonatal death.

And then there are parents who did successfully bring up a child, invest a great deal of themselves and their money in their boy or girl's life and education only to hear, one day, that they have been killed in an accident or died of some unanticipated disease. Their shock can only be guessed at by those fortunate enough never to have had such an experience. Yet, among these bereaved people we find more than a few whose psychological, social and economic resources trigger a proactive response to ensure 'that something good can come out of' what for them is a tragedy. A similar expression speaks of a death 'not being in vain'. Numerous funds and charities have been created by bereaved parents to provide for research into the conditions that killed their children or to continue their life interests. Through such ventures the parents often find some meaning, not simply or even primarily of a rational kind, but of a moral kind, where 'moral' refers to the socially created and community fostered values that sustain engagement with others and gives some hope for the future.[13]

They encounter goodwill and emotional support from those they recruit or who come to assist them. New and deeper friendships are formed, sometimes with the friends of their deceased son or daughter. These charities furnish their own form of 'words against death' and ensure that parents simply do not lapse into a hopelessness which is the moral outcome of rational meaninglessness.

Lifeline's identity-curve

One final dimension of meaning, meaninglessness and mortality that stands out in contemporary society spotlights illness, incapacity or a redundant old age. One way of expressing this dimension is to take the familiar notion of a lifeline and represent it as a curve describing degrees of significance of identity, understanding significance as meaning the value of a life to itself set in a social world.[14] As the curve of life's social significance passes its peak and moves to a tailing-off, many express the wish not to have to live on in pain and a 'meaningless life'. In such a contexts 'meaningfulness' involves not only a sense of social involvement that sustains a valued sense of identity but also a sense of being to some significant degree in control of one's life. The fact of a longer life has not been greeted by uniform celebration, for many qualify its prospects with thoughts of incapacity and lack of control. This has become a most contentious issue over the question of assisted or doctor assisted suicide in cases of seriously debilitating prognosis. There are those, albeit few at present, who seek help to end their life before their anticipated pain becomes unbearable or their condition creates an entirely unacceptable indignity of identity. Their decision to do this is understandable given the economic-political ideology of market-led consumerism in which the very idea of 'choice' became the much advertised watchword of the early twenty-first century. Politicians of all parties underpin their public-facing policies over healthcare and education on the 'choice' of patient or parent, with largely enforced league tables of performance being widely reckoned to furnish some basis for choice of hospital or school. Meanwhile, commercial agencies seek to embed choice in a much advertised focus on individualism. Still, at the time of writing, the social line is firmly drawn such that we may choose where to educate our children, where and what to purchase for our daily needs and where to get medical treatment for our healthcare, but we may not in any official sense choose to die. This is, of course, a complex issue and it is understandable that politicians are loath to speak on it. The medical profession, too, stands in a difficult place since it would need to be the agent of 'doctor assisted death', something that very many doctors see as contradicting their professional commitment to the preservation of life. Many argue the notion of the thin end of the wedge, thinking that if today's choice is for me to desire the end of my life for reasons already mentioned then, tomorrow, it might be my family or others who might wish me to die sooner rather than later for reasons of inheritance or convenience. Yet, there are many whose lives have taken shape under market forces and the ideology of choice and consumerism who do not see why their choice should be blocked over the matter of their death. The prime factor underlying all these issues is that of 'control', a concept integral to a contemporary sense of identity but one that is, frequently and conveniently, overemphasized in a market-driven economy. For, in any social world, the choice of individuals is restricted by the power of the state at some point or other. Laws exist and if I exercise my choice to break them then I am likely to forfeit my right to freedom. The prison service will take charge of my body. And in a similar sense, a hospital takes charge of my sick and dying body and does not leave me with the choice of how to die; though it is perfectly possible that we will see legislation change over such issues before many years pass.

These issues of identity, control and choice are all deeply significant for natural burial for it is, at present, the quintessential expression of choice in relation to our bodies, albeit after death. We may not be able to choose how or when to die but we can choose a whole series of things regarding our post-mortal social presence in addition to the long established practice of writing a will that will enact one's life-wishes when one is dead. These, paradoxically, also influence some people's sense of themselves while still alive. Here natural burial shares in a wider attitude to death that has, very largely, developed alongside it, namely, the fact that significant minorities plan their own funeral in advance of their death. This is, at least, one forward-looking activity that an individual can engage in, especially if it is a person who has been diagnosed with a terminal illness and, in that sense, has nothing to look forward to. Choosing hymns, songs, music and readings, as well as pondering who might take part in the event, has become an established activity, or at least one that is no longer found strange. It is one of today's most obvious *memento mori*. It is in constructing one's *memento mori* while still alive by choosing how and where to be disposed of that people often learn of natural burial as one such option.

Lifestyle and death-style

One way of bringing some focus to these ideas is to link lifestyle with what Davies has previously called death-style, and has discussed as a process of lifestyle and death-style coherence or incoherence. This theme concerning the assonance or dissonance between values of life and of death is a natural development of the phenomenology of the everyday life-world alluded to above in Davies' work on meaning and salvation. As we will see in subsequent chapters, there is much to be said for approaching natural burial as a practice that increases the assonance between lifestyle and death-style and, in that sense, giving an individual a greater sense of integrity of identity than would be afforded in a form of funeral that compromised a person's lifestyle. The dynamics linking life values and death are, of course, very complex, not least because they exist within ever-changing social worlds. What we have intimated above and discussed in greater detail elsewhere would suggest, for example, that traditional churchyard burial afforded high levels of congruence between an individual's view of death and a Christian afterlife; that cremation mirrored concerns over social hygiene and over views of death as the simple end of human existence, and that the private ritual placing of cremated remains afforded some fulfilment of identity of a life lived and of the memories retained by survivors.[15] With social changes, however, and especially with new attitudes to ecology and lifestyle the issue of death-style can also be expected to take a different turn. And this we think is the case for both some aspects of traditional cemetery burial but most especially in regard of cremation. What the late nineteenth and early twentieth century regarded as sanitary and for the social good, namely, the use of cremation to avoid overfilled graves and wasted land, is now questioned in terms of crematoria gas emissions, potential harm of the atmosphere and damage to human well-being at large. Dissonance replaces assonance over cremation for what is, at the time of writing, a very small minority but which may well expand as this form of burial becomes increasingly well-known through formal marketing and media publicity but, perhaps most especially, through the snowball effect of personal experience of the natural burial of family and friends.

Symbolism, identity and death

One feature of lifestyle that needs some additional introduction for this study of people's construction of a meaningful identity in relation to death concerns the role of symbolism and ritual. Over the course of our lives we accumulate a variety of symbols, some growing in their depth of significance over time, others simply being accumulated through our involvement in a growing variety of pursuits. Some take a very material form in objects we have been given, bought or simply come to share, others take the form of words, poems, songs or sayings that carry with them memories of other persons and times of significance to us. While the passage of time renders some symbols redundant, others are lost or intentionally abandoned, but there are periodic moments when symbols that are crucial to our sense of identity are multiplied or are intensified in significance. Birthdays offer one such example when our individual life is singled out by our family and friends for special attention. So, too, with various life or relationship anniversaries or when we gain some new qualification, status or sporting achievement. At Christmas, too, many families and other groupings celebrate their own well-being in the complex interplay of being together, giving gifts and sharing food and drink.

The role of such symbolic and ritual activity in the ordinary growth of our lives then acts as a background to their significance in end of life care, death and funerals. It is their potency during our lifetime within our life-world that gives them such a potential for significance towards and after the end of our lives. Many individuals possess deeply rooted symbols that are, practically, part and parcel of their identity and that families wish to incorporate within funeral or memorial rites, often including objects, music, songs and poems that bind or represent a person to their children, partner or friends. These things capture the meaningfulness of life, not least in its emotional tones. Yet, the attention we give such identity-symbols may vary greatly. When we are younger and in the process of establishing ourselves upon the stage of life they attract great attention, later they may be taken for granted, while later still many may cease to be important as life energy decreases and an individual's attention becomes increasingly narrow-focused on but a few. If sickness and serious illness beset someone that is even more likely to be the case as attention withdraws from the wider world into the circle of the self. Then, lifeline contact and desire for support from intimates may become intense though, for some, the desire to be quiet and die alone is far from unknown. It is as though many of us live on an arc of life, beginning with nothing, then rising in significance as our world-involvement grows, only to decline in older old age. The physical spaces that match this arc reflect this process, the child starts with nothing but parents and the parental home, gaining much with maturity and family responsibilities, often in a new home, he or she probably reaches a high identity-point as older relatives die and not only leave items of inheritance, replete with their sentimental value, but also a new sense of independent responsibility for kin as well as in occupational and other social worlds. With time this situation, too, changes as retirement and increasing old age may involve another change in place, not least when the older old person moves from their object-full and memory packed home into a retirement home where there is only room for a relatively few 'personal belongings' – itself an enormously telling expression.

It is against such a changing background of shifts in location of identity that, for recent centuries, the next step would be either into a civic cemetery, for some 25 per cent to 30 per cent of the population, or through a crematorium for the other 70 per cent before one's ashes are interred, scattered or placed in some site of personal significance. With the advent of natural burial, however, the choice changes. Through the options already mentioned and others yet to be discussed in the ensuing chapters, individuals have the opportunity to 'rethink themselves' in and through their death, while that expression will require some explanation as this study proceeds it is important at the outset to pinpoint the theme of imaginative depictions of personal identity through particular locations. As we will see, the cultural innovation of natural burial allows for this, not as some entirely new concept, but as a creative alignment of pre-existing cultural motifs. The fact of individual identity and gardening, of British motifs of woodlands and meadows, of birdsong and animal life, as well as motifs of peace, rest and safety that have had their echoes in traditional cemeteries and churchyards, have opportunity to coalesce in natural burial. Here the multivocality of symbolism, the multiplicity of 'nature' as a symbol of natural burial, will emerge as significant. So, too, is the opportunity to be creatively involved in planning one's own burial service, an option of 'choice' that has been quite limited in traditional church funerals but had already begun to emerge from around the 1990s, encouraged by insurance agencies and their advocacy of forward planning over one's death. Pre-planning applies not only to the choice of hymns, songs, music, poetry or readings but also over the services of priests, secular, or a mixed economy style of ceremony leader who will give an individual or family what they request and not simply what a church liturgy prescribes. In the case of our Barton Glebe burial site all of these things are possible, despite the fact that this is a consecrated site, meaning it carries a legal force allied with the Church of England, as well as a church-based reference point relevant for those with church links.

Gift and emotion

There is a potency in such symbolic ideas, offering a pool of potential orientations and an allure and cultural attraction for those whose lifestyle finds echoes in ideas of self-organized funerals. For them, landscape and sound-scape cohere in furnishing an attractive scenario in which some find it easy to imagine themselves when dead. Such imaginings relate to the complex themes of identity and meaning-making, of relationships between family members and others, and of the patterns of values, beliefs and emotions that prompt and pervade our lives, all within wider cultural images of self, society and environment.

So, too, with another factor underlying the life-curve of identity mentioned above, and which contributes markedly to our theoretical analysis in this study, that is, the theme of reciprocity. Sometimes called gift-theory, this perspective on the way people relate to each other is of utmost significance for our approach to death and, most especially, to natural burial. Theoretically rooted in the anthropology of Marcel Mauss and subsequent scholars, gift-theory is a way of describing and analysing the many ways people create and maintain relationships through a great variety of exchanges. As we will see in later chapters, the key issue of exchange can easily be identified in objects given and received, but more complex aspects of relationships can also be understood through ideas of trans-generational transmission of objects or of objects that are symbolic of potent ideas. We will see this apply to the human body itself when thought of as a gift of the corpse that may benefit future generations. Just what kind of a gift this entails is something we will ponder later.[16]

As for the divide between life and death itself, the many accounts of human existence that dwell upon its sharp distinction may, at first glance, easily give the impression that life is of positive value while death is entirely negative. But this is deceptive, not only because life is seldom always positive for everyone, but also because, as a person ages new contexts of ill health or relative incapacity bring distinctive constraints. This is of particular relevance as life-length extends in some contemporary societies bringing the question of death in its train as something desired by some as an exit from an unbearably painful illness or even from an increasingly dragged-out tedium. That tedium-factor is, of course, quite different from the desire for death and glory that inspires martyrs in many traditions and highlights but one setting in which life is given a strongly positive valuation. Still, for many, life is a mixture of positive and negative experience brought about by individual circumstance grounded, not least, in the impact of our close relatives, of the arrival and passing of personal success and failure, and of our own emotional dynamics and responses to these events. Death is often one of the most potent of these, sometimes drawing near to herald periods of grief, but sometimes arriving abruptly to deliver death to our doorstep. Ironically, the part played by emotions in such experience is easily ignored in studies of death despite the fact that grief has occupied a central role in modern accounts of bereavement. This is because 'emotions' become focused on grief and restricted to a narrow range of interior reflections. Some recent studies have addressed themselves to this in terms of the part played by aspects of the material culture of death in cemeteries and in the belongings of the deceased.[17] Later, in this book, we will take this theme further as when, for example, exploring natural burial sites as 'therapeutic landscapes'. In all of this work our exploratory study will draw ideas from a variety of academic disciplines, including anthropology, sociology, psychology, linguistics, history and theology.

To hint at something of the complexity of this task we end this introductory chapter with a single example lying beyond our site and cultural domain but, nevertheless framing many of the issues we will take up throughout this book. It concerns but one aspect of life and death related emotions in the

Norwegian philosophical artist Edvard Munch. Born in Norway in 1863 and universally known for his painting 'The Scream', he described his ' "whole youth" as "worm-eaten" by his father's religious anxiety'. But, as for himself, he experienced two deeply influential vision-like experiences that helped redirect his life and thought.[18] One of these came, in the French environment of Saint-Cloud, as he gained some deep sense of the 'spirit of life' or whatever it is that holds 'a body together' while it still changes and develops: this is associated with what came to be called the Saint-Cloud manifesto. It tells of an experience associated with climbing the hill at Saint-Cloud on a warm early spring day when he hears a cock crow, smells a bonfire of leaves and sees new shoots spring through the soil. These mixed sensory stimuli led him to give an account of a transformation in his awareness.

> I felt it as a sensual delight that I should become one with – become this earth which is forever radiated by the sun in a constant ferment and which lives – lives – and which will grow plants from my decaying body – trees and flowers – and the sun will warm them and I will exist in them – and nothing will perish – and that is eternity.[19]

Following this experience he felt able to paint a representation of his dead father, something he had previously been unable to do, a constraint that may well have been linked to the fact that he was not present at his father's death, something that had been 'a great obstacle to him'.[20] Though entirely withdrawn from anything like the Lutheran religious orthodoxy of his father and of his own boyhood he now thought it 'necessary to believe in immortality' albeit described in terms of 'the atoms of life or the spirit of life' that 'must continue to exist after the body's death', despite his inability to account for that inevitability.[21] Munch's cameo reveals the complexity of individual emotions set amid personal social history, psychological biography and geographical locality. It will stand as a reminder that (a) the idea that we may persist in nature after our death is not a new one exclusive to natural burial and (b) of factors that will not always be captured or capturable in later chapters, whether by lack of space, by absence of intimate knowledge or by our analytical skills. Nevertheless, moving on from Munch's mixed European personal chemistry we now pass to a very English world of reflection, countryside and the natural domain of burying the dead and anticipating our own future in death.

2

Varied sites and changing rites

This chapter focuses upon describing the innovative practice of natural burial and provides detailed material from one particular site that has been studied in some detail. As a consequence of being free of constraints experienced in more 'traditional' disposal locations, natural burial offers not only greater choice in how the living ponder their own future funeral but also how the living may engage with their dead, all through the landscape where they lie.[1] This chapter maps these diverse landscapes in order to illustrate what sets natural burial grounds apart from other disposal locations. It then discusses the implications of these new landscapes for mourners and funeral professionals through material drawn from ethnographic work and aligned interviews[2] focused on Barton Glebe; a consecrated Church of England affiliated woodland burial site managed by the Arbory Trust in Cambridgeshire.[3]

Introducing a typology of natural burial provision

The gradual increase in the number of natural burial grounds in the United Kingdom, following the first natural burial ground opened in Carlisle in 1993, has prompted an array of interpretation of landscape and management strategies.[4] This diversity means that, apart from a broad conceptual definition, an all-encompassing definition for natural burial grounds seems impossible. One intriguing yet key perspective upon this difficulty lies in the fact that whereas many may speak conceptually of natural burial in terms of what happens below ground, it is what happens above ground that frequently seems to set the image and popular perception of natural burial practice.

Whereas some natural burial grounds, like Barton Glebe, are consecrated, with graves randomly placed in woodland glades with minimal memorialization, other sites are not consecrated and may occupy a small area within an existing cemetery with graves in rows and some memorialization permitted.[5] Yet others may look to the casual observer like an overgrown meadow or field with very little else to distract the eye.

At the time of writing, there are 207 natural burial sites in Britain, mostly located in England, with a further 24 sites planned and another 11 sites proposed across Britain. Ireland's first natural burial ground, located near

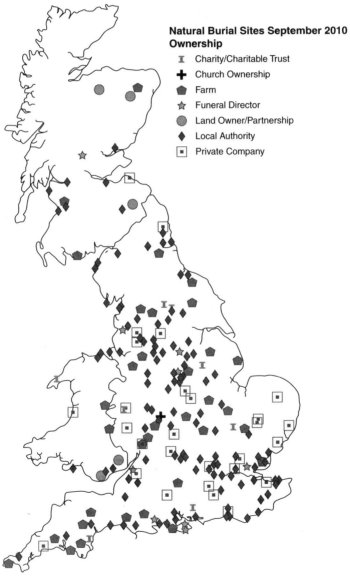

Natural Burial Sites September 2010 Ownership

- Charity/Charitable Trust
- Church Ownership
- Farm
- Funeral Director
- Land Owner/Partnership
- Local Authority
- Private Company

Figure 2.1 Distribution of natural burial sites in the United Kingdom by ownership and type

Killane in County Wexford, opened officially in late 2010 with a second Irish natural burial ground soon to open[6]. A team of researchers at Sheffield University have surveyed and mapped a significant number of designated natural burial grounds and it is thanks to their survey work that we have a better understanding of the diversity of distribution, ownership and landscaping of Britain's natural burial grounds (Figure 2.1).[7,8]

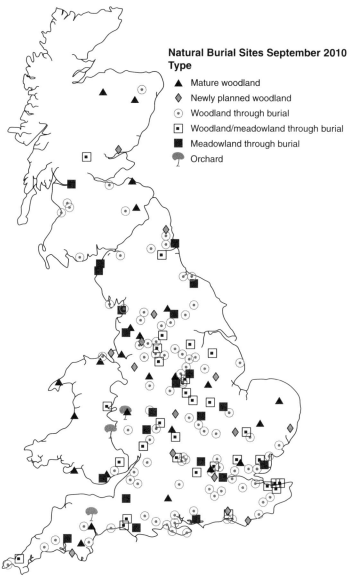

Figure 2.1 Cont'd

Clayden reported that 'farmers, individuals and private companies manage approximately 30 per cent of natural burial grounds as businesses'.[9] This percentage has increased over the last 6 years by 8 per cent if those sites listed in the Natural Death Centre's (NDC) database are used as a guide. The current Manager of the NDC stated that there were 208 'active' natural burial sites in the United Kingdom as of February 2010, of which 120 are municipally owned, 79 are privately owned and 9 are owned by charities or trusts.[10] This would mean that 58 per cent of natural burial provision is offered and owned municipally.[11] Although local authorities dominate in terms of ownership of natural burial grounds, it is the privately managed natural burial grounds that occupy the largest area in hectares of natural burial ground.[12] This is probably because local authority natural burial provision tends to be located within an existing cemetery or grounds of a crematorium. In addition, each natural burial site's physical character or landscape varies greatly, irrespective of ownership, because the landscape's character is partly dependent upon the site's history of land use and any aims for the site held by the owners or managers in addition to offering burial.

The exclusive or inclusive designation of land for natural burial subsequently affects management practices so, for example, the influence of regular cemetery management prevails in sites that are part of inclusive local authority provision. This sometimes results in graves arranged in rows, where each burial is marked by a memorial tree instead of the customary headstone. Indeed, by far the most common expression of natural burial in local authority sites is to plant a tree upon each individual grave, with the idea of creating woodland through burial. In this context, visiting is often inscribed upon the landscape by visible objects (not always biodegradable) being left upon graves; as is customary in the rest of the cemetery or garden of remembrance. Some view the instances where regular cemetery management practices are transferred onto natural burial provision as impeding the realization of the concept of natural burial as a member of staff at a municipal cemetery illustrates from Rumble's (2010) research below:

> [Named natural burial ground] is a whole woodland area: it's professional and encapsulated by its own privacy, whereas this isn't. We're selling a bit of a cemetery as part *of* a cemetery! And I think it therefore dilutes the whole green burial bit. So I've no idea how they're going to react here [possible clients] but again, we're down for offering choice . . .

Time has shown that local authority provision of natural burial often cannot compete with the privately or trust-owned natural burial provision. As the cemetery operator states above, this is probably because the provision is conceptually undermined by the close proximity of more traditional graves, which very often, are disapproved of by those who are choosing natural burial. Moreover, visible headstones in various states of upkeep also undermine popular expectations of a 'natural' landscape by those seeking a natural burial. There are some municipal cemeteries that offer natural burial such as Hexham (Figure 2.2) and Brighton and Hove City Council that have been successful, but a number have not been as successful as their privately owned counterparts.

Privately owned and charitable trust sites tend to offer the greatest diversity of locations and management practices, partly because they usually occupy a larger area and therefore experience fewer spatial constraints. Moreover, they probably have different budgetary constraints from local authority providers, experience greater self-accountability and control over landscape management and regulations. Something of the variation in the landscapes of privately owned natural burial sites can be gained from the following illustrations. Figures 2.3 and 2.4 show privately run natural burial grounds that are visibly less manicured and regimented than the local authority provision in Figure 2.2.

Not only do natural burial sites differ between landscape and management practices but also with regard to what is allowed to be buried in the grave plot. Around four natural burial grounds in Britain have secured licenses from the Environment Agency to allow owners to be buried with their pets.

Figure 2.2 Hexham cemetery's natural burial provision
Source: Rumble (June 2008).

Figure 2.3 Graves in a green field burial ground owned by a farmer in Co. Durham
Source: Rumble (June 2008).

Figure 2.4 Privately owned Epping Forest Burial Park
Source: Rumble (April 2008).

We suspect that given the British tendency for domestic pets that this may prove a very popular option for people in the future. Moreover, the extent to which a site will regulate the pro-environmental practices of natural burial also varies enormously, prompting Clayden's assertion that, for the benefit of consumers, natural burial ground providers 'must be explicit about what is and is not permitted' by 'clarifying the environmental aims of the burial ground and how these are going to be achieved through ongoing management'.[13] This is particularly relevant with regard to types of coffin or urn and memorial items permitted at the graveside.

Nevertheless, despite the diversity that we have listed above, it is possible to generically classify UK natural burial sites in three ways:

1. With regard to *ownership*: private, local authority, Church of England, charity/charitable trust, etc.

2. With regard to the *physical landscape*: mature woodland, copse, green/ meadow field, newly established woodland. Very often the physical landscape is also an outcome of a particular natural burial ground's aim to do one or more of the following: reclaim, preserve or create native habitats.

3. With regard to *'green' credentials* that usually dictate the purpose and future role of the site in relation to explicitly conserving biodiversity and native habitats.

For comparative purposes we can note that in the United States, the Green Burial Council identifies three types of 'natural burial cemetery', a taxonomy derived from a focus upon land conservation as opposed to burial, namely,

1. conservation burial ground,[14]

2. natural burial ground and

3. hybrid burial ground.

Harris claims the 'greenest' in this taxonomy is the 'conservation burial ground' with the 'natural burial ground' offering 'a green burial that may or may not involve ecological restoration of the land'. The 'hybrid burial ground', in turn, as with many of the natural burial grounds in the United Kingdom, is 'a conventional cemetery that accommodates green burial'.[15]

Other countries appear to be propagating their own versions of natural burial, though far from the extent witnessed to date in the United Kingdom. In Japan, people can choose tree burial (*jumokusou*).[16] In Taiwan, the local government of Taipei are promoting 'tree burial' alongside 'flower burial' and 'sea burial', available since 2003 as a 'result of enquiries into disposal practices in Australia'.[17] New Zealand,[18] Australia,[19] Canada,[20] Netherlands,[21]

Germany,[22] Ireland and Italy[23] also have one or more natural burial grounds.[24] Legacy Parks is the latest natural burial company to appear on the scene and opened South Africa's first natural burial ground in spring 2011.

Looking across cultures and time, the current innovation of 'natural burial' shares practices in common with the 'sacred groves' of rural India, garden burials of British Quakers in the mid- to late seventeenth century and the Orthodox Jewish tradition of interring a non-embalmed corpse in a shroud or plain wood coffin to honour an interpretation of the biblical motif of 'dust to dust'.[25] Harris concludes that natural burial in America is little more than a return to long tradition with much of what constitutes natural burial once being standard practice in this country, the default, not the exception'.[26] However, a subtle but significant comparative difference in the evolution of the practice lies in America typically using a concrete-reinforced vault and an embalmed corpse.[27] When Ramsey Creek, the first American 'conservation burial ground' opened in 1998, both the location and the mode of burial offered a radical break from Jessica Mitford's renowned 1963 portrayal of the American funeral industry with its proclivity for embalming. In Britain however, embalming is not obligatory practice[28] and, because graves are not constructed as cement-lined vaults they make natural burial less obviously distinct from cemetery or churchyard burial that came before. Developing this perspective, Rumble has previously argued that, in two ways however, natural burial sites are qualitatively distinct from other burial places in contemporary Britain.[29]

First, they have an explicitly dual purpose, both as a place to inter ashes or a corpse, and as a place deemed to contribute to ecological preservation or improvement to be enjoyed by the living. This makes a natural burial site 'unlike a cemetery with its singular mortuary purpose',[30] and in Britain this is encapsulated in some providers' ambitions for making natural burial sites protected ecological places to be managed by environmental or wildlife trusts once burial sites become full. In America, Joe Sehee, Executive Director of the Green Burial Council even wants to use natural burial grounds as a 'fundraising strategy' to purchase and create public open spaces to be enjoyed by the living.[31]

Secondly, beyond a place of interment and ecology, natural burial may be identified as providing a contemporary therapeutic landscape for mourners. Contributing to this quality of place is the fact that, at Barton Glebe, for example, there is minimal visible presence of the dead when compared to an average cemetery. Here, in a sense, the creation of a burial place has not accorded a sovereign status[32] to human beings but, perhaps, to the preservation and flourishing of the natural environment. Some respond in criticism to this configuration of significance arguing that natural burial is a recent cultural development indicative of death denial. For example, in reference to Forever

Fernwood cemetery's green burial section in California has been described as 'only a park' that 'has lost all connection with the personal and cultural memorial function of a cemetery'.[33]

Such criticisms demonstrate that what is at stake here is the perceived cultural function and appearance of places of burial. Forever Fernwood's green burial provision is being evaluated using fixed notions of what a cemetery should do and look like, but do such distinctions and fixed functions of place matter? As Rugg and other historians of cemeteries have so clearly demonstrated, the meanings and purposes of burial places are highly mutable, being subject to the sensibilities and tastes of the living.[34] So, despite the fact that in England the most common mode of disposal is cremation, the informants of the present project tended to see funerals at crematoria as of the one-size-fits-all variety, a factor they thought made for artificiality. But, on the other hand, cemeteries and churchyards are, themselves, sometimes seen as places of neglect and monuments to death. This ever-changing historical trajectory with regard to how places of the dead are valued and therefore used has inevitably meant that for some the recent option of natural burial holds much allure as we shall see in the next chapter. However, it is interesting to note here that even in countries such as the Netherlands, where cemeteries are still perceived as 'dynamic spaces' with grave reuse ensuring that cemeteries are regularly used for interment purposes, some Dutch people are moving away from this mode of burial to choose natural burial and prompts us to ask what factors are motivating these people to do so? Perhaps it rests on one of the distinctions of the *place* of natural burial, in other words, that natural burial grounds tend to prioritize 'nature' above burial and ash scattering; a priority that influences the overall management and long-term objectives of the natural burial ground as well as influencing how people behave within and perceive the natural burial ground.[35]

Defining the place of natural burial: Distinctions and continuity

So, be it in a woodland setting, a former set-aside arable field developed into an overgrown meadow or a copse surrounded by landscape vistas – all encountered when visiting sites around Britain – a defining characteristic is that of seeking to 'naturalize' what is essentially a burial ground. However, these most recent British burial places are not unique in doing this as Tarlow's archaeological research on nineteenth-century British garden cemeteries showed with '[t]he popular appeal' of this type of site lying in its 'naturalistic landscape, less ostentatious memorials and its emphasis on living plants rather than cold architecture'. She argued that these qualities were valued as 'Protestant virtues of simplicity' in which 'nature was a central part of British identity in the nineteenth century'.[36] It would appear that to a large extent nature is still an integral part of the identity of those choosing natural burial, though the emphasis on nature has shifted so that:

> ... engagement with 'nature' from the gradually more distanced perspective of urban living, has resulted in an understanding of the natural world as something from which human beings have become set apart. Thus, when people choose natural burial this reflects a sense of themselves as somehow separated from nature, and a desire to be reconnected with it. This view is likely to be espoused even among those who live and work in a rural location, so revealing its contemporary hegemony.[37]

In the present project it certainly seems as though natural burial appeals as a new option in a mobile society where many may lose a sense of belonging to a specific place while still valuing 'nature'. Here, the much valued aesthetic veneer of a natural landscape with varying degrees of human activity inscribed upon it provides the most persuasive means by which natural burial sites achieve their contemporary dual purpose as burial place and aesthetic place for passers-by, dog-walkers and bereaved visitors.

A naturalized burial place encourages therapeutic moods such as tranquillity and reflection and which reflect historical continuities in society–nature relations where landscapes have been designed for spiritual uplift, therapy and recuperation.[38] Loudon's garden cemetery designs were, for example, believed to foster moral vigour and reflection,[39] as were picturesque parks and gardens of the eighteenth and nineteenth centuries,[40] the American 'rural cemetery' movement,[41] and the pursuit of gardening for leisure or therapy by *all* social classes offering an 'escape' from life's circumstances.[42] Just as British 'garden' cemeteries throughout the 1820s–40s fostered 'the creation of an aesthetic and sentimental landscape of remembering which had particular emotional resonances for the bereaved of the nineteenth century'[43] so our newer 'natural' burial sites also serve to a large extent as twenty-first century therapeutic landscapes for the bereaved.[44] Natural burial grounds inspire bereaved visitors to claim, as one visiting widow expressed it, that natural burial 'touches something in people which they don't know is there'. However, for a number of those interviewed in relation to Barton Glebe, the sites of churchyards, cemeteries and crematoria have come to appear as 'soulless' and, or, 'neglected' places.

> I find seeing a churchyard with a load of gravestones very *depressing*. And they get so neglected. Nobody looks after them. And I think that's

so depressing. I mean, don't get me wrong, I love churches, but outside, when you see all these down and out sort of graves it's depressing. But when you look at Barton Glebe up there, and I remember we went on the open evening there, and we walked around and there was this lovely, lovely, lovely place where somebody had planted their own seeds and it was just all wild flowers. And to me, that's what it *should* look like! And you know, does it really even matter that you haven't got these tomb stones and that, which are really . . . I mean they do fall to pieces! As I say, that to me is back in Victorian times. (A woman who is preregistered at Barton Glebe)

A cemetery would never appeal to me *at all!* It's just . . . it's just . . . well, not *anything*! It's not associated with the church, and it's not associated with anything particularly beautiful really. It's just a lot of grave stones isn't it? But I mean, this tree thing is *lovely*! There's an *atmosphere* when you're there of peace and with trees . . . longevity! (This woman's husband's ashes are interred at Barton Glebe)

It would appear that burial modes prior to natural burial have come for many to represent inanimate landscapes, whereas for those who visit or who have preregistered at Barton Glebe, the place seems animated, the very opposite of a cemetery as a 'monument to death rather than remembrance of the living person', as one grandson said of the place where his grandmother was buried. This comment could imply that some people seeking woodland burial do not want to be part of the detritus of history in old gravestones as a churchyard or cemetery might intimate. Perhaps some people do not see themselves as part of such an order of things, or at least not enough to draw them there when newer options offer more compelling attractions, including the sense of being a 'living memorial' and allowing 'a return to nature'.

Nevertheless we should not forget the socio-historical and psychological contingencies and continuity between natural burial grounds and preceding places for the dead, an issue insightfully commented upon by the priest serving the parish in which Barton Glebe woodland burial ground is located.

In the same way people were buried in churchyards, then in cities churchyards filled up with no land available to expand around the church, so then we get separate cemeteries. Then cemeteries fill up, new technology allows cremation and crematoria, then people begin to feel that cremation is a bit soulless perhaps and then recognise that its environmental impact is very negative. People begin to care about the environment a bit more and as I say, there's a spirituality without particular religious affiliation, which would find a crematorium soulless, so again, alternative burial sites are popping up. So I think they kind of evolve out of each other!

The evolution of places for the dead has meant that, through time, some churchyards, once full or abandoned, are now being retrospectively cultivated as public gardens and wildlife habitats for rare species. Worpole lists some examples: the Begraafplaats Te Vraag in Amsterdam is a nineteenth-century cemetery now maintained as a public garden, while Lambeth churchyard in London and Little St Mary's in Cambridge are also kept as public gardens. In spite of the enduring 'landscape aesthetic of the churchyard'[45] that is deeply embedded in our cultural landscapes for the dead, churchyards are being appropriated for other uses. Furthermore, cemeteries,

> . . . may acquire the characteristics of local parks. The ownership of the
> site may change, and management practice will alter as each generation
> defines its key reasons for seeking to dispose of the dead in a particular
> type of cemetery landscape.[46]

Any definition of natural burial as a place for the dead is, then, inevitably subject to change, but quite what direction the mutability of natural burial sites will take in the future remains to be seen. At present, what is emerging is a view that a natural burial site, located within mature woodland that prohibits memorialization upon graves, constitutes the greatest display of integrity to ecological values and the most authentic kind of natural burial landscape. Despite 'natural burial' as we know it today being, to a certain extent, an 'invented tradition'[47] it would appear that a demonstrably 'natural' landscape constitutes the greatest integrity to the prevailing cultural conceptual expectation of what natural burial grounds should be and look like.

Creating the 'natural'

One significant source of tension or conflict in natural burial provision derives from the diverse expectations and values that are brought to a particular natural burial ground. The tensions between ethics and aesthetics in particular make managing a natural burial site fraught with difficulties, especially with regard to graveside memorials and planting. For a good number of site operators the 'wild' or 'native' is prized above the 'domestic', 'cultivated' and 'non-native' as the extract from one natural burial ground's newsletter illustrates:

> Now that we have completed the clearance of all ornaments and other non-
> permitted items from graves, we must turn our attention more particularly
> to the plants on the site. We have a Wild Flower Guide to indicate what
> is permitted, and we will now be beginning a thorough audit of all plants
> to ensure that what is planted is in keeping with the natural woodland

appearance we are creating, and is in line with the Guide . . . As with the ornament clearance, we do hope you will be understanding if you find that plants are removed from a family grave. It is not a process intended to cause additional grief, but it is intended to ensure that the Rules are properly enforced again for the benefit of all.[48]

However, it is not just natural burial ground operators who have a tendency to prize the 'wild', so do bereaved visitors. Although natural burial ground staff may 'police' graves, visitors to a natural burial ground acknowledge the success or failure of attempts to manage graveside activity as with the woman below, whose mother and sister are interred at a natural burial site.

> It's supposed to be a woodland, you know, you don't want bits of, I mean I look around and look at what people have done and I tut tut to myself sometimes – you know, somebody's planted *quite* inappropriate flowers and I do a little tut because I think *they're* not wild flowers!

When considering the significance of flowers in gift-giving at large Goody claims that 'wild flowers are essentially the play things of children', whereas domesticated flowers are reserved for adults.[49] Here we have a distinction between the wild and the cultivated/domesticated, distinctions that fall under a hierarchy in gift-giving with the most prized being purchased flowers, followed by cut garden flowers and finally, wild flowers.[50] It is interesting, then, that at first glance, natural burial practice sets the 'wild' above both 'garden' or cut flowers indicating a shifting hierarchy as wild flowers become increasingly rare with some even being protected species. However, even if the value status of wild flowers is changing, there will always be those in Britain who feel that wild flowers are simply disrespectful as grave markers to the deceased. Unfortunately however, it is not only flowers but also memorial objects that can cause disputes because of individually held notions of what constitute 'natural' things as this extract from a natural burial site newsletter illustrates:

> . . . Although it is somewhat early to be thinking about Christmas, this is our opportunity to mention the adornment of graves at that time with seasonal decorations . . . Tempting as it may be to bring a little tinsel, balloons, baubles, or even a small tree, they are not appropriate, and will be removed.[51]

As Cowling incisively expressed it, 'ethics and aesthetics are not always reconcilable'[52] in natural burial; an issue that surfaced time and again in natural burial providers', users' and affiliated professionals' comments during Rumble's ethnographic research at Barton Glebe:

> . . . there's a *balance* between *true* woodland burials – people who *want* all that eco – but I think it's half and half because some people *want* it, but then they add on things that are not *compatible* with the eco thing. (Area manager of a funeral company)

> The only *true* woodland site I have seen is [named natural burial site]! And it's a *managed* woodland, so they're looking after the trees as much as they're looking after the graves. And they're *very, very strict* on what you can have there, even in terms of the flowers you can have in the floral tributes. But rightly so, as they're keeping it as a managed woodland. Maybe you can call yourself a woodland burial site if your *vision* is that it'll be a woodland! But I know there are those that *are* woodland sites, those that'll *become* woodland sites and then there are those that I can't actually *ever* imagine being woodland! (A civil celebrant who conducts funerals at natural burial sites)

> There's one or two that have crept in recently [graves that look like managed gardens]. Words will have to be said, but I try to wait a little bit of time and then I will have to write to them or try to contact them and say: *look*, this *isn't* what's done . . . it's not *meant* to be a garden, it's *meant* to be completely natural. . . . I don't let on that there's a period of grace but *I* would not find it easy to immediately pounce on someone as soon as they're mourning the loss of a loved one and say: I'm sorry but you can't do this, this isn't what it's about . . . the odd little bit that appears around an anniversary or birthday, *fine*, so long as it gets cleared away pretty quickly, otherwise my man will remove it. On the whole it's not badly abused: there are some up there who seem to think daffodils are natural, wild flowers! [chuckles] Somehow I'm finding the best way for them to have an accident! [smiles] (Owner of a privately run natural burial site)

These comments demonstrate how the practice of natural burial involves both a conflict over what constitutes the 'natural' and a tension between the anonymity and presence of individual graves; the former is a frequent concern of natural burial site providers and the latter of the bereaved as they make meaning and invest value around an individual grave. Some foresaw this tension when natural burial was still in its infancy in the United Kingdom:

> The idealists of woodland burials have visions of a rural idyll. But the reality of behaviour by the bereaved has not been considered. Numbers will want to mark the grave and even where traditional headstones are banned, grave markers, flower vases and other monuments will appear.[53]

Landscapes are 'self-consciously designed to express the virtues of a particular political or social community'[54] and natural burial grounds are no exception. In designing and establishing natural burial grounds it would, then, seem that the 'authenticity' of each British natural burial site is directly proportional to the perceived 'naturalness' of the site.

> I can *see* the appeal at [named natural burial site] because that seems to me, to be the essence of what a woodland burial is all about: to bury *in* woodland *between* the trees. I can see that. But I don't really see where some of the other sites are actually coming from or what they're trying to achieve! (A civil celebrant)

It would appear that an authentic natural burial ground connotes one in which the natural context is genuine and unadulterated, despite this being an unachievable standard given that, in a technical sense one might argue that the moment nature comes into contact with culture it is no longer natural and unadulterated. Thus, there remains a tension in natural burial grounds in which, to varying degrees the natural element is an artifice. Nevertheless, the degree to which the 'natural' context is manifested is pivotal in creating an authentic place on the one hand or an inauthentic place on the other. The latter is aligned with placelessness[55] derived from 'natural' elements being but superficially or mediocrely manifest in the natural burial ground. In all of this, differences of understanding reflect ongoing social change in Britain involving social class and individual tastes.

Barton Glebe

As for Barton Glebe, the relative success of its woodland burial ground's topography is enshrined in the 'character' of the place derived from an 'aesthetic integrity' that contributes to the landscape's cohesiveness.[56] Aesthetic integrity is enshrined in the Arbory Trust's ambitions to create deciduous woodland comprising native trees, as well as the choice of lodge design and materials selected by the Trust. The lodge was specifically chosen because of its natural materials and 'rustic' look (Figure 2.5).

Rather than providing a shelter and ritual space that was aesthetically more modern, utilitarian or urban for example, the 'rustic' lodge was understood to be more 'in keeping' with the cultivated landscape at Barton Glebe. A 'condition of placefulness' is achieved at Barton Glebe because the architectural and landscape planning of Barton Glebe was consciously informed by the 'specific culture of the region'.[57] This focus upon aesthetic integrity in designing Barton Glebe reflects national British prescriptions and

Figure 2.5 The original, smaller lodge at Barton Glebe
Source: Rumble (2007).

procedures concerning place-making: 'national park regulations . . . confine the use of building materials to those available, and long used, locally'; a practice Porteous contrasts with America's 'bogus assemblages of historic artefacts'.[58] The conflicts over graveside memorials for example, epitomize contested understandings of the authentic and 'bogus' in relation to the material culture of natural burial and its perceived aesthetic integrity in terms of the overall landscape and values invested in the place. Nevertheless, the paradox remains that neither Barton Glebe's landscape nor the 'rustic' wooden lodge are naturally occurring. Both have been created to form something of utility to humans that enshrines particular romantic values. Natural burial grounds inherently epitomize the natural-but-not-quite landscape; for example, partly derived from the bereaved being allowed to plant flowers upon graves at Barton Glebe, yet they have to be ones that would naturally occur. In short, the variety of natural burial sites seen in Britain today is a reflection of the tensions between notions of a cultivated nature and naturally occurring nature and our aspirations to nurture one or the other.

To a certain extent, the illusion of the natural is an integral part of creating a natural burial site, with sites gaining high media profile often being examples of successful illusion-making and 'theme parking',[59] they fulfil people's socioculturally informed expectations of woodland or nature. In this they can be likened to the notion of businesses in 'late capitalism' understood as 'staging experiences' in an 'experience economy'.[60] A few private natural burial companies offering exclusive woodland burial and funeral ceremonies on their sites epitomize how the site of 'consumption, rather than production or exchange' is where money is to be made.[61] By commodfiying 'woodland' and 'experiences' in a Disneyland-like fashion, these companies can charge high fees for their 'natural and more meaningful alternative to traditional burial and cremation'.[62] Natural burial provision therefore, is an example from within the funeral industry of a themed, memorable experience engaging all five senses to be sold in the late capitalist marketplace. It could even be argued that natural burial is an outcome of colonizing our imaginations through 'Disneyfying' the environment.[63]

Natural burial providers can even grade the quality of their theme-park experience by charging different rates for reservations depending on where one is buried in the forest or woodland and the views one is privy to from the particular chosen grave location in the woodland. So place is also very much a commodity in natural burial.[64] It can be designed and produced by 'experts' or professional 'specialists' in order that it may be consumed through market forces; a facet of many places designated as natural burial grounds in England. The success of commodifying woodland or a 'woodland' experience by 'judicious landscape planning'[65] is evident in the fact that a number of funeral professionals spoke of a particular natural burial ground as being *the only true woodland burial site*. Other sites were merely poor imitations of woodland or meadow requiring funeral directors to 'prepare' clients' expectations by warning them that they *need to have vision* in order to avoid disappointment from unmet expectations upon first visiting a natural burial ground.

Managing disappointment

Although some visitors might not discern a difference between Barton Glebe and a churchyard, their landscapes can be markedly different. At anytime of the year a cemetery and/or churchyard always has something to distract a visitor in addition to the natural landscape, usually in the form of headstones, memorabilia, a building and plastic flowers. A natural burial site in winter, by contrast, can be bleak with the seasons marking a barren landscape affording little comfort to the bereaved visitor. Still, sites within existing mature woodland do tend to attract more custom precisely because there is something growing in the landscape all year round. The natural burial sites that have received large financial investment and are located within existing mature woodland tend to offer a stage-managed theme-park experience capable of offering its own form of comfort upon the bereaved all year round. They cultivate a product that meets people's expectations of 'woodland', by being located within mature woodland. Moreover, these sites tend to have facilities and buildings in addition to the place of burial.

By sharp contrast, a field or newly planted woodland, lacking any facilities or buildings, can be extremely barren when exposed by the seasonality of landscape, sometimes being even too much for grieving relatives to bear as they feel heartless and disrespectful in burying someone in a landscape that suggests abandonment or isolation from the living. Quite the opposite is usually true of cemeteries and crematoria which are replete with evidence of human activity so that:

> The tidiness and upkeep of the grounds tacitly signify safety, confidence and support – the landscape demonstrates that both management and mourners are prepared to take care of the dead in respectful ways.[66]

Meanwhile, a funeral director said of the privately owned green burial ground in her town that when it first opened and she took funerals there, she would advise families that *'you've got to have vision, because it was just a field of weeds'*. Other funeral directors and civil celebrants have been equally keen to manage their clients' expectations of woodland or green burial to avoid disappointment or anger on the day of the funeral. Such a management of emotion underlies a great deal of professional work with the bereaved.

'Natural', 'woodland' 'eco' or 'green burials', link idealized visions of nature in many people's minds. The 'green' associated with 'eco' and woodland, as well as the green of nature that waxes and wanes due to the seasons, are expectations held in parallel by those talking about natural burial. Therefore, disappointment and expectation both need to be managed should these expectations not be met. As a result, funeral directors try to avoid disappointment through managing their clients' expectations by advising clients to visit their preferred natural burial sites *before* finalizing funeral plans:

> When I first heard of green burial sites I got a vision in my mind that it's woodlands and lovely plush grass, you think of [named natural burial site], but all we saw when we arrived at this site in, it was just what looked like big mole hills. Apparently what they do when they fill in the graves is that they literally mound them up and put a tree in the centre and as the ground settles it gradually levels out. So now, if somebody comes in and says they want a green burial . . . I always advise them to see the site *first*, rather than to say 'yes, that's what we want', because, you know, whatever you talk about you get a vision in your mind and then when you actually see it up close, it's not like that *at* all! . . . And others come in and say they'd like to be in [named natural burial site] and I'll say: well, have you actually *seen*

it? And they'll say: *no*. And I'll then tell them: well I *suggest* you *do* look at the place *first* to ensure that this is what you actually want to do! So as I say, you're not turning up on the day, you're not thinking: oh blimey! I didn't think it'd be like this! Because it is a bit of a shock isn't it? (An independent funeral director)

It is, perhaps, worth pointing out here that if funeral directors were only motivated by profit, a negative image often ascribed to them, then this funeral director would not be concerned whether his clients liked the natural burial ground or not. However, the success of this funeral director's business demands that he be sensitive and aware of his clients' emotional needs.[67] Having realized that some of his clients are disappointed by the 'reality' encountered encourages them to look at specific sites before settling on the natural option.

Another funeral director quoted below, in speaking about the steps he has taken to avoid disgruntled customers, also demonstrates the importance of the concept of time in natural burial. Initially, there appears to be a cultivation or expectation of an image for a natural burial site to be *'a wonderful woodland where graves are dug between the tree roots'* but over time, acceptance of the 'natural' prevails, in all its seasonality:

> For families that sometimes do come and ask what are their choices and what are the alternatives, I give them the information and tell them that they *really* ought to go and have a look. If it's a very nice brochure, that's all very well and good but they've got to really feel comfortable to go and see how it's set up. And you've got a wonderful contrast because families that are not sure, I tell them to go to [named natural burial site] *and* to [named natural burial site], because some like one and some like the other! [giggles] And it's amazing what different vibes you get and what people think when they come back because they're completely different aren't they? One's already established, there and ready, and the other one's just a complete field and in the wintertime they don't cut the grass or anything and people come back and say: You're right, we're not going there now! And they have completely different thoughts really. [Named natural burial site] is an open field with a little cut path round the edge isn't it? And they don't realise that the concept is then to *plant* the trees and make a *wood*! Which some people like; some people are set against it when they go and look. . . . So it's a kind of Catch 22 at the moment . . .

There is a tendency for people to expect an established forest, but it is only through accumulated burials over time that trees are planted upon graves in some cases, thus it is only over a duration that the concept becomes clearer and visible. As the funeral director suggests, some clients accept nature's seasonality and woodland's different stages of growth, others prefer the cultivation of an image most often met by privately run, well invested natural burial sites. However, even the funeral professionals have been surprised by their own reactions upon visiting natural burial sites. An independent funeral director who has been in the business for 60 years stated that natural burial:

> . . .Wasn't what I was expecting . . . I was a bit . . . not upset . . . a bit . . . not disappointed, I was . . . surprised shall we say. It wasn't what I expected. I expected something that was neater and tidier. . .

People's expectations are partly the result of their own lived experience and cultural familiarity. This funeral director had much experience with cemeteries and churchyards, subsequently he was expecting something 'neater and tidier' because that is what he is used to with regard to the landscape the dead occupy, indicative of his acquired cultural values with regard to where and how the dead are located. The reactions, either by the professionals or anecdotes of their clients' reactions, demonstrate that 'woodland' is a concept replete with cultural expectations making natural burial sites rich in symbolism, partly originating from historical and sociocultural constructions of landscape. These symbolically loaded places are pervaded by life-giving and life-cycle metaphors, quite unlike a crematorium, which is a symbolically neutral or depleted landscape according to many who chose to use Barton Glebe. For example this widower's views on cremation are shared by a number of bereaved people interviewed by Rumble:

> I've got nothing against it [cremation], it's just I've never met anybody who likes going to a crematorium . . . it's *too austere!* . . . and it's *too clinical*. And I've been to a number of funerals and they're all *exactly* the same.

Davies's view that the possibility of removing ashes from crematoria to privately dispose of elsewhere has diverted 'attention from the crematorium and reinforces its role as a transient place of utilitarian necessity'.[68] With increased options it may well be that the attraction of crematoria is diminishing because they are becoming 'non-places'. Davies uses Augé's (1995) term 'non-place' to refer to 'places of transition – places that people pass through but which carry no personal significance for those individuals'.[69] Such places are usually necessary to our lives but lack symbolic depth or enduring meaning, accordingly, some see crematoria as 'a necessity as part of someone's 'journey' but . . . devoid of particular significance'.[70] In considering the spectrum of allurement within crematoria, Davies refers to the hermeneutical analysis of sacred architecture by Lindsay Jones who argues that some architecture, as with art, invites expectations within us; invitations to participate in a building through an 'identificatory pull' or 'allurement' motivated by 'self-reconciliation'[71] that something in a building or place is close to us; has something to do with us.

> Unless this quality of allurement or magnetism or invitation, this so-termed perception of similitude, is present in the architecture in one form or another . . . passers-by will not feel compelled to pause and invest themselves in hermeneutical reflection on that architecture.[72]

A woodland or natural burial ground, like sacred architecture, can inspire visitors' expectations so that they can bring 'their hopes, joys and sorrows'[73] to the site and make connections between their experience and the place itself; investing their expectations in the natural burial ground. The place becomes symbolically loaded, exciting perhaps, and therefore much more significant than a crematorium, unless that is, one's expectations of a natural burial ground are not met in the landscape. Then, people can feel disappointed as discussed above and illustrated below:

> I must say when we first made the arrangements I went a couple of times and then it was a couple of years until my recent visits to [named natural burial site] and when I did go I was disappointed. I thought it looked pretty *scruffy* compared to what I expected. Well, obviously trees take a long time to grow, but it was all sort of rough grass and no sign of real trees. I mean I can see that in the end the trees *will* come and the grass will be in better shape. So, yes, I expect it will improve but there was a time I was rather disappointed about the general way it looked. (A preregistered widower whose wife is interred at Barton Glebe)

Disappointment raises an interesting possibility; perhaps there is a distinction between 'real' allurement when one is confronted with a particular space or building and some 'imagined' allurement? Moreover, initial disappointment when first visiting Barton Glebe, indeed any natural burial site, suggests there is a strong cultural expectation of 'woodland' in Britain, fostered by the cultural and axiomatic allure of trees for example. Certainly, there appears to be an element of romanticism in the cultural allurement of woodland burial (real or imagined) and subsequently woodland and other aspects of 'nature' have a cultivated emotional geography.

Speaking of how landscape is used to evoke particular moods and emotions in relation to cemeteries, the historian, Mark Schantz employs the term 'melancholy pleasure' to describe the intention of reformers behind America's rural cemetery movement in the nineteenth century. These reformers sought to elicit a mood of 'melancholy pleasure' in visitors to their cemeteries by inducing a 'transformation in the hearts of the living'.[74] Melancholy pleasure was 'a disposition to be savored': part 'mystical, emotional and pleasurable' cultivating 'feelings and sentiments' beyond mourners' own horizons 'and more worthy of Christianity'.[75] The moral and emotional imperative behind America's rural cemetery movement in the nineteenth century mirrored the garden cemetery movement in other parts of Europe at the time, as well as the ideas associated with the Scottish botanist and cemetery designer, John Claudius Loudon (1783–1843) in Britain. Moral and emotional transformations in mourners were deemed possible and beneficial through the creation of beautiful landscaping and serenity, far removed from people's experiences of overcrowded churchyards and 'scenes of profane commerce'.[76]

'Nature's' emotional geography

One attitude commonly held by those who choose natural burial is that it will provide a more positive experience for the bereaved if, and when, they visit such places. One local resident who attended a funeral at Barton Glebe said a woodland burial would *definitely* provide a positive experience for the bereaved in her opinion, because:

> You can touch and hear and feel: it's the leaves and the trunks and the shapes and the fact that everything is *alive* and lush and green and to me, that's very spiritual. If you're anxious or worried about something, to go for a walk in a wood is very therapeutic because of that life and the *energy* that that wood gives off: the light, the colours, the smells, the noises . . .

The belief that a walk in a wood is '*very therapeutic*' because it grounds one's emotions, as implied by the lady above, is an example of how a cultural pre-adaptation has fostered the uptake of natural burial in Britain. Cultural associations towards woods, trees and nature are imaginatively appropriated, both implicitly and explicitly, in establishing the value and practice of woodland/natural burial. There is an embedded popular perception of woodland as therapeutic in Britain, with certain aesthetic qualities of nature and landscape being morally conceived as inspiring positive emotions; often deemed 'healthier' and cathartic.[77] Preferences for burial in a natural setting, as opposed to formal, manicured, serried ranks, often encompass an attitude that natural burial enables a catharsis in grief because of a sociocultural assumption that trees, in particular, embody therapeutic value[78] and:

> . . . appear to have personal significance for most social groups in British society . . . Woods and trees are seen as affording particular settings for tranquility and bodily relaxation, where one can escape the perceived

stresses of modern life. Trees remove the presence of modernity, and provide a setting for intimate social relations, for therapy, for play, for fantasy, for revitalization.[79]

This is exemplified in the cultural notion that going for a walk is good for calming the mind, relaxing and aiding meditation and has recently received the attention of evolutionary psychologists keen to demonstrate and measure our connectedness to nature in relation to positive emotional expression.[80] Meanwhile, Rumble's work shows that 'nature' and landscape at large rather than trees in particular were often taken as the prime focus for renewal and therapy by the bereaved, and she sees the fact that the Arbory Trust does not include a tree as part of the grave sale allows that wider natural environment to be drawn upon in the imaginations of users and visitors at Barton Glebe. This may sound paradoxical for 'woodland burial' contexts especially when we hear voices such as that of West saying that: 'It is my experience that where a tree is included as a component of the grave sale, the appeal to grave owners is increased. For many people trees have a romantic connotation.'[81] Familiarity with tree planting, something that became widespread in the later twentieth century context of planting standard roses as memorials in crematoria grounds, has to some extent served to filter out some of the wider features of the plant world, as well as the animal sounds that may frame the human perception of funerary sites.

Emotions and the therapeutic context

What then of the emotions and ideas of grave-related experience, especially in terms of 'therapy'? Milligan argues that the perceived therapeutic value of 'people-landscape transactions' is predicated upon four cultural framings of 'nature' that foster therapeutic value: nature restores, nature provides a site for reflection and diversion, nature facilitates competence building and nature carries symbols that affirm the culture or self.[82] The following comment by a funeral director, who stated that he saw natural burial sites, as opposed to the cemetery provision he was offering, as an empowering experience for the bereaved demonstrates this cultural framing of 'nature' as a source of restoration and reflection:

[Natural burial is] more cost effective for the public, it's kinder. It's the natural choice to me. It's more friendly and kinder. . . . Whereas I class the memorial headstone as tat because it's on that headstone that you get that tat. . . . I just think it's personalisation in your face whereas a woodland burial, I think it's more natural, there's more contentment, and when you visit it's like a wood you visited three or four days past – it's just a continuation! You don't get that same kind of grief element; you don't feel like you're in the same boat as everyone else. It kind of makes you more empowered . . . with a woodland burial you don't have to put your glad rags on to visit: but most of the time you can't anyway, its wellies and boots or whatever! So it actually brings you down to that kind of level of environment whereas here [the city cemetery] everybody puts their own issues on it [death/burial]. I just think it takes away from the cemetery *feel*.

Note the number of positive 'emotion/feeling' words this funeral director uses in relation to natural burial: *contentment*, *kinder*, *friendly* and *empowered* for example, and what is this *cemetery feel* he speaks of? Cemeteries, crematoria and graveyards are more exclusively associated with being places of death where a visitor's purpose often centres upon visiting a grave[83]: to '*hover there and then go*', as a man who desires a woodland burial intimated. Another individual, one whose grandmother is buried at Barton Glebe, echoed this sentiment when describing his mother's visits to his grandfather's cemetery sited grave:

> . . . it's always been about *doing* something. We went to my grandfather's grave and we cleaned the headstone and made sure all the plants were right and that, and then we left. So in some respects it was more a *duty* than a spiritual journey . . .

At a natural burial ground, however:

> . . . if people choose to go back it's a very natural, very *positive* sort of atmosphere. Whereas graveyards, you know, people don't *go* there! It's a separation. It emphasises the separation between life and death, and it emphasises, to me, even more, that we want to sanitize. Whereas for me, death is part of life . . . life comes out of something and goes back into it. It seems to me, of what I've read, that although there is a separation in that it's a designated site, it's *not done* in the same way. I mean, me walking along the road there I just think that there's a field with trees – you know, it's a *part* of nature! Unless you knew it's there, you wouldn't think: 'Oh! There's a graveyard!', whereas you do with a cemetery. So that distinction isn't quite as strong with woodland burial. (A lady who has preregistered for a grave space at a natural burial site)

In this sense then, natural burial offers an alternative to the *cemetery feel*. As numerous interviewees indicated, the primary emotional focus of natural burial sites need not be derived either from the grave or from death, rather from the powerful potential of the natural landscape behind it replete with more positive emotions than they imagined customary places of burial entailed:

> There's a sense of walking in . . . a meadow amongst the trees and the sun's shining – a *pleasantness* of a *place* rather than lines of *hard rock* and stone with different names etched in them. It's just a softer picture to me than a cemetery . . . If you go to a graveyard there is only one purpose for you going to a graveyard, but if you go to a woodland burial site you can walk round and enjoy the flowers, the trees and the birds, and you can go for a walk and you can remember and mull over without necessarily thinking: I'm going to visit the grave of so and so. So if she [his wife] did go there . . . it would be a more positive experience: more of a place just to *be* rather than *tend* a grave and put flowers on it and all that sort of stuff. You know, the focus is very much different that just going to a place and walking around it, which you do when you go on country walks and enjoy the surroundings – you have time to think. If people *were* to visit [his grave] you'd want to have that sort of experience rather than one where they thought they *had* to come: a) to tend a grave and b) that they'd come to that *specific* spot and *hover* there and then go!

This man's perception of going to a cemetery or graveyard with only one purpose is a cultural one whereas Barton Glebe offers him *a softer picture*, not only because of the landscape's 'natural' aesthetic, but because there is some freedom in going to a place where one can just *be* rather than fulfilling sociocultural obligations to *tend a grave and put flowers on it*. Additionally, since the sovereign status in a natural burial ground is often granted to 'nature'[84] this facilitates *a more positive experience* for those visiting because death becomes muted but life does not.

Redefining the boundaries between life and death

Perhaps then, one of the defining characteristics of natural burial grounds is that they help redefine boundaries between life and death.[85] Rumble argued that this is part of the appeal of natural burial grounds; for example, a preregistered woman stated: *I wouldn't want to be part of something that seems to separate life from death and I think cemeteries do that*. Here our earlier concern with the seasons returns, for it is the impact of the changing seasons within the landscape of natural burial grounds that fosters the symbolic connection between mortality and nature expressed within the annual cycle of death and rebirth, decay and renewal.

> [Barton Glebe] is very seasonal. I mean there's another grave of a person I actually knew there who died earlier this year, and when her grave was fresh and new, it was literally *covered* with flowers because it was in the summertime. It was *gorgeous!* But now all those flowers you see have died and there's nothing very much there at all now, so I don't know whether they will also be planting plants that come up every year . . . [slight pause] . . . that's much the best thing to do: not annuals, but perennials. So there's something very . . . speaks very much of life and death in nature, you know, and that's really rather lovely.

The widow quoted above, demonstrates how 'the restorative character of living trees and plants' provides 'a vehicle for transforming the turbulent emotions of loss into a more fixed hope in renewal and regeneration'[86] that can empower the bereaved in coping with a death. The widow is also clearly a keen gardener and it is interesting to note that her observation of the distinction between annuals and perennials itself acts as a motif of existence. Perennials blossom for years while the self-defined annuals have no such longevity. The memory of her husband and her continuing relationship with him is embodied by the perennials she has planted for life and enduring memory. Similarly, one natural burial site administrator reported:

> We get people saying: 'oh! They'd love to be among these trees!' It makes them feel that *life* is continuing and *that* I think is what the *woodland does*: it gives you that feeling of 'it's not ended!' . . . we have such *joy* up there and people say: 'isn't this lovely!' And in summer you'll get a dragonfly just flit past and 'oh! That's my wife!' or 'that was my daughter' . . .

A Baptist minister who is keen to preregister at a natural burial ground also articulated how natural burial landscapes are replete with symbolic motifs of cyclical renewal:

> Death is an inevitable and natural part of life. But we tend to treat it like its unexpected and unfair. So if woodland burial helps to make a connection with nature and the understanding of death's inevitability – the seasons you see in the trees and the leaves falling what have you – if we can connect our own mortality with what we see in nature, then there's a sense that woodland burials can be positive [for mourners].

Rumble has argued for two channels through which the ontological categories of life and death are brought closer together in natural burial grounds: one through the physical and non-human aspects of the place itself and another through human activities and modes of engagement within these places, often deemed therapeutic. We will address both of these channels for redefining the dichotomy of life and death considering how death has, to some extent, been naturalized permitting the activities of the living to come closer to places occupied by the dead. While natural burial grounds relate life and death in increasingly complex ways death seems to be muted as life is emphasized.

The therapeutic natural place

While nature's physicality at Barton Glebe is replete with both life and death motifs, it is the living dynamic that most often predominates for the bereaved and those preregistered for burial there. This reflects something of Davies' idea of a landscape of hope cultivated in the mode of 'ecological hope' underpinning the continuity of identity and memory.[87] That is not to say that for some bereaved visitors their loss is not accentuated by the natural world's vitality nor that the life of the natural world is felt to be more significant than the lost life of someone dear. Nor, indeed, is it to say that people's attachment to Barton Glebe is static or always pleasurable.[88] Nevertheless, as we have demonstrated above, the life-symbolism engendered by the natural world clearly confers a sense of *peace* or *comfort* to visitors.

It is, of course, also the case that churchyards, cemeteries and memorial gardens occupy the natural world, but in them death's presence is visibly marked through erected headstones, tombs and plaques, often in serried ranks.[89] The spatial organization and materiality of these markers are constant reminders of human intervention in demarcating appropriate and separate places for the dead, all apart from the living. Barton Glebe on the other hand, has less conspicuous memorials set in a dynamic seasonal landscape in which anyone is welcome to walk their dog or wander along the paths between the glades. In this sense the landscape could be said to be therapeutic,[90] but only for as long as the landscape exudes vitality and life; there is little of therapeutic value in observing tree saplings withering on their stakes or wild flowers wilting from disease. Observing the vitality of the natural world confers some sense of security that puts visitors at ease and grants a *cosy feeling*; allowing us to speak of Barton Glebe's landscape as therapeutic because it is perceived as comforting.[91]

> I suppose in a sense, what I'd expect is, just very much like in any other quiet place where people can just sit, relax and just be. That it's not out of place. The sort of place where somebody could just take a book, or their sandwiches and just sit down! Not *radically* different from another part of

nature that you were comfortable to just sit and be in. Now, I might be very disappointed! (Though she is preregistered, this woman has never visited Barton Glebe)

Similarly, a woman who is bereaved and preregistered describes Barton Glebe as:

> . . . a very nice, peaceful place, reminiscent of a . . . flowery meadow or woods if you like, where you can be buried peacefully without any sort of adornment. It's just thoroughly peaceful, and to sit there and reflect is . . . something really quite *special* I think. It just gives you a really nice cosy feeling I think. A comfortable place to be!

This woman associates the *peaceful* quality of Barton Glebe as a place where she can *reflect*. Her encounter with the place fosters a shift in her cognitive and sensory perception so that the place has a *special* quality set apart from everyday routines, where she can secure a slower rhythm, stillness and reflect.[92] The value of stillness is something capitalized upon in many domains, not least in the travel industry's advertising of retreats as locales of tranquility and renewal.[93] Renewal is also much in symbolic evidence in the 'natural' world at Barton Glebe. Rumble described how one widow took great comfort from a toad living upon her husband's grave. Other visitors spoke of Barton Glebe as encapsulating life's dynamism, its *holistic rhythm*, human *kinship to the natural world* and how it embraced the *circle of life*, all despite the fact of their grief. This site is therapeutic, then, because its naturalized landscape provides a contemplative environment for mourning that is visibly not a cemetery, but rather a place in which abundant life in the 'natural' world is the main feature, as opposed to memorials to the dead:

> I think it's a question of people wanting a burial but wanting it in a *nicer* environment than a cemetery that's full of stones and hundreds of other people! Very *obviously* a cemetery! Maybe people like the idea that there are graves dotted around amongst trees and you're never *absolutely* sure where a grave is and I think that's part of the appeal *and* the natural surroundings. And actually, it is one of the things I focus upon when I do a woodland burial; we do talk about these beautiful surroundings where the squirrels will play and what have you, because it's part of the *feature* of it I suppose. (A civil celebrant)

Whatever *'feature'* of the living world is used metaphorically within a funeral service, its crucial impact is that the chosen feature be symbolic of the dependency of life and death and their integral place in the world: in the example above playful squirrels in beautiful surroundings achieved this goal. So while mourners feel the loss incurred through a death this context fosters a shift of focus from that death to the living environment and its continuity of life. With that in mind much could be made liturgically of symbolic elements that pervade the natural burial ground itself. A few clergy made similar observations as a result of conducting funeral services at natural burial grounds, but as yet, the Church of England does not have a funeral liturgy explicitly for use at natural burial grounds such as Barton Glebe, represented in Figure 2.6.

One issue arising here concerns what some critics of natural burial have identified as the potential psychological problem of death denial in which death is masked by 'nature'. Critics have argued that death needs to be integrated with life and that this is only possible with death's visible integration in the world of the living, not least through the use of burial markers. On the contrary, the elimination of burial markers in some natural burial grounds is seen as a 'subconscious attempt to deny or exclude death by making it invisible'.[94]

To us, however, Barton Glebe does not deny death, rather, the Arbory Trust has created an alternative time and place where grief may be facilitated through the 'natural' landscape unencumbered by conspicuously marked rows

Figure 2.6 A view from the main pathway in South Glebe
Source: Rumble (April 2009).

of headstones, curb sets or plaques. Although their absence does, admittedly, render the dead more invisible, it also helps convey a sense of location outside of daily life's bureaucracy in a peaceful liberation from fewer 'external intrusions'.[95] This is why we see Barton Glebe as a therapeutic landscape of personal restoration, reflection and hope. The pursuit of therapeutic place or practice in the event of death may, of course, also be found in other cultural practices around the world. The Hadza, for example, conduct their *epeme* dance shortly following a death in an attempt to 'establish and maintain a state of well-being and good order'; a psychological state more valued at the time of death when death threatens to bring chaos.[96] Still, 'therapy' does not imply the absence of all troublesome experience, for while death may not be marked by visible headstones it is evident through the impact of the seasons as we have already observed, and nature's agency can itself be distressing enough for some bereaved visitors, especially when plant growth is seen as stubborn or unwanted in smothering (and so transforming) an attempt to garden or manicure a grave.[97] Take this widow's comment by way of illustration:

> It can be very bleak there in the wintertime. But that's okay I think: it's the seasons, it really reflects the seasons . . . For the first two and a half years he [her deceased husband] was there, I needed to do something. I needed and wanted to make a garden in memory of him, which is why it was such a shock when I went there last November and it was covered with all these bramble things, and I thought: well, it's not what I wanted! But I think my views are gradually changing so that I can see that the seasons are part of life and death; and they're illustrated at Barton Glebe in a beautiful way! . . . [pause] . . . And I don't think I have to do any more . . . [pause] . . . I'm glad I did what I did, but I don't have to try to create something myself, because the place itself does that.

The seasons and nature's unwanted growth, as in these brambles, threaten to mask the identity of the deceased and their locality, often held dear by the recently bereaved. Funeral directors also acknowledge the occasional unsettling impact of the seasons on the bereaved and their expectations of natural burial:

> . . . the winter it's all drab and then there's a change and in the summer and spring it's lifted again: and I think, if you can get that into your mindset, that's what it's about! Whereas, I suppose, for a normal burial, there's more of continuity because it's manicured, it's looked after, you can cheer it up with some flowers on the stone, you can wash the stone, er, but with the woodland, that's the reality![98] And the reality of life is like that: you know, sometimes it's down here, and then it rises up and comes back

down again. It's like a circle, you know, and for some people, that's what they want! But I think the true woodland burial people know that and accept that – they don't question it – it's where people are of two minds and then they have that realisation that 'ooh! That's not quite . . . I was here in June and it was glorious! Birds flying around, and the sun and blue skies' and then you've got a thunder storm, or in autumn when all the leaves are blowing and things are dying, you know, and people 'oh! That's not what I had in mind at all!' And then the thought that they're out there in this bleak land, you know, so, it is difficult for some people. But, you know, once you've made the choice, that's it!

When the 'drab' landscape does elicit strong negative emotions for visitors they often resort to trying to garden the grave; to intervene with 'nature' and produce new life symbolic of continuing memories and the identity of the deceased. As the widow stated above:

For the first two and a half years he was there, *I* needed to *do* something. *I needed* and *wanted* to make a garden in memory of him . . . But I think my views are gradually changing.

This reflection, shared by a number of the bereaved, is not only a reaction to changing emotions elicited by the seasonal changes in landscape but also to emotional changes occurring over time since bereavement, something that is also evident in decreasing frequency of visits to a grave that diminish over time: similarly with the importance of the grave's location and the felt need to garden the grave.[99] This behaviour echoes Robert Hertz's classic observations on the psychological transformation of the bereaved over time paralleling to some degree the transformation of the buried corpse from its society-bound identity to an identity related to some form of afterlife status such as ancestorhood. As for the widow just cited, she is beginning to comprehend the natural burial site as a whole rather than just her husband's grave within it: a psychological transformation reflecting the transformation of the grave. Her husband's imagined corpse seems to be undergoing a change in character as reflected in the widow's changing concept of and relationship to the grave. Initially, the discrete separation of the deceased in his grave was marked by the widow's desire to make a garden of it in memory of him but now a change allows her a broader view of the entire grounds and of the trees growing at Barton Glebe. In more technical terms, bereaved visitors who are focused upon a grave and feel a need to garden it may be identified as of a liminal status as newly bereaved just as the corpse is liminal in the deceased person's transition from 'living' to 'dead'. In this natural burial context that transition as integration into the soil is idiomatically referred to as going 'back to nature'. The symbolic parallels at work here align the deceased's return to nature with the bereaved person's reintegration into society, itself a status reflected in acknowledging the natural burial site as a whole.[100] The psychological transformation in the widow is indicative of the necessity of time to allow her to make the separation between the living and the dead.

> The brute fact of physical death is not enough to consummate death in people's minds: the image of the recently deceased is still part of the system of things of this world, and looses itself from them only gradually by a series of internal partings. We cannot bring ourselves to consider the deceased as dead straight away: he is too much part of our substance, we have put too much of ourselves into him, and participation in the same social life creates ties which are not to be severed in one day.[101]

The therapeutic human place

Just as the significance of a grave and of a person's grief are mutable and changing, so too with the honouring of and engaging with the dead. Here natural burial grounds, as one of the latest disposal innovations to be widely available across Britain, are having an impact upon the rites and attitudes associated with funerals and grave visiting. As one administrator of a natural burial ground explained in an interview:

> I have had people come to me and say: 'Well, they won't let us do that, or we can't do that somewhere. We wanted to go into our local church, but there's not room for me or my husband'. That's very often one of the things. 'They won't let us have music by the grave, they won't let us do this, we can't reserve next to each other' . . . I've been to friend's funerals and they're just so soulless and morose and awful, and I'm not exaggerating this, but a burial up there [the woodland burial ground] isn't! It isn't, and I can't put my finger on why it isn't. I think it's because people are having what they want. I think that's what it is! People are able to do what they want to do. And they don't feel inhibited there, whereas in a graveyard they can. Certainly, 'oh! I can't walk on that grave there!' Those taboos, whereas walking through there [the natural burial ground] you don't actually feel like you're walking through a graveyard, you're walking through a forest or a wood. A wood! And I think it's all those little things that put people more at ease and therefore give them, they go back and have picnics up there! On people's birthdays families have gone up there and had a picnic with the children in the summer and . . . [slight pause] . . . would you do that in a graveyard or in a cemetery? Probably not, but you can up there.

The suggestion that people would not ordinarily picnic in a cemetery but that it is somehow facilitated and acceptable in natural burial sites is not simply a service provider's rhetorical advocacy for natural burial. Bereaved visitors to Barton Glebe have also made similar comments in suggesting that there is less inhibition and greater latitude for individual expressions of grief as this widow explained:

> I used to go and lie where my grave is next to [my husband] and I'd take a sandwich quite often actually, but I don't do it now. There's a little shop in Barton and they do take-away coffee and I sometimes used to go early in the morning on my bicycle and buy a croissant or something and they do take-away coffee, so if you're very careful you can balance it in your bicycle basket and I'd just go and sit and have my coffee and croissant next to [his] grave. Or I'd take a sandwich out and just go and lie there and read! If there's somebody else around I don't do it, but most of the time there isn't somebody around, so, you know, if it's a nice day I just take a sandwich out there. It was mostly in the first year. I don't do it so much now. I only did it once or twice last year. But actually, it is a place that I love! I used to lie down where I'm going to be buried and I'd be thinking: Gosh! This is where I'll be!

Another widow describes how frivolity also has a place at Barton Glebe.

> I've taken my grandchildren over there and they just run around and create mayhem and they don't know what it means but they talk about it and say 'this is granddad's place' and I think that's great! I mean, that was the whole idea of what it's all about.

These comments emphasize how Barton Glebe is as much about informality as it is about environmentally sensitive practices, with the absence of architectural and traditional constraints creating a less controlled environment that fosters informal behaviour; a widow can take a sandwich and read or lie beside her husband's grave while children can run around and 'create mayhem'.[102] Just as the architecture of crematoria 'allowed a broad band of cultural commitments to find expression in their own decade or stylistic period and, in so doing, to make some firm assertion on the nature of life and death in ways that have not been determined by the direct patronage of churches',[103] so we now find the same applying to natural burial grounds.

Natural burial grounds offer individuals in Britain 'far greater choice, first about how they might deal with the deceased and secondly, about the style of burial landscape within which they and the deceased can be accommodated'.[104] In particular, Barton Glebe seems to enhance options for public and private rituals and grant greater freedom in visiting behaviour with the diminishing visibility of graves creating opportunities for this when compared with the image of municipal cemeteries:

> . . . in a cemetery you're invariably being buried *so* close to the next person that we're all standing on someone else's grave and people find that quite difficult sometimes . . . I always think that cemeteries are made up of individual little beds, whereas in a green burial site there's so much room between them [the graves] and one could just go and sit on the *grass* next to mum there and be able to *feel* close. And I actually think people go more to visit at a green burial site than they would do in a churchyard. (Funeral director)

Perhaps the reason for a higher frequency of visits is because a green burial site is not seen as such a distressing place nor, indeed, as a chore?

> You know, I went to [named natural burial ground] and I thought: this is *perfect*: bluebell woods, the RSPB are there and there were kids racing about looking for Easter eggs. You know, it's a place you want to go! You don't think: "Oh gosh! I better go and clip round the grave and lay some flowers": it's not a *chore*, it's actually somewhere that you want to go. (Founder of an eco-coffin company)

> I've also been up to [named natural burial ground] with my husband on a day I wasn't working and just walked around the grounds because they're so beautiful and I've seen families just sitting at graves having a picnic! And I just think there's something very special about that. You know, that continuity of life and that people can feel comfortable to go into a cemetery and have a picnic with their relatives; how beautiful, and you never see that at municipal cemeteries! (Civil celebrant)

For those who have attended or anticipate attending a natural burial ground one commonly voiced view is that the funeral is more relaxed for mourners:

> I think it [a woodland burial site] allows your emotions to be played out much more naturally than in a crematorium or in a church . . . [slight pause] . . . I think there would be less freedom for you to think and reflect at a crematorium and churchyard – it's a more controlling environment than I would imagine at a woodland burial site. I mean some people like the control as it helps them cope and get through it – from the moment they get there to the moment its finished everything is organised, and they just have to do very little. And others might find the woodland burial

approach – which I think does give you more freedom and flexibility and creativity – might be harder for some people. (Local resident who attended a funeral at Barton Glebe)

I think it's easier for people to grieve in that sort of context [natural burial ground] than in a crematorium . . . I think it makes death a much more natural thing, you know part of the natural process. (A preregistered woman)

For those who preside over funerals at natural burial grounds it is commonly noted that the timekeeping is more relaxed:

. . . people stay longer there than they do at a normal cemetery – well obviously at the crematorium you've got to get out because you're on a time limit; it's a sausage-making mentality! [giggles] You know, you're always watching the clock when you're in a crematorium, but I was amazed (it wasn't a particularly sunny day or hot, but it wasn't wet) we stood there absolutely for *ages* afterwards. We stood there probably for half an hour talking and chatting! (A civil celebrant who conducts funerals at natural burial grounds)

. . . when we have a funeral up there – a burial or a funeral – people stay for ages! (A woodland burial site administrator)

I think people felt a little more comfortable lingering afterwards; after I'd pronounced the blessings and the final words. Maybe because it's an open space: there's more of a chance to just pause and take breath after the funeral has finished, but a churchyard is a bit crowded and stepping on other people's graves. I mean, I think there was a slightly more relaxed atmosphere afterwards at Barton. (Anglican curate who has conducted funerals at Barton Glebe)

There was no hurry. 'cos normally when you go to a crematorium you've only got half an hour . . . but at [a natural burial site] nothing was hurried . . . There was *no* hurry. We weren't timed or anything like that . . . everyone just lingered on you know. In fact, it took us a whole day and it was really, really lovely! . . . there wasn't any hurry – there was no time factor coming into it, which was good . . . 'Cos as I say, if you go to the crematorium you can't always do what you want to do in half an hour. (An independent funeral director)

Time appears to be a crucial factor that enhances the public and the funeral professionals support for natural burial because, it would appear that a funeral at a natural burial ground is deemed to be more relaxed because there are no time restraints for the mourners or the funeral director; subsequently funerals can take an entire day rather than the allocated time-slot at a crematorium or church for example. Moreover, repeated suggestions that people 'stay longer' or 'linger' at the graveside in a natural burial ground suggests a relaxed atmosphere and more positive mood than is customarily expected at a funeral. This quality is valued by those who support natural burial, as a woman who has preregistered for a grave space at Barton Glebe demonstrates by comparing crematoria and woodland burial sites:

> I mean it's a soulless place! [a crematorium] It's the sort of place where you feel you can't chat, you can't relax. Again, this difference: You know people are quiet, in the wrong sense of being quiet. Whereas I hope it would be very natural just to be yourself when you're going to a woodland burial and the funeral.

The association of a natural burial ground with informal behaviour and feeling comfortable serves to bolster the allure of natural burial sites as people are put more at ease and this aids the creation of a therapeutic environment. By creating a place for behaviour that is sometimes far from sombre, life is once again reaffirmed and hope permeates many narrative vignettes of mourners' grave visits to Barton Glebe. Here again we learn how the geographical proximity of the dead with the living in a place that does not discourage the activities of the living such as dog-walking, reading, picnics and child's play, and in a landscape and soundscape that accentuates the natural world, has perhaps brought the conceptual categories of life and death closer together. It has certainly made the distinction between them more ambiguous in this latest place of burial and, in doing so, the designation and function of burial places are being gradually contested and redefined. It would appear for example, that natural burial grounds often have a utility beyond that of burial: some are investments in social capital or enterprises, others permit the grazing of livestock in the burial ground and others intend to generate revenue from coppicing trees in the future.[105] Moreover, natural burial grounds demonstrate that the living are still not willing to get too close to death. Rather than 'naturally' leaving a corpse out in the open to decompose at the whims of the elements and animal kingdom, a corpse is still interred and so rendered invisible, so that the living can return to the burial ground to sit or walk a few meters from corpses residing below ground. So although we observe that the activities of the living and the place of the dead are brought closer together in natural burial grounds, especially in opposition to cemeteries, the living still maintain a distance from the dead by rendering them more invisible in these naturalized burial grounds. However, by making the dead more invisible via the absence of headstones or grave markers, the options for what can be done, said and felt in natural burial grounds increases, as funerals and grave visiting become more aligned with celebrating life, and therefore, less restricted or bounded by duty or etiquette.

The array of landscapes, management practices, visiting behaviours and funeral forms found at natural burial grounds is fostered by a bewildering array of social, 'spiritual' or religious, ecological, consumer and ideological concerns that underlie the motivation either to set up a natural burial site or to choose one in the event of death. The following chapter therefore, attempts to identify the range of values that prompt a person to choose natural burial as opposed to more traditional disposal options currently offered in Britain.

3

Options and motivations: What people say

Chapter 1 drew attention to 'choice' as a widespread contemporary motif much advocated by politicians for healthcare and education and much advertised commercially for body-care, pleasure and luxury. In the light of the previous chapter's material on Barton Glebe's natural burial site, this chapter will not only highlight choice in the funeral options available to people but also highlight the range of motives and factors that lead them to choose natural burial for themselves or their relatives. Among those factors we will, for example, encounter the influence of the internet upon the wider, non-professional public.

Once more, ethnographic and interview materials play a significant part in allowing us to identify recurring categories of values underlying people's rationale for supporting natural burial in general and Barton Glebe's provision in particular. Environmental, romantic, family, aesthetic, consumer and religious–spiritual values are all evident, even though no two people will share all of them.[1] Indeed, not only is there no single 'burial culture' in Britain, as the previous chapter made clear, but the development from the tradition of church-linked burial into the innovations of civic cemeteries in the mid-nineteenth century and cremation in the late nineteenth century and onto the natural burial in the late twentieth century have also provided opportunity for further, and as yet, experimental options. Processes such as the freeze-drying and composting of corpses or alkaline dissolving of the corpse are currently advertised commercially as Promession and Resomation respectively.[2] Though each is a relatively odd term, as neologisms they seem to take 'cremation' rather than natural burial as their model while, as technical processes, they also resemble cremation in utilizing engineering technology rather than the more hands-on means of burial. However, any serious analysis of these innovations lies beyond the scope of our present study.

Diversity and choice in the funeral industry

It is against this background fact of there being no single 'burial culture' in the United Kingdom that the online advocacy of natural burial by consumer organizations such as the NDC, Cowling's *Good Funeral Guide* blog, the journalism of Harris and the publicity by writers such as Beal from within the British and American natural burial industry comes into its own.[3] Facebook lists two or three natural burial advocacy groups,[4] while YouTube is often used to disseminate short videos and films made by those in the alternative funeral industry. Eco-coffin suppliers, owners of privately run natural burial sites and a good number of privately owned natural burial providers have Twitter accounts that allow them to self-publicize their activities and keep the public informed of the latest developments and issues in the funeral industry. So although 'people seldom' choose to be buried in ways that are 'completely culturally unfamiliar',[5] it seems that many, especially Americans and Britons, are using the internet and social media to personalize existing funeral norms through funeral choices that reflect the lifestyle of the deceased or the bereaved consumer and are consistent with their values.[6]

Moreover, alternative funeral providers and consumer advocacy groups are shaping natural burial in much the same way that consumer demand, organic farmers and food producers have changed the agricultural industry in recent decades.[7] Those in the natural death movement who advocate the use of 'eco-coffins' have, for example, fostered a revival in small businesses offering hand-woven willow or wicker containers. A prime example is that of the family-owned Somerset Willow Company in England that offers hand-woven, home-grown willow coffins.[8] There is a burgeoning range of 'natural' materials replacing more 'traditional' materials for funerals with today's funeral directors and independent suppliers offering coffins, urns and shrouds made, for example, from organic cotton, wool, hemp, silk, water hyacinth, willow, bamboo and jute.

As already intimated, the impact of the internet is also considerable not only for the bereaved responsible for organizing a funeral but also for individuals pre-planning their own future funeral. These people can now research their funerary options and even buy coffins directly from the supplier or producer without ever needing to approach a funeral director or funeral home. Additionally, in the 'green' funerals sector, small businesses such as the Somerset Willow Company are able to move into the funeral industry as new suppliers through the public presence offered by the internet. The traditional monopoly held by funeral directors and 'traditional' funeral suppliers and professionals is, to a large extent, challenged by the natural death movement and by internet possibilities. Indeed, the 'green' funeral sector offers far more sophisticated advertising than the 'traditional' funeral industry.[9] Natural burial providers also take their advertising into non-traditional industry outlets such as country shows and 'green' exhibitions, with many of the providers' websites including extensive online 'know-how' literature and self-help guides. All this enhances the general public's knowledge of options concerning death and funerals as well as creating opportunities for a new breed of cemetery operator:

> . . . inadvertently, the natural burial movement has opened the door to new operators including charities and not-for-profit groups . . . whose motivation for providing burial space may be very different from the Local Authority or Church. These providers bring with them different motivations and relationships with the landscape which may or may not be informed or confined by a working knowledge of the cemetery or professional experience of caring for the deceased and bereaved people.[10]

These new burial-space operators, with their investment in offering natural burial provision across the United Kingdom have, inadvertently perhaps, created a commercial opportunity for individualism and creativity in the secular and/or 'green' funeral industry, for example Green Fuse or Urbi et Orbi.[11] Funeral directors, who are also civil celebrants and/or natural burial providers and those who choose to train as civil celebrants, often bring to their training prior knowledge from a diversity of careers. This cumulative repertoire fosters ritual innovation, culminating in a plethora of funerary-related ritual services that can be marketed as bespoke events.[12] Perhaps this trend is partly fostered by the influence of the New Age, which uses mainstream funeral rites to validate New Age ideas and redirect the New Age towards social activities. A prime example of this is the recent, though still numerically very small, creation of 'Soul Midwives', non-medical companions to the dying who reckon to use a knowledge of the dying process (physical, emotional and spiritual) to bring relief from fear and suffering and to ease the passage caused by factors such as pain, distress and unresolved emotional issues. The initial natural burial and soul midwifery advocates, as to some degree also with the more established champions of palliative care, share the desire to de-medicalize death and instigate a more, as they see it, compassionate, authentic approach to death and disposal. It is at the point where palliative care, the hospice movement, New Age ideas and natural burial provision meet that a potentially rich and diverse array of bespoke, independent ritual specialist and funeral services have arisen. Again, the internet has largely enabled these recent funeral related services and specialisms to gain some credibility, public demand and media coverage, as well as providing a commercially viable business or sustainable income for someone who sets up a new independent service. This situation is, however, fraught with potential difficulties at the point where qualified professionalism, especially within the British National Health Service, meets some formally unqualified individuals who may be driven by their own bereavement experiences to wish to help others. However, these critically significant issues lie beyond the scope of this present study whose concern lies less with the motivation of natural burial providers and more with the motivations of consumers. To these issues we now devote the remainder of this chapter.

Environmental values

Environmental values offer an immediate starting point given that, as Peter Owen Jones, the clerical pioneer behind the Arbory Trust's woodland burial site, expressed it, 'environmental issues have captured the imagination more persuasively than eschatology': indeed, he went further to criticize the church for being 'predominantly disengaged from these issues.[13] If the church was slow to appreciate the importance of environmental issues many others were not, especially those who saw a commercial advantage in linking environmentalism with human needs, including the anticipation of death and the need to deal with the dead. It was against that background that this new 'product', natural burial, came to be presented as a consumer 'choice' motivated by newly emphasized ecological concerns.[14] Though we will return to these issues in Chapter 4 our immediate interest lies neither with analysing the 'green' merits of natural burial nor with the Church of England's provision as such, but with those who specifically choose to utilize natural burial because of environmental values.[15]

Reforestation and nature conservation

The explicit articulation of the perceived dual purpose of Barton Glebe as a place to bury the dead and conserve 'biodiversity' demonstrates how natural burial incorporates social and scientific agendas.[16] The Forestry Commission Advisor to the Arbory Trust said that, '[R]ight from the outset the concept was to have it good for wildlife as well as good for people'.

Natural burial grounds are widely perceived to be of benefit both to the human and natural world, an outlook existing within a cultural milieu where a concurrent belief in scarce resources has led to them attaining an intrinsic value that then creates or drives new cultural practices and value systems. For example, one reason that great value and public spending has been invested in initiatives to reforest parts of Britain with native deciduous woodland is because of a belief that Britain inherited a post-industrial deforestation legacy. Natural burial is tied to this legacy because natural burial was originally 'seen as an opportunity to recreate regionally appropriate native woodland that would enhance the environment and local identity.'[17] This would, then, be a means of addressing concerns over the United Kingdom's sparse native woodland cover. Similarly, the cultural value placed upon 'wilderness' increased in Europe at the end of the twentieth and beginning of the twenty-first century, and did so precisely because 'wilderness' has disappeared as a geographical and material phenomenon.[18] Perhaps inevitably then, those natural burial grounds that involve planting native trees to nurture new woodland act as a conduit for both stalling the disappearance of 'wilderness' and 'woodland' as well as for eco-political agendas driven by deforestation concerns.

The environmental preservation or enhancement possibilities presented by natural burial grounds are perhaps one reason why local authorities were keen to support this provision because it offered implementation evidence of 'sustainable' development in accordance with Local Agenda 21.[19] Indeed, the perceived fostering of natural habitats for local flora and fauna is advanced by site providers keen to advertise their environmental credentials as a reason why people should utilize natural burial provision. One large commercial site actively encourages educational nature-days for children and furnishes extensive lists of its biodiversity activities on its website to support the image of an environmentally friendly mode of burial that fosters biodiversity programmes and protects local habitats.[20]

'Green' rhetoric is, perhaps, most explicit in the advertising of natural burial sites and aligned products such as biodegradable coffins and caskets. For the majority of those interviewed, environmental references were more likely to surface in romantic values expressing 'a return to nature' or 'giving something back', albeit with a few notable exceptions. David, for example, has a friend interred at Barton Glebe and has preregistered himself. He describes himself as being 'pretty green without being fanatical about it'.

> I don't like PC greenness and so on, but I do like to be green. I don't like wasting fuel. I don't like polluting things. And the idea of woodland being preserved and with graves in it seemed like a very good thing . . . a few woodlands and things are not *bad*. I mean England hardly has any now apart from the New Midland wood which they're now putting up. You know, it's a good thing to have woodlands around for all sorts of reasons.

David makes a connection between natural burial and opportunities for reforestation, anticipating that by being buried at a natural burial site he is also preserving it. He does not perceive his decomposing corpse to be a source of woodland pollution yet, interestingly, this was one reason why the Forestry Commission Advisor opted not to bury people among trees but to develop the glade format at Barton Glebe. Nevertheless, it is not only corpses that are perceived by some to be sources of pollution: cremation, too, has come to attract some negative appraisal which champions of natural burial have been quick to highlight.

Reduced pollution and energy consumption

I had always thought cremation would be what I want. But gradually as the years went by . . . I started thinking about cremation! All this *pollution*: the wood, the coffin, it's all just burnt and added to the toxic waste whatever, not quite, but you know what I mean. (A preregistered woman)

This woman, who had preregistered for burial at a natural burial site, was clear that cremation represents 'all this pollution' and that for her the products of cremation mark a toxic body more than a sacred body. For her, having a natural burial avoids creating 'toxic waste' and allows the body to remain sacred. However, it is not only those choosing natural burial who articulate concerns about the toxicity of the cremation process,[21] for the Government has also implemented nationwide regulations for crematoria through the introduction of the Environmental Protection Act 1990 and Integrated Pollution Prevention and Control (IPPC) measures adopted under the Pollution Prevention and Control Act 1999 subject to European Law.[22] Concerns regarding an activity's impact upon the environment have filtered down from government legislation to individual consciousness in daily life, as the Forestry Commission Advisor to the Arbory Trust indicates:

. . . you know, I like to think that my wife would come and walk the dog in here [Barton Glebe] . . . much better than traditional town cemeteries and of course most of the rural churchyards are full up nowadays, so yeah, it's all about that getting back to nature experience and the fact that your final impact is lessened and we all think about our carbon footprint nowadays . . .

Government initiatives for lowering carbon footprints have also penetrated the wider funeral industry with the introduction of mercury abatement initiatives for crematoria. Highlighting the airborne emissions from crematoria is capitalized upon in advertising for seemingly 'greener' practices and consumables from within the funeral industry. 'Let your last footprint be a green one'[TM23] is a salient example of how advertising from within the 'green' sector of the funeral industry takes the preoccupation with carbon footprints to the grave in order to sell a product.

The pioneer of natural burial in the United Kingdom, Ken West, writes retrospectively that:

> When I first introduced the concept of woodland burial in Cumbria in 1999 [sic], global warming and carbon footprints had yet to be recognised . . . As woodland burial evolved to become natural burial, being buried under a tree or wildflowers became, for some, a personal statement in support of the environment and their opposition to the problems of conventional burial and cremation.[24]

Ken West's original idea for natural burial was predicated upon a pragmatic decision to create an 'alternative' in disposal options for people in his own area in the north-west of England. Over time, however, natural burial has developed a sales pitch within the 'green' funeral industry that focuses upon the ideology of ecological sustainability culminating in a debate over the relative 'green' merits of various company products and disposal practices. One result of this is that many natural burial providers come to oppose cremation and other burial provision.[25]

One eco-coffin provider invested in research in order to claim on the company homepage that 'our coffins use less energy at crematoria',[26] while a natural burial provider attracts custom through an interactive 'Essential Guide to Green Funerals' website.[27] Similarly, Green Fuse contemporary funerals are members of the Association of Green Funeral Directors and publish '10 tips for a green funeral' that encourage potential clients to, 'make a carbon offset from your estate', 'avoid chipboard veneer coffins' and 'choose burial rather than cremation'.[28] The Association of Green Funeral Directors itself fosters competition among its members with regard to their 'greenness', as well as directing the public towards those funeral directors who are credited with being the most environmentally caring and aware. In America, the Natural Burial Co-operative's homepage has links entitled 'the truth about conventional funerals' and 'incineration/cremation', outlining the negative aspects of formaldehyde used in embalming and the consumption of non-renewable fossil fuels in cremation, as well as listing the perceived detrimental airborne emissions of cremation upon the environment.[29] The Natural Burial Co-operative, the American online Centre for Natural Burial, claims that 'the high heat of cremation converts our body's nutrients into air pollution' and in its preference for natural burial suggests that 'perhaps a molecule from your body will end up in a berry that a bird eats'.[30] Here, then, commercial interests attempt to convince and invite us to 'use your funeral as a conservation tool' with no mention of the religious authorities that have for centuries provided the framework through which death and disposal are managed, understood and practised.[31]

However, the environmental values of those choosing natural burial provision, as opposed to those commercially providing it, are frequently more allied with romantic values and a certain sense of 'integrity' and 'authenticity' existing between this mode of burial and their ordinary attitudes to life and afterlife.[32] Natural burial then, encapsulates how typically,

> Environmentally beneficial actions may also follow from non-environmental concerns, such as a desire to save money, confirm a sense of personal competence, or preserve time for social relationships.[33]

There is, then, a complexity surrounding the uptake of natural burial with some people appreciating its perceived environmental benefits and many others seeing in it a means of expressing significant social relationships, a desire to save money and even the opportunity to become a source of new life. It is to these more intangible, relational motivations that we now turn, beginning with the idea of romantic values.

Romantic values

When alluding to the influence of romantic values behind the appeal of natural burial in Britain we are thinking more of a particular worldview than of any specific historical period. Here Veldman's historical critique of a post-1945 'greening of Britain' is particularly insightful in arguing both that the early Green movement was an example of a romantic protest against post-war affluence, and that romantic values are often central to British middle-class identity.

> The romantic tradition supplied these protestors with the concepts and criteria they needed; its long history of suspicion of the scientific method, revulsion against the social and cultural by-products of industrialization, and effort to restore humanity's links with the natural world proved easily adaptable for the fight against technology and technocracy.[34]

Though traces of this romantic, middle-class related, tradition resurfaces in the idioms and rhetoric currently used by many speaking of natural burial it is likely that as natural burial gains popularity it will encompass a wider range of people from various classes and ethnicity so that the currently embedded values of anti-materialism and a desire to restore moral vigour and authenticity are likely to change. Although some recent research indicates that those choosing the highly specific forms of private land or garden burial are 'middle or upper class' the predominant socio-economic class and ethnicity of natural burial users in Britain remains largely inconclusive.[35]

Irrespective of socio-economic class, another pertinent conclusion drawn by Veldman is that the 'romantic critique' of contemporary Britain, which offers 'continuing vitality . . . amidst changing economic, social and cultural conditions',[36] appears all too evident in contemporary British death rites such as 'garden burial' and natural burial. A slightly different angle is evident in Beck's analysis of Germany's ecological protest. Beck's analysis saw advanced industrial society as fostering a yearning and search for its antithesis, with 'nature' becoming 'the bolt-hole of anti-modernism, keeping open to its dissidents (those weary of modernism and convinced anti-modernists alike) the option of modernism as a variant of itself'.[37] In the context of natural burial, one man's comment that woodland burial 'is about as far away from the industrialisation of death as you can get', resonates both with Veldman's identification of romantic values and with Beck's quest for the antithesis of modernity. So, too, with another widower's opinion that natural burial grounds have 'a greater pastoral, naturalistic element to them'.

Where, only a century ago, modernity, industrialization and the age of progress furnished a source of moral vigour and enlightenment for elites, today those with romantic values see in modernity all but sources of erosion. Consider the changing associations with Victorian cemeteries for example; for some, what were originally landscape designed to inspire reflection and encourage recreation[38] are now associated with dilapidated, neglected modernist false hopes. This is a cultural perception that the NDC and some natural burial ground providers have been quick to draw upon for by highlighting that with the passage of time there is a shift from what were once well-managed cemeteries into a wasteland of neglect that reflects in its decay 'our own transience'.[39] By contrast, a natural burial site is presented as a landscape abundant with growth that promises continuity, renewal and, ultimately, symbolic immortality.[40] Where once Victorian values stood proudly inscribed in stone they now topple in neglected and overgrown cemeteries where the passage of time not only reveals changes in the landscape but also in values.

Romanticism first influenced death narratives in the nineteenth century, especially when focusing upon ruins and nature, much as with the advertising used by some natural burial providers. The grave memorials of the nineteenth century began to depict motifs that emphasized nature's regenerative, transcendent and cyclical qualities.[41] These notions constitute a cultural legacy still apparent in natural burial's allure in Britain today,[42] despite the fact that natural burial does not incorporate the use of stone headstones. This cultural legacy is preserved by an attitude that encapsulates something of the 'romantic Rousseauian nature symbolism adapted to an English love of deciduous trees'.[43]

Simplicity, no frills and back to nature

While Veldman identified anti-materialism as an aspect of a romantic critique Rumble saw it exemplified in the 'no fuss, simplicity' ethos and appeal of natural burial and its aligned preferences for eco-coffins.[44] Peter Jupp, for his part, offers another interpretation of the 'no fuss' idiom when referring to Woodburn's anthropological fieldwork among the Hazda:

> . . . when death involves major social readjustments and the risk of conflict and disorder, death beliefs and practices will be more elaborate and more ritualized than where such adjustments involve no reallocation of authority or of assets but are largely a matter of personal feelings.[45]

Jupp, then, sees the modest procedures and requests for simple funerals in contemporary Britain as indicative of the fact that 'death typically takes place in retirement and old age'.[46] While this is an astute observation it remains partial, for other cultural ideas also inform people's preferences for modest funerals. Take Janet for example, whose preference for a modest funeral is also connected to a moral judgement about the value of money. She has preregistered for a grave space at Barton Glebe and alludes to a belief in an existence where money is deemed to have little value, for money is not her 'priority' in life and, in moral terms, neither should it be for society.

> You know, I'd go for a cardboard coffin because I think that it's eco-friendly because you're not cutting down trees and that sort of thing.[47] I also think, on one level . . . like everything else . . . celebrating important moments in our life has become extortionately expensive! And to me, these things are part of natural life, so to me, it's about simplicity. I don't think that's got to do with money. We need money to live, I'm not saying we don't, but it's not my priority in life. I don't think that it should be a priority of our society and we need to get back to a simple way of living and being that resonates with the whole of creation. And I think, that does it [woodland burial] – to a certain extent.

Janet's sentiment resonates deeply with romantic critiques of industrialization, capitalism and mass production, all of which are understood to oppose and threaten moral values in romantic discourse and thus threaten those livelihoods and identities constructed within and through romantic thought. By avoiding excesses of commodification by choosing simplicity for her burial, she is consciously attempting to restore or further relations between herself and the whole of creation, as well as with her immediate environment.[48] Her comment also suggests a sense of belonging that extends to 'society' and 'nature' so that, rather than perceiving her own identity through religion, community, profession and class, she locates her belonging within the whole of creation.[49] Such an identity of belonging is integral to the romantic notion of returning to nature. Indeed, those familiar with or considering natural burial often say they like the idea of being in nature or put back to nature as with this lady who is considering preregistering at Barton Glebe:

> Well, I just think it's natural that you go back to the earth. It's how things are: everything is born, lives, dies and they go back to nature. It's like in India, you know, where you scatter your ashes on the Ganges – you just go down the Ganges.

Similarly, a funeral director who is also a self-employed civil celebrant articulated this sentiment of an inevitable but harmonious union between humans and the earth:

> There are so many people conscious of ecology these days. They quite like the idea of becoming part of nature again. Amazingly it's not just young people; it's people you know in their 80s and 90s who feel like that . . . But what a wonderful thing! You've become part of the earth that's sustained you. That's a lovely thing. And you cost the ecology of the world very little.

To become 'part of the earth that's sustained you' appeals to many engaged with natural burial. Romantic notions of human or society's interconnectedness with nature and cycles of life are implicit in desires to be 'blended back to nature' and choosing a mode of burial that represents 'just going and becoming part of the earth'. In theoretical terms it could be argued that these sentiments echo Freud's principle of a forceful death drive towards dissolution and dissociation; from life back to the inanimate state that he described as part of the 'ego-instincts'.[50] One preregistered client of Barton Glebe expressed such a thought when saying, 'We will all die, we are all buried. It's part of what life is. You know, we go back to what we were.' One Founder Trustee of the Arbory Trust articulated similar ideas:

> I have no empathy with regimented cemeteries . . . or burning or cremation and having your ashes dissipated somewhere . . . like your own back garden. That doesn't really appeal to me. I think I would probably be blended back to nature. If I had my choice I think I'd be staked

out naked and be stripped bare to my bones by birds of prey and that sort of thing but unfortunately that's illegal! So I think I'd just like to be buried in a woodland setting and just blend back with nature.

Or, as this sentiment was expressed by one Humanist celebrant,

I think also, people would describe it [natural burial] as minimum fuss, just something simple: the idea of just going and becoming part of the earth, and there's no marker – nothing to show where you've been. It's kind of slipping away quietly without making a fuss.

This appeal of 'becoming part of the earth' suggests a desire for 'slipping away quietly' from the social world in order to seek 'authenticity' without the fuss of obligations, duties and ritual which society demands; to go back to 'how things are' as one woman articulated above. To locate one's authentic self in an authentic life is an ideal implicit in the desire to 'just blend back with nature'. In a questionnaire from an anonymous 83-year-old woman registered for a grave space at Barton Glebe, she responded to the question, 'What appeals to you about woodland burial?' by saying,

In the woodland I feel Martin Luther King's words: 'all life is interrelated and all men are interdependent.' I feel part of the natural world too; far removed from the fast moving, noisy environment which pressures us today. One is able to reconnect with values that really matter in life.

Like those quoted above, this woman discerns a connection or interdependence between human beings and planet earth. There is also a sense that she recoils from the pressures of modern life, also shared by another preregistered woman who felt that in response to 'feeling rather tired . . . I thought how nice to just lie down under the trees'. Here we find a desire for temporal or spatial distance, of freedom almost, from perceived social pressures and felt demands. One way of understanding this is through life being lived through a net of obligations that underlies the social world embedded in reciprocities of many kinds.[51] Natural burial seems to imply fewer social obligations and debt so that the essence of a good life is achieved through connecting with values that really matter in life; one simply slips 'away quietly without making a fuss' as the Humanist celebrant identified above. So it is that Barton Glebe appears to offer a refuge from daily life, a place apart.

The 'natural' world to which the woman above refers is not, of course, nature *per se*, but a projection of a nature that constitutes a kind of utopia, a wish-fulfilment and a yearning for something other than advanced industrial society. Nature becomes a means to discover and foster 'self-evident truths',[52] and, in this way, the natural world of Barton Glebe assumes a spiritual dimension for the bereaved or preregistered individual.[53] One local resident spoke of the site as being,

> . . . very simple but quite spiritual – very peaceful. I think it looks very gentle and green and just very relaxing, and certainly when I drive past it most days, I always look! It's funny really! And I very seldom see anyone there, so it just looks like a peaceful haven.

Or, again, in the words of Arthur, one preregistered man.

> It's not like the hustle and bustle of everything around. As soon as you walk through those gates you seem to enter a different world.

Arthur's comment highlights how the 'spiritual refreshment' of Barton Glebe is attained through a temporal and spatial separation from daily life and a quality of landscape lying beyond words. Together they make the burial site a 'peaceful haven', devoid of the obligations, responsibilities and stresses of day-to-day life. Arthur's clear articulation of a separation between Barton Glebe and the usual realms of his daily life raises the question of whether the site is, for him, perceived as a place of separation or transition, a distinction of deep theoretical significance in Van Gennep's long established anthropology of rites of passage.[54] In another example, drawn from an anonymous questionnaire, an elderly woman stated she had chosen Barton Glebe because she felt 'a deep sense of pleasure from the spiritual refreshment it gives . . . In Barton Glebe one can feel close to life which has gone before, touching us within ourselves: an indefinable something.' Barton Glebe's natural landscape presents an opportunity to give material form to immaterial qualities of life and therefore, a means of talking about the ineffable qualities of life, death and beyond. To these important themes we will return in Chapters 4 and 5.

At a theoretical level, Prendergast and his colleagues have argued that those who privately dispose of ashes are 'drawing upon cultural repertoires' such as the 'legacy of nineteenth-century Romantic values' in a contemporary trend 'towards the re-enchantment of the everyday world'.[55] While there is, clearly, an element of re-enchantment evident in the practice of natural burial, some care is needed with this kind of analysis lest it depart too far from what some people say and appear to feel. There is always a challenge involved in attempting to interpret what people say and, in this case, we doubt whether romantic values and re-enchantment can explain the whole phenomenon's appeal, not least because science-influenced ideas of the world and nature have added whole dimensions to what is often identified as eighteenth-century romantic notions of the sublime. To be at one with 'nature' in a scientifically framed sense of the 'natural world' of ecology is not the same as an aesthetically framed thrill of the wild that holds such a firm sense of place in European cultural history. As we will see below, there are other reasons, too, why we would not overly deploy the romantic model of sentiment and value in explaining natural burial. Still, such dispositions and values of 'nature' are aligned to some degree with contemporary critiques of science and capitalism's perceived culpability in nineteenth-century industrialism, one effect of which was 'the centuries-long nostalgia for rural life in Britain'[56] expressed in the words of David, a bereaved and preregistered contributor to our research findings:

> I like the idea of leaving my bones in England for a generation, or two or perhaps five or something! I just like the thought of it. It's not quite 'some corner of a field that is forever England' but you know, there's something of that. You know, this is my country.

His sense of Barton Glebe as – 'not quite "some corner of a field that is forever England" but you know there's something of that' – is rooted in a socio-historical motif of 'Great' Britain embracing, war patriotism, romantic heroism, the beauty of youth in fighting for the green fields of home as encapsulated in Rupert Brooke's idealistic war poem 'The Soldier'.[57] David's cultural reference reveals how he perceives his own identity, 'this is my country', bound within Barton Glebe and a mode of burial located within 'forever England'. So it is interesting that, in comparing the advertising strategies of the 'green' and 'traditional' funeral markets, King argued that the main theme in the green funeral market advertising focused on 'nature,' in which:

> Suppliers of green funeral products are promoting an air of calm and peacefulness to consumers by placing their products in quintessentially 'British' backgrounds. This also helps to evoke a feeling of localness and, by extension, a continuation of contact between the living relatives and the deceased.[58]

Remembrance in nature and giving something back

In adding to the explanation of romanticism we think that one significant feature of natural burial lies, both symbolically and materially, in a sense of continuity between the deceased and their living relatives expressed in the often mentioned notions of 'giving something back' to nature and of being remembered in and through nature. But why might this perspective be so alluring to those who choose natural burial? One approach to answering this question lies with the social psychiatrist and psycho-historian, Robert Jay Lifton[59] who developed the theory of symbolic immortality to explain how and why 'healthy individuals seek a sense of life continuity, or immortality, through symbolic means'.[60] For him, such an attainment constituted 'an essential requisite for mental health and the realization of a vital and enduring self' in confronting our own inevitable mortality.[61] Achieving symbolic immortality becomes 'one possible way of assuaging the certainty – and oftentimes fear – of death by transcending the most potent conception of what death signifies, namely the severed connection to the present and future and to the world of the living'.[62] Symbolic immortality is inherently a means by which, in facing mortality, human beings can bring a 'sense of ontological order to the challenges and uncertainties of life'.[63] Lifton was not conflating a need to transcend death with denial but rather arguing that the 'need to transcend death . . . represents a compelling universal urge to maintain an inner sense of continuous symbolic relationship, over time and space, with the various elements of life'.[64] Lifton proposed five pathways for humans to achieve symbolic immortality by which he meant a 'sense of immortality' that expresses 'ties' to other human beings, as well as to the past, to history and to the future. He did not mean an absolute immortality since, as he said, 'even in our unconscious lives we are by no means *convinced* of our own immortality'.[65] His five pathways mark possibilities by which any individual could pursue one or more of these in seeking to 'attain a sense of continuity'.[66] The five pathways are as follows: Biologic, Creative, Religious, Natural and Experiential.

> . . . the pursuit of symbolic immortality gives meaning to our existence by preserving our connection to others in material ways in this life while ensuring our continued symbolic connection to others once we have left this mortal coil.[67]

Lifton suggested that the varied ways human beings have created a 'sense of deep connection' between themselves and nature allows the perception of self to become 'part of a larger bionetwork' under the 'Natural' pathway.[68] This notion is encapsulated in natural burial advertising that promises a 'return to nature' that fosters a connection between one's decomposed body and one's potential to give life as, for example, to a tree. One preregistered man's questionnaire response said that natural burial interests him 'because in the natural decomposing process nutrients will be released into the soil to sustain nature and so, I can be sure my body is helping in the future'. In speaking of a continuing utility beyond his physical death this individual exemplifies something of symbolic immortality that also carries with it a notion of reciprocity. Another case reflects such a reciprocity when in a woman, wishing to give herself to 'replenish the earth', expresses an emotive understanding of 'nature' that goes beyond any strictly material concept to speak of relationships between the human and non-human in a way that does suggest romantic values and an enchantment with the world. Her rhetoric espouses a belief in natural burial as enhancing continuity and embodying a deep connection with the larger natural environment, it also echoes Lifton's natural symbolic immortality theory.

> For me, it's about being buried *naturally* with very little protection and being able to be part of nature and nature's lifecycle and for all that transition of nutrients and energy and life and soul, whatever you believe, that is all very free to move around and be reused, re-energised and revitalised. Whatever happens to your spirit and your soul that's how I feel. It's about being able to replenish the earth and the tree thing for me is just a symbol of all of that, because trees are marvellous really, they're life really and fresh air and freedom and fullness, and dignity and grace and all of those things. Whereas going through a pair of curtains into an incinerator or being shelved in a rather grotesque gilded coffin, somehow seems a bit false and not so natural.

Lifton's symbolic immortality, echoed in this desire to 'replenish the earth' and be a part of 'nature's lifecycle', can also be applied to those who market natural burial through an appeal to the human desire for continuity by literally promising symbolic immortality in 'a place where life goes on'.[69] Or, again, by those marketing a site where one may create a 'living' memorial. Here people harness what Lifton saw as a natural pathway to achieve symbolic immortality as well as engaging the biologic mode in which the created memorial acts as a symbol of continued existence in the memories of one's offspring. By planting a tree upon a grave in the hope of establishing new woodland one pursues the creative pathway towards symbolic immortality in an anticipated reforestation project or nature reserve. Continuity is promised in the landscape. So, too, with a 'living memory' in which 'the memory of a loved one will always be remembered . . . as the woodland develops and evolves it will turn into a lasting tribute to all who rest here and for all future generations to enjoy'.[70] One anonymous questionnaire respondent who, along with his wife, is preregistered for burial at Barton Glebe spoke of how 'somehow, we feel our 'presence' will live on in such a place'. He included the information that their younger son 'was concerned that the environment should be managed to benefit future generations', and told how that younger son had, himself 'died in 1991 before Barton Glebe was established, but his ashes will be interred with whoever is first to die'. This is a good example of how contemporary funerary options may interplay with each other as, in this case, cremated remains have been retained for inclusion in the burial of whichever parent is first to die.

Beyond kinship links, allusions are also frequently made to the choice of natural burial as something of value for one's offspring and for wider society since one will 'leave this world a better place'.[71] Indeed, we draw attention here to this form of memorialization and to the way natural burial providers are, by speaking of 'living memory', creating and fostering a new cultural concept. They not only begin with the widespread cultural assumption that memory is important but also invoke the allied sense that it can be viewed in a negative way as 'dead' or in some transformed positivity as 'living'. This implied opposition is then deployed by setting the dynamically 'living' memory in the symbol of a tree framed by natural burial against the passively inert 'dead' memory encapsulated by the stone memorials in cemeteries and gardens of remembrance.

Family values

Despite this marketing emphasis on creating a 'living' memory and a 'natural' place worthy of visits from one's offspring, the theme that predominated among those interviewed was that of the cultural obligation of visiting and maintaining graves. Natural burial reveals a spectrum of socio-cultural obligations over kin visiting and maintaining graves. As one widow put it,

> If you bury somebody, someone has to look after the grave – there's nothing worse than an abandoned grave!

This telling cultural idiom of an abandoned grave becomes all the more significant when the next of kin or close relatives are geographically dispersed and deciding where one's final resting place should be, and whether one's choice places further obligations upon close relatives, becomes an issue. But, it is this very issue that seems to be largely circumvented by the natural burial option as these quotations from a civil celebrant and a preregistered widow, respectively, make clear.

> From a personal point of view, the reason why I want to be in a woodland burial site is that my family . . . they're not going to have to come and pretty my grave up: they're not going to have to put flowers . . . The fact that my sisters don't have to worry about making sure the grave's alright or that it's tidy because I mean, I'll have the wild flowers that are there when it goes to meadow! So I think that's quite nice: that's one of the reasons I know I want to go there!
>
> . . . there is not the upkeep of a grave. Whereas in a churchyard you do tend to look after the grave . . . it's not the same. It's not an issue for me whilst I'm alive but when there is no family left erm . . ., there's erm . . .,

no one to look after it! I mean there are people who normally look after the churchyard and tidy it up, but I mean, it's not the same. Whereas here, there is no longer any worries about looking after the grave. When I'm gone, if the children don't want to come, then they don't have to.

Yet another individual in the process of planning his funeral arrangements expresses a similar view to this widow:

> . . . I didn't want to inflict a burden on the family to keep the place tidy. So a woodland burial site is natural, left to grow naturally. So that's another reason: people can be buried in an area where they can forget it, forget going and having to look after it all.

While people still refer to 'tidiness' in natural burial, such orderliness is something rapidly rendered invisible when there is no obvious grave to tend and the advantage of this is that it renders any sense of neglect redundant. Here, then, we encounter two significant cultural notions that affect family decisions over choice of disposal, namely, a tidy or neglected grave on the one hand, and grave visiting and headstone maintenance on the other. Certainly, in interviews with over 60 individuals, people frequently stated that grave visiting and maintenance is what is socially expected, something also evident in a local parish priest's reflections.

> . . . you know my parents are going to be buried there [Barton Glebe] and part of their thought was . . . knowing that I'm an unmarried only child – with a woodland burial their remains will be respectfully dealt with but it won't matter that there's nobody there to lay flowers on it afterwards because that's not what you do with a woodland burial. So I think that's something that's perhaps not immediately obvious but is important to people.

Perhaps older subscribers to natural burial articulate a strong expectation of grave visiting because of personal experience framed by a cultural legacy driven by the expectation of cemetery or churchyard grave maintenance. Certainly, there was a tendency for those with children, who are preregistered or considering preregistering for a grave, to perceive grave visiting as burdensome to their offspring, especially if they wanted to be buried as opposed to cremated. And those without offspring, spouse or siblings, tended to fear the possibility of a neglected grave, as with Amy, aged 69, who was attracted to Barton Glebe and away from cremation after attending a friend's funeral there. She perceived natural burial both in terms of its being ethical and also leaving no neglected grave; an absence all the more obvious since she has no children. After attending her friend's funeral at Barton Glebe she changed her prepaid funeral plan.

Initially I went for cremation because I didn't want an unattended grave. But when I heard about Barton, well, flowers can grow over me and I can fertilize the field! I put down for a cremation you see, because not having any children, I didn't want a neglected grave . . . And then, eight years ago at the beginning of this week, a friend across the road, her husband died and he had a woodland burial at Barton. One of the first . . . I was very . . . [pause] . . . taken with the idea because somewhere like Barton there's no neglected graves so I changed my mind and I thought: I want a woodland burial!

Unlike Amy, Jane is a French Catholic aged 77 and has remarried with children and stepchildren, all of whom are geographically dispersed across England, Italy, France and America.[72] Her concern was of not wanting to burden her children, something she feels she has done prior to arranging her funeral:

I was absolutely obsessed with trying to sort things out for them because life hasn't been that easy: you know, there's been quite a lot of commotion and traumatic experience throughout our life, with my divorce and so on.

Despite being Catholic:

I don't like burial. I don't like coffins . . . [cremation] is quickly done, it's perhaps not very environmentally friendly. I mean if you could be burnt, that would be fine, like they do in India. Besides that, burial is all very well, but if everyone were buried there would be no space. So you have to be dug up and put somewhere else afterwards: it's awful! No, I just don't like the whole system of a coffin. I don't like cremation really either!

Though she is neither in favour of cremation nor traditional burial, what appealed to Jane about natural burial was the potential invisibility of the graves, especially having offspring in several countries which makes grave visiting difficult:

. . . it is very difficult to visit the tombs of the people you loved, and you say: 'Oh yes, yes, we'll go and visit', and then you don't because you have to travel miles.

Neglected graves

Jane's past experience of visiting 'tombs' – as she puts it – makes her mindful of the perceived duty of grave visiting by kin and of that as a problem for her children and stepchildren spread across four countries. She does not wish to burden them, too, with the guilt that they did not 'travel miles' or with the demand that they should do so.[73]

This weighty sense of responsibility of visiting graves was something that Jupp recorded as one of the 'active choices' favouring cremation as a solution to people's 'fear of neglected graves'.[74] Though his research was conducted before the first British natural burial ground had opened we can, now, see something of that fear motivating natural burial, at least when the practice is known and accessible. In our case it is interesting to see that when pressed people often stated that if they had not known of the Arbory Trust's provision, or presumably of some similar choice, they would have opted for cremation over cemetery burial. As we have seen, some had even changed their prepaid funeral plan from cremation to natural burial after learning of Barton Glebe.

Natural burial thus offers a solution for people's fear of a neglected grave or of being a burden to survivors charged with the responsibility of grave visiting and maintenance. The very goal of having a 'natural', non-maintained grave, becomes a new cultural value as the widespread yet largely implicit cultural assumption that an unattended grave is testimony to a forgotten memory is rendered redundant, replaced by wild-flower meadows and with trees as the 'true symbols of life and eternity' while 'graves are symbols of death and fading memory'.[75] One subtle power of natural burial lies in the fact that the grave's position fades as trees and wild flowers mature: death is sequestered by life and a form of 'eternity', for what will survive is a tree or flowers rather than a grave. This is the perfect materialization of symbolic immortality with nature creating continuity from death back into life. Here, too, at least for some visitors, the tree or wild flowers have the capacity to do the work of memory.

The emotional dynamics associated with an unkempt grave in a traditional cemetery are complex yet instructive. The scene of dereliction, of being forgotten or uncared for in death, seems to be partly associated with an element of shame. But beneath that there may, perhaps, lie the equally complex association that many make between their worth in life and their worth when dead. Many traditional societies have stressed the role of ancestors and of the proper performance of post-mortem rites to keep the ancestors happy and ensure their ongoing blessing. Not to honour them is to court their annoyance and their potential to curse or harm their living descendents. Though we certainly do not wish to draw any parallel of that kind, it is worth suggesting that, at another level of understanding, such ideas of the link between the living and their dead is but another way of expressing the importance of society itself as an ongoing venture whose rootedness in past members is but one source of its power to exist today and survive tomorrow. For symbolic immortality should not simply be seen in terms of the identity of the dead, but as an attribute of society that transcends each of its individual members.

Disputes over disposal preferences

'Society' is, of course, a difficult concept to handle in theoretical terms because it refers to that complex patterning of values and clustering of allied emotions that relate and help integrate individuals and groups within identifiable communities. Moreover, many of these elements are subject to change. And one feature of social change as it relates to contemporary families and other social units is that not all members accept shifting values, adapt to dynamic changes or engage with newly preferred emotions and moods.

The emergence of natural burial, just as of cremation more than a century ago, is likely to appeal to some members of a family and not to others. Indeed, having spoken of those who feel positive towards natural burial it is perfectly obvious that there is real debate within some families over a person's expressed preference for this form of burial. Though Barton Glebe may satisfy and, indeed, overcome a number of fears involved in some people's preferred mode of disposal, there remain those whose preference is not shared by kin, most commonly the spouse. This situation is not, of course, limited to natural burial, for funerals may often trigger disputes within family politics. Funeral directors know this well enough, as highlighted in this long citation from an area manager of a funeral company:

> You know, if you get two or three people in a family, there's always some degree of disagreement and it's generally because memories fade you know: 'Oh I remember Dad saying this two Christmases ago, that he wanted cremation' and somebody else will say: 'Well, I spoke to dad six months ago and he said burial!' But there's nothing written down! And I think a lot of it is down to the people who're left having a battle in their own mind about what is right and what is wrong, and it's generally about people's own prejudices you know: 'I can't bear the thought of dad being cremated!' 'I can't bear the thought of Dad being in the ground!' So there's always that going on [whereby there may be disagreement amongst family over the deceased's mode of disposal] You know, there's a compromise. One of the compromises with this woodland thing is that 'Yeah, we'll have the wicker coffin but we'll have a cremation as well': so, in a way, balancing out the needs of the people left behind.

One local resident described the dissonance between her own preference for natural burial and her daughter's dislike of it as the outcome of her daughter's negative experience of a young friend's funeral at Barton Glebe. Contention can also exist between spouses whose differences are often reconciled by the funeral preference of 'whoever goes first'. While Jupp's cremation research claimed that, 'The general rule was that marital partners usually chose the same mode of disposal as their partners',[76] what we do not know is just how much this outcome is a process of dialogue and compromise. But compromise can take a number of forms and is facilitated to some degree within the context of the Arbory Trust which accommodates both the interment of ashes as well as whole-body burial. This allows for spouses divided in opinion over burial or cremation to find a compromise through the purchase of adjacent burial plots at the site itself. In one particular case one spouse desired burial in order to possess a memorial in witness to personal faith, while the other spouse abhorred any memorialization and preferred cremation and the scattering of ashes. Again, Barton Glebe became the preferred disposal location through spousal compromise because one could have a wooden plaque in witness to their faith, while the other could have an unmarked grave. Still, these wooden markers do decay in time unlike the much more durable materials of cemetery headstones.

Location

Alongside dependent kin, location is also a significant factor in people's consideration of natural burial. Once more we encounter a complex scene where 'location' alludes to geographical and emotional aspects of place, to a temporal and spatial closeness to 'home' and to a continuation of memory. The attraction of Barton Glebe being close to home and therefore, one assumes potentially more accessible to bereaved visitors, supports a sociological claim that:

> . . . Dedicated burial grounds of whatever nature are conducive to societies that are relatively fixed geographically and stable socially. These may be characterised by unilinear lines of descent whereby the dead are placed in the local graveyard or cemetery, visited by the living and form part of the nexus between the society of the living and the world of the dead.[77]

The 'society of the living and the world of the dead', especially when associated with churchyards and cemeteries, have often been relatively close to each other, and this juxtaposition also impacts upon natural burial. That is to say, the location of a natural burial ground has to be discussed in relation to its proximity to other modes of disposal, as an Archdeacon who formerly served in the Diocese of Ely explained:

> I think having a woodland burial site near a major city centre, as Cambridge is, is a major advantage. If you had a site in my part of the Diocese, which is the most rural part – I'm talking about my Archdeaconry which tends to

be going up to King's Lynn and the Wisbech fenland area, you could easily find a piece of land there, but I don't think it would have the same sort of appeal or attraction that it does in Cambridge. For a start, there's just not the size of population that would warrant a site like that unless there was a very long term commitment to that site – you know, just because of the geographical spread of the population you might only have two or three funerals a year. And I think in many rural areas the parish church and churchyard – an ancient churchyard – is still a powerful magnet for people to be buried in: whether that's burial strictly or whether that's burial of ashes. And again, where the churchyard remains open – and in a lot of my rural parishes the churchyards are remaining open – then that is probably going to be attractive for people who have lived in the village and associated with the village for a long time. The centre of a population that has loose affiliation to parishes, where people don't actually belong to an area as such, actually having a burial site outside of the city that people can belong to, whichever parish they belong to, is attractive . . .

Certainly, in visiting the other natural burial sites in Cambridgeshire, Barton Glebe has a good take-up rate by comparison, begging the question whether this is because of the site's easy access from Cambridge. Moreover, recent survey research of Britain's natural burial grounds has concluded that natural burial sites offering on-site facilities, continuity of care and a high quality of landscape proved to be the most popular.[78] The Arbory Trust's provision fulfils these criteria, not least over the last, and it is to that theme of landscape quality that we now turn.

Aesthetic values

To speak of aesthetic factors is to enter the realm of named human emotions readily available for local use in the shared understanding of a community. But human perception is such that there is much within individual experience that is not always shared, and perceptions exist that are difficult to put into words. Moreover, with time and social change, innovative contexts emerge that bring their own opportunities for experiences that either have no immediate frame of reference or demand an integration of previously separate frames. In the later nineteenth, and early twentieth centuries, this was the case with cremation and, from the 1970s, it also came to be true of cremated remains. Just how to respond to cremation, and later, how to deal with cremated remains in a personal or family based rite of disposal, became an issue, albeit one lying beyond the scope of this present study of natural burial where, in a sense, the options are easier. The long tradition and cultural framing of burial, of woodlands and of 'nature', now allows these domains to begin to unite in an aesthetic clustering of emotion-pervaded ideas much fostered in the explicit commercial marketing of this practice and widely evident in the responses of those interviewed, albeit in words seeking some acceptable expression. That very struggle to find the right words to capture what a person feels is evidence both of the deeply implicit emotions of individuals surrounding death and of a social change that has not, as yet, generated its own well-worn paths of expression. Nevertheless, we can go some way in describing the situation as it appeared to us in this particular context of Barton Glebe at the time of study between 2008 and 2011. This we do through the motifs of 'peacefulness', 'tranquillity', 'simplicity' and of things being 'basic'.

A peaceful, tranquil place

Peace has long been attributed to cemeteries as the location where the dead 'rest in peace', an idiom that properly reflects the idea of a cemetery as a place where the dead 'sleep' and whose peace should not be disturbed. In many societies this restfully peaceful state contrasts with that of the dead who are restless because of obligations unfulfilled by living kin or because of some personal moral malaise that may require ritual attention by the living. This is all the more important since the dead should, if anything, bless the living and cause them to flourish and not, as may be the case if their restlessness, rebound in a curse that distresses the living. Speaking in general terms, something of this link between the living and the dead is evident in the small yet significant minority of people who visit Spiritualist churches or other mediums after a bereavement to see if all is well with their dead.

To the idea of peace, understood almost as a psychological state or condition of emotions or moods, we should also bring the theme of place as the context of mood, for here the notion of tranquillity comes into its own as an interplay between mood and place. Perhaps we might say that 'tranquility' is even more relational than the idea of somewhere being 'peaceful'. Both ideas should, however, not be divorced from the fact that while certain types of places are credited by a society as possessing the capacity to foster peace or tranquillity there often remains personal and idiosyncratic factors that draw individuals to certain places. Certainly, the location of Barton Glebe is regularly associated with peace and tranquillity and seems to possess sufficient factors to strike the cultural classification of an appropriate resting place, as well as striking some individuals as 'their' place. This is reflected in the words of a terminally ill woman who felt drawn by the peace of Barton Glebe to preregister for burial there.

I just know it still is the place for me! . . . You know when you just go somewhere and you just know like when you go to look at a house or somewhere, you know that is the house! You just get those first few seconds: I've never had it before! You know it's been a trauma the last seven months coming to terms with what's happening, but I actually know where I'm going to be at peace! And I'm going to be resting and it's beautiful and it's . . . natural and it's just tranquil!

Another person, a widow, described how – 'We thought it was very beautiful, we could hear the birds singing and we thought that would be a nice place to be buried'. However, it is not only clients who are attracted to the 'tranquil' nature of natural burial, for some funeral professionals also expressed such sentiments as in the case of a civil celebrant describing funerals at St Albans woodland burial ground:

It's lovely with that breeze so you can just hear a rustle; it's just a very comforting sound and then of course when the flowers come out it's just lovely! It's just lovely. It's so natural, it's like woodland! . . . You can't really ask to be buried anywhere more peaceful . . . so tranquil up there. . . . it's not difficult to describe: it's just a beautiful, peaceful place and I can't think of anywhere better to be!

As already intimated, these sentiments are inextricably linked to romantic values and cultural associations of nature that allow for a therapeutic construction of nature. Cognizant of that, such moods are reflected in names typically given to natural burial grounds around the country as in 'Greenhaven', 'Eternal Forest', 'Green Lane', 'Oakfield Wood', 'Birdsong', 'Springwood' and 'Acorn Ridge'. These names help constitute a grammar of discourse drawing from romantic and aesthetic qualities of 'nature'. Far from being accidental, these names help constitute the material process of creating a natural burial site's landscape as well as endowing it with meaning.[79] To call a natural burial site 'Oakfield Wood' for example, is to creatively conjure up and impart a certain character to the place.

Basic and simple

Another dimension of life emerges when we move from the peace and tranquillity of a funerary location to thoughts of a funeral and its ensuing site being 'basic' and 'simple'. Once more we encounter a sense of self reflected in the desired form of funeral. One widow, for example, stated how her husband would not have wanted a lot of 'pomp and ceremony', itself a phrase redolent of explicit social activity. She thought that, had he known about natural burial before he died, he would have preferred this mode of disposal. Another person, the owner of a private natural burial ground claimed, 'we don't try to sell it as anything other than what it is you know, which is a natural burial ground: no frills, you know'.

But are references to a lack of 'pomp and ceremony' idiomatic of the same sentiment behind that of 'no frills'? To answer this brings other factors into the social equation, for if the references to a lack of ceremony and the absence of frills or fuss are expressed by the bereaved then both expressions tend to allude to a desire for something that is neither too expensive nor replete with the commodities and rituals demanded by consumer society. However, when providers of natural burial speak of 'no frills' we wonder whether they are not implicitly alluding to a perceived lack of obligation on their part to exchange services in return for custom. In this commercial context 'no frills' and 'basic' are metaphors for the absence of services, mainly maintenance procedures, in natural burial practice. 'No fuss' is therefore a cultural idiom for desiring or providing commodities and services that are low cost and low maintenance. As the founder of an eco-coffin company explains: '"No fuss" is a clever phrase to use because it means '"not too expensive." It's a more polite way of talking about money'. This cultural idiom, then, reveals a subtle variation in meaning depending upon the speaker's interests and intentions. For the owner of a natural burial ground 'no fuss' suggests minimal services and grounds maintenance; for the consumer it may carry the sense of a relatively inexpensive purchase or a desire for minimal memorialization. Part of the power of the idiom lies precisely in this potential for a variety of meanings. In technical terms, such multivocality is typical of the symbols utilized in rituals dealing with the core values and life-concerns of a group.

Furthermore, in conceptual terms at least, natural burial can also be aligned to the cultural notion that 'less is more', a phrase frequently commodified in the marketed concept of 'organic' food, 'downsizing' or 'back to basics' as a lifestyle choice. 'Less is more' has a material and a spiritual dimension, so perhaps for the widow who claims her husband would not have wanted the 'pomp and ceremony', the 'spiritual' aspect of 'less is more' might well have predominated, since it implies a degree of authenticity in negating 'pomp and ceremony'.[80] To some degree the sociologist Max Weber's correlation between a Protestant ethic of thrift and a denial of consumer excess resonates with interview comments over attempts to keep the funeral simple and without fuss, as well as with the mode and place of disposal.[81] In America, too, some have observed how changing sensibilities of taste relate to funeral rites, so for example, cremation practices 'have swung back and forth between austerity and ostentation, the plain and the gaudy',[82] despite American cremation being historically rooted in Protestant values.[83] Still, in Britain, natural burial appears to appeal to those who wish to see some distance from 'ostentation' and 'the gaudy' in funerary practice as expressed by this civil celebrant:

> I suppose I see it [woodland burial] as an alternative to the conventional burial but with an eye to ecology. . . . without the showiness if you like. With the *gravitas* of the actual ceremony but with the marking of that spot in a much more natural way. . . . if I wanted to be buried, that's how I'd choose to be buried. I think aesthetically it's more pleasing.

In all these essentially aesthetic expressions there is, inevitably, an association with social class,[84] for just what and how we consume are frequently class related and, indeed, identified.[85] Class affects choice because it underlies the formation of aesthetic judgement and emerges quite naturally as when the civil celebrant just cited claims one mode of disposal to be 'more pleasing' than another. Yet another telling expression of lifestyle values is evident in the choice of coffins.

Contemporary sensibilities of taste

One very particular coffin-choice that has burgeoned and become rapidly available over the last 20 years or so is that of eco-coffins. Although not exclusively available or sold for natural burial, these are powerfully symbolic of this disposal mode. Indeed, the symbolism of coffins is of special interest not only as an expression of the material culture of death but also in terms of theology and their place within funeral liturgy.[86] But, just as with the landscapes utilized for natural burial, eco-coffins are natural, but *not quite*. For, eco-coffins, like the concept of 'nature' in natural burial, are 'natural', in a controlled rather than in any 'wild' malevolent fashion. The coffin and the landscape both rot but look good beforehand; each is 'manufactured' and express the relative nature of the 'natural' in natural burial practice, each is also strongly symbolic in that they participate in that which they represent. Indeed, West describes biodegradable coffins as the outcome of 'artistic and technical innovation' in the funeral industry and as having become 'a funeral icon' extending beyond natural burial.[87] A preference for eco-coffins was something mentioned a number of times by funeral professionals as one that is not bound to the practice of natural burial in the United Kingdom but also, for example, being increasingly chosen for cremation as this Baptist minister and eco-coffin supplier indicate respectively:

> But what I have been aware of is people using more and more eco-coffins but not necessarily in woodland burial! . . . I think the idea of using different coffins is part of that personalizing of funerals, so if people have a connection with nature – which a lot of people do as they're involved with wildlife trusts

or what have you – the idea of using an environmentally friendly coffin is more appealing – and they're quite attractive as well I think!

Some people don't actually care whether our coffins are eco-friendly or not, that's just a bonus, it's the design they like. And yet other people want something that's eco-friendly and very simple.

Then we have a Humanist celebrant who has conducted numerous natural burials since she started in the industry 10 years ago, also thinking that eco-coffins are more appealing.

I've definitely seen an increasing number of eco-coffins at crematoria and I'm all in favour of them: I think they're lovely! I think they look nicer. Visually they're more agreeable. But I don't like cardboard coffins and I understand they're not very ecologically sound! . . . I think the aesthetics, you know the beauty of them, is also important.

It is likely that eco-coffins are not aligned solely with natural burial because they encapsulate more than just the materiality of a new cultural practice. Eco-coffins also represent contemporary sensibilities of taste in which the fashion, food and home-ware industries have also been moving towards more 'natural', organic, 'fair-trade' products, packaging and manufacturing processes. Products and materials produced from small-scale, skilled and environmentally friendly processes sell at a premium, especially products that claim to be handicrafts or that originate from a 'cottage industry'. The same applies to eco-coffins as epitomized by the family-run Somerset Willow Company, which advertises its coffins as being 'intricately hand woven'.[88] Consider also, the bespoke handmade felt shrouds produced by two felt makers who market themselves as 'part of a long tradition, making use of past knowledge but taking it forward into the twenty-first century' with their company Bellacouche. They align their products with 'life cycle textiles', 'thinking outside the box' and 'staying close to nature'.[89] Again, this sensibility of taste and espoused values are arguably class-based in a middle-class direction.[90]

By refusing to consume the funeral industry's standard coffins, purchasers of eco-coffins can use the coffin to 'make a real statement' at the funeral, as one eco-coffin supplier suggested. Their promises set the buyer or deceased apart from perceived consumer standards and homogeneity as this eco-coffin supplier expressed it:

So the coffin's not just like a McDonald's meal: it's not just the same every time, it's not just the standard coffin that the funeral director wants to sell you. The fact the family can seize back some control of the whole process, and again it comes back to choice: they can get more choice, take more control and have what they think reflects the person's life, much more so than just a standard chipboard veneer coffin. And it's two things working in tandem: people wanting more choice and the industry providing much, much more choice . . . our slogan is: 'let your last footprint be a green one' in that, yes, it is environmentally beneficial to have an environmentally friendly coffin over a chipboard coffin but the actions of one person doing that isn't going to have a huge impact – obviously if the masses start doing that, it will have a big impact – but where it does carry a lot of weight I think, is that it makes a real statement at your own funeral if you choose an environmentally friendly coffin to future generations: you've gotta' look after the world.

Also aiding the rising demand for eco-coffins is a general view that they are cheaper than more 'traditional' designs, just as there is a perception that natural burial is cheaper than 'traditional' burial and cremation, issues that merit some consideration here.

Consumer values

Cost

Although there is a popular view that 'green burials confront the high costs of conventional burials'[91] our research could not offer conclusive support for that opinion. What it did show was that 'cost' is not simply a monetary concept, but is allied with identity and notions of 'taste', as with this lady who is considering preregistering at Barton Glebe.[92]

'I'd want an eco-coffin . . . I'd want to go simply! We're not glittery people, we don't want to be.' Here we have an explicit conflation of consumption preference with the construction of self-identity, a fundamental integration through which individual and group identities are created and maintained in modern society.[93] This woman's desire to go 'simply' in seeking lower costs to avoid ostentation encapsulates anti-materialistic, romantic values. By aligning material thrift with subjective self-appraisal, implicit alignments between self-identity, a desired mode of disposal and consumption are inextricably woven together in a reflexive evaluation of self. She attempts a continuity and integrity between her life values and an articulation of a desired 'death-style'[94]; a desire that is facilitated and fostered through media and advertising.[95]

For others, a desire for a cardboard coffin represents a political consumer resistance to a view that the funeral industry has wrongly commodified a ritual act. This is expressed here by Jane who has preregistered for burial at Barton Glebe where she already has a friend buried:

> . . . [woodland burial] should be accessible because the whole process of dying is expensive . . . it's horrendous to think of that and I know the undertaker has to make a living, but in the end I just want a cardboard coffin, because I mean what's the point? And anyway, I would never want one of those big, brass-handle things. It doesn't disintegrate and I think that's important. I think it's going to be expensive anyway, even with a cardboard coffin! I hate all that! I don't mind giving money if I have it, but what do people with no money do? It's just horrendous that for some people they have to think about all that [money] before they die you know!

Speaking on behalf of his industry, an independent funeral director and civil celebrant offered his opinion on consumer expectations of cardboard coffins:

> When people come in wanting a cardboard coffin, they always want one because they think it's cheap, but when they come in they get absolutely blown away by the prices. I mean they retail for about two to three hundred pounds with our normal markups, which is a lot of money for people to pay. I mean I can buy a veneer for a fraction of that cost and sell it for a reasonable markup and people are quite happy to pay that, because they're getting something solid for their money.

An eco-coffin supplier rightly identifies the conflicting perceptions of consumers who want 'something solid for their money':

> We try and price ourselves so that we're comparable to chipboard veneer. A lot of it is perception and the fact that it's cardboard means a lot of people think it's a supermarket box! A lot of what we try to do in our market is to educate because a cardboard coffin is as expensive, if not more expensive to produce because it takes more time. But there's still the perception that a chipboard veneer is a more premium product than a cardboard coffin. So that's one of the challenges we've got.

Below is an exchange between a married couple who have preregistered at Barton Glebe:

> *Caroline*:   It's simple . . .
>
> *David*:   It's probably as cheap as any.

Caroline: Although, they do say that cardboard coffins are more, as expensive as wooden ones I've read! Whether that's true I don't know. Yes! Erm . . . it's . . . natural.

Here again, one can identify the perception of a simple product or practice with lower cost and the advantage of being 'natural'. Time and again we observe how 'simplicity' is conflated with being 'natural', as constructs loaded with qualified romantic values and capitalized upon whether in advertising 'ethical' or 'green consumerism' or in the attitudes of users of natural burial.

Ethical consumerism and 'natural choice'

When moving from the material culture of coffins to the context of funerals we are confronted by an even more dazzling array of consumer choice. Viewed positively, the Arbory Trust Administrator spoke of how:

. . . People have become more aware of their choices. We've found that they are therefore not afraid to take them. And this new style [woodland burial] is therapeutic and it is lovely people have a choice and are freer to take them [in funerals].

Choice and preference for 'green consumption' demonstrate how individuals may act as ethical consumers with a felt responsibility towards themselves and the planet while feeling empowered to engage with articulated environmental risks. Green consumption is often seen as a 'politics of choice' that can 'unambiguously form part of a strategy for environmental reform'.[96] However, though there is an element of moral responsibility implicit in such decision making, in which environmental values can be expressed through market-based processes of consumption patterns, natural burial is not exclusively the domain of green consumption choices. For many other consumer attitudes involved in this practice also contribute to a 'responsible dignified choice' and its associated consumer experience.[97] Here, the 'hypersensuality of the contemporary marketplace',[98] tied to the 'experience economy',[99] commodifies notions of 'nature' and 'woodland' to offer a funeral experience deemed ethical, therapeutic, authentic and personal, to create a statement about the deceased and their integrity to environmental issues and, by extension, to humanity. Natural burial therefore becomes much more than simply 'an alternative to the municipal cemeteries which are soulless', as a founder of the Arbory Trust originally conceived of their aim.

It has been argued that the 'sensual logic of late capitalism' operates through *hyperesthesia*[100] in a rampant branding of the senses and with 'experiences' being sold as, and appealing to, a composite of the five senses, makes consuming the 'natural' appealing. A 'natural' product thus becomes akin to an authentic product and some people who engage in such consumption benefit through the 'authentic' experience of making a statement about the order of things or the way they should be:

> Despite its variety of uses and its potential for misunderstanding, the concept of nature seems to do its work by pointing to a quality of givenness, whether in the way things are, the way they used to be, or the way they ought to be.[101]

Natural burial may once have been conceived as an 'alternative' choice in burial provision but, after almost 20 years since the first site was established, it is now equally about seeking a spiritual or authentic experience as an ethical consumer, for natural burial is also an example of consumer revalorization of 'the endless innovation in the 'senses' (meanings and uses) of things', especially of nature.[102] Here the issue of 'spirituality' in relation to traditional forms of religion and to innovative forms of self-authentication raises significant questions. We will consider some of these below and again in Chapter 5.

Religious–spiritual values

Some of those who had preregistered with Barton Glebe had actively chosen it because of its endorsement by the Church of England and so clearly expressed through the act of consecration. A few people expressed how the Trust's concept bore out their faith, and they certainly did not see woodland burial as compromising their religious beliefs; others had interred a spouse at Barton Glebe because it reflected a continuity with the deceased's faith or church life.[103] Take Jim for example, who is preregistered and a member of the United Reformed Church:

> The environment is important and I try to get to concern groups with various areas of social responsibility. One of the things I do in my retirement is I convene the Church and Society forum which is part of my church – the United Reformed Church, so I do consider social issues and social responsibility as being a crucial expression of part of one's faith I suppose.

For those who identified themselves as having no faith, all felt that they were not prevented from utilizing Barton Glebe simply because it was a consecrated Church of England affiliated site. The priest who serves Barton parish believes this is because natural burial represents,

. . . a circle of life kind of thing that even if people are not religious they can identify with our kinship to the natural world. We are part of the natural world and to go back to it in that way [natural burial] seems appropriate.

For those with a conviction of faith, God's creation is often associated with natural burial. One of the authors had previously suggested that this would be the case on the basis that, '(t)he theological tendency, where it exists, is likely to relate more to the earth than to the cross . . . to engage the doctrine of creation than of salvation and to envisage salvation in terms of the natural processes of life and death.'[104] This 'theological tendency' is illustrated by the widow who said that,

[Natural burial] probably reinforces my faith really, because you're very close to creation. I dunno! But I have no problem with woodland burial: none whatsoever . . . every time I go I think 'Oh! This is lovely!' When I see the flowers I think it's lovely and it's so peaceful.

This preregistered woman who was in a religious order for 20 years overseas sees a continuity between her faith, God's creation and choosing to be buried in a natural burial site.

For me . . . [pause] . . . choosing a woodland burial site as opposed to . . . erm, a traditional cemetery, was really about the fact that this is much more in . . . [pause] . . . in contact with the whole notion that we're part of the whole of creation you know. It's not about these great monoliths and what goes on after. It's much more simple . . . [pause] . . . it, it, it fits in with my understanding that we are one with the whole of creation. You know, we go back into that oneness with creation again as far as I'm concerned.

These comments regarding creation and a sense of kinship with the non-human world supports Owen Jones's suggestion that Barton Glebe's woodland plan, with open glades managed for the benefit of local flora and fauna, enables people to feel 'a little closer to our imaginings of heaven (as a restored Eden) than a graveyard or a municipal cemetery'.[105] 'Nature' has become a locus through which some people choose to project their continuity and express hope. This suggests not simply that there is 'a renewed sense of the sacred located within the natural world' but that natural burial is a dynamic means of framing symbolic immortality and revitalizing hope, and this may qualify or replace the fact that hope was one predominantly expressed through a religious narrative.[106] 'Nature' proves to be a dynamic symbol because people's understandings of life and death are relatively easily encapsulated in the transience of flowers, the effects of the seasons upon growth and the vitality of an animated non-human world.

Barton Glebe's provision is understood to allow people of all faiths and none to 'identify with our kinship to the natural world . . . to go back to it in that way seems appropriate' and permits being 'very close to creation'. These sentiments can be understood whether within a diversity of religious traditions or none and explains why religious values were not commonly articulated by those taking part in this study.[107] They did not need to be, since religious values are neither threatened nor explicitly fostered through natural burial practice. Jupp's research on cremation versus burial preferences similarly concluded that religion played a minimal role: 'Religious preferences were rare' in people's decision making.[108] However, the 'natural' world easily aligns with religious–spiritual values so that people can perceive 'truths' of their faith or spirituality being validated in or through the 'natural' order. Subsequently people are able to make claims that natural burial 'roots the community in what really matters'.

Value coherence and 'death-style'

This chapter supports the claim that 'people's experience of a natural burial ground as a place of ceremony, commemoration and communion with the dead goes well beyond its greenness or its aesthetic appeal and is highly personal.[109] As we have seen, multiple values are conferred upon this practice and motivations are complex.[110] Indeed the very fact that there is a diverse array of values underlying people's preference for natural burial explains something of its broad-based appeal. Certainly, from the interviews quoted above we see people creatively constructing a 'death-style' from the values they espoused over a lifetime spent constructing a meaningful lifestyle. One of the authors has argued extensively for seeing a relationship between lifestyle and death-style, and for degrees of coherence or incoherence between them as manifest in funerary practices. This has included the idea of the fulfilment of identity gained over a lifetime in the rites and beliefs framing funeral rites, whether in beliefs in a heavenly afterlife with its eschatological fulfilment of identity or, for example, a retrospective fulfilment of identity achieved by interring or scattering the deceased's remains at a natural burial ground or some place that resonates with the deceased's life values and interests.[111]

In definitional terms Giddens identifies a 'lifestyle' as 'a cluster of habits and orientations' that reinforces our individual sense of ontological security; habits, values and behaviours that offer a cohesive narrative of meaning-making about our lives. 'High modernity', as Giddens speaks of contemporary society, presents human beings with a 'plurality of choices' in which we are less able to draw upon more singular sets of dispositions that came with the orders of 'tradition'. 'In a world of alternative lifestyle options, strategic life-planning becomes of special importance.[112] And this, it seems to us, is no less true in death-style options. Some interviewees were, certainly, considering their mode and place of disposal and taking steps to ensure that their preferences were met through funeral planning and prepayment plans; a demonstration of Giddens' 'life-planning'. Rosie, for example, chose Barton Glebe because of its proximity to her beloved parrot sanctuary.[113] Rosie wants her funeral 'to be a celebration of her life with animals and birds' and has chosen a cardboard coffin 'because the birds like to play with cardboard boxes!' Rosie's reasoning demonstrates just how she is engaging in 'the reflexive constitution of self-identity'.[114] So, too, with Arthur and Ivy below, who explicitly construct continuity between their lifestyle and desired death-style in the course of their life-planning by preregistering with the Arbory Trust. Barton Glebe was their 'natural progression' because of a perceived self-identity and lifestyle orientated around 'country life'.

> We're both into country life as you can imagine living here because go out of our front door due north, and there's nothing for five miles! We're both very keen on birds, as you can tell from all those bird feeders and the wildlife what have you, so it seemed a natural progression to go and be buried in a wood!

Individuals not only seek continuity for themselves through a reflexive constitution of identity in lifestyle and death-style choices, but also on behalf of the deceased when deciding their mode of disposal and place of memory, especially if the deceased did not express a preference when alive. This 'retrospective fulfilment of identity' is clearly exemplified by this person's thoughts on her dead husband[115]:

> He'd be happy with Barton. He delighted in things. [He] had this sense of God abundantly pouring forth in things. And I feel Uttoxeter cemetery with the kerb stones, [He] would've hated to go like that. I feel the idea of a toad living on his grave and all these little insects buzzing and crawling around, you see, I think [He] would've loved that!

This widow retrospectively articulates a continuity between the place and mode of burial and her husband's personality and life values. The fact that 'he delighted in things' and saw 'God abundantly pouring forth in things' is materialized in the living, natural world of Barton Glebe and encapsulated in the toad and insects. By placing his remains in Barton Glebe she retrospectively fulfils her husband's identity and creates continuity between his lifestyle and death-style. Similarly Andy, who not only buried his grandmother at Barton Glebe but also presided over her funeral service, also demonstrates how people seek a 'retrospective fulfilment of identity' in which a person's life values are honoured in death. This can be expressed in the choice of disposal mode, the extent to which a funeral is or is not religiously framed, the location of interment, aesthetic preferences in funeral consumables, and in conceptions of continuity beyond the grave. In Andy's opinion, the retrospective fulfilment of his grandmother's identity is encapsulated in the concept of woodland burial.

> ... [O]nce we'd got the concept of a woodland burial, *that* seemed incredibly fitting because my grandmother's life in the last few years involved going out around the garden putting down chickens' eggs for the foxes, nuts for the squirrels, feeding the birds, watching the animals coming down to the feeding stations, and . . . gardening . . . nature . . . she was happiest when she was out in the middle of nowhere . . . So, it just seemed ideal: we could bury her in a way that was suitable to her . . .

By articulating a post-mortem identity authentic to a nature-aligned life both Andy and the widow were able to discern a continuity of identity for their deceased kin. While this shows how symbolic immortality may be sought or fulfilled by nature that is not to say that it is necessarily secular or a replacement for a religiously informed eschatology. Indeed, this widow's husband, for example, had spent much of his life in a monastic order while her reflections on life were also influenced by theological ideas. So, in this, as in many cases of life values and afterlife beliefs, we often encounter a clustering of ideas that express a variety of perspectives.

The social coherence and contestation of values

Despite this variety of cultural values associated with natural burial they all operate within webs of social relations sustained by core values that help maintain social kinship. Moreover, the environmental values informing preferences for Barton Glebe often arose from the way individuals perceived their responsibility to subsequent generations in terms of their current responsibility towards the planet. There seemed to be an implicit desire to root 'community in what really matters' and to improve social relationships by way of getting to the 'true things of life'. Even so, family values were expressly concerned with reducing or overcoming a sense of burden upon surviving close kin, whether in cultural expectations of funeral planning or in visiting and maintaining graves. Aesthetic values of what is considered 'good taste' also exist within a web of social relationships as do consumer values. Finally, the religious–spiritual values informing preferences for Barton Glebe also reflect the social relationships maintained with a religious institution and a person's valued personal relationship to God. So, sociologically speaking, all the core values identified in this chapter only exist with the potential to bear upon natural burial preferences because they are established and perpetuated by social relations.

Though diverse, the values invested in natural burial practice become the means through which natural burial becomes defined and set apart from other modes of disposal and places of burial. One way of thinking about these differences is through certain key conceptual binary oppositions that seem to be implicit in the values identified in this chapter. Though we offer the Table 3.1 with a degree of caution, aware of the over-simplicity that such tables may induce, we think it to be valuable as a shorthand description of the territory of natural burial and of what constitutes the concept and practice.

It is worth noting that while we confidently place cemeteries and crematoria in the column for things negatively valued by supporters of natural burial, private ash scattering and churchyards presented an ambiguity and we could not confidently place them in either column. Churchyards, for example, are often valued because of romantic connotations[116] that often carry family histories of burial, while ash scattering is valued for a variety of reasons including the opportunity to personalize disposal by interring or scattering ashes in places that are highly significant to the individuals concerned. It is also worth noting that Prothero's excellent account of cremation in America deployed a similar listing of dichotomous values for 'The World According to Genteel Cremationists'.[117] In his taxonomy those things that were valued in relation to cremation in America were, among others, 'simplicity', 'purity' and the 'spiritual'; the same qualities that are positively valued by natural burial supporters today. Meanwhile, some of the qualities that were valued by American cremationists, such as 'progress', the 'high tech', 'modern', 'future' and 'science', are not valued by today's natural burial supporters in Britain. In part, this is because supporters of natural burial are motivated by values and ideas that form part of the romantic legacy of Britain[118]; a legacy now suspicious of technology, science and modernity but which in the later nineteenth century inspired many supporters of cremation across the world.

In retrospect, we have seen how funeral practices change over time with cultural trends offering new opportunities for individuals to express their personal identity amid their social obligations and consumerist options. We have also observed, in Chapter 1 how innovation may develop in ways that lead to potential conflict with personal or family interests, and this is also true of natural burial practices. When either individual or family users on the one hand or management and institutional providers on the other, assert their intentions or rules, some conflict may occur as each assert the integrity of

Table 3.1 Symbolic and material expressions of values invested in
the concept and practice of natural burial

Positively valued	Negatively valued
Material element	
Natural burial	Cemeteries, crematoria
Life	Death
Trees, wild flowers, animals	Headstone, non-biodegradable plaque
Eco-coffin, shroud	Chipboard coffin, plastic urn
Wild flowers	Cut flowers, plastic flowers
Animals, landscape	Stone or plastic memorials, personal ephemera
Nature	Techno-science, modernity
Glades, randomness	Plots, serried ranks, rows
Non-maintained grave – obligation free	Maintained grave – obligation
Symbolic quality	
Egalitarian	Hierarchical
Life and death combined	Life and death separated
Personal, unique	Anticipated, formulaic
Allurement	Non-place
Authentic	Contrived
Facilitates positive emotions	Facilitates negative emotions
Anti-consumer	Consumerist
Simplicity	Ostentation
Cathartic, positive	Isolating, soulless, negative
Tasteful, modest	Tatty, brash
Expressive, creative	Conformist, restrictive
Peaceful, secure	Disruptive, insecure
Regenerative	Sterile, polluting
Multipurpose utility	Sole-purpose utility
Humanist, holist	Materialist, anthro-centric
Natural death	Sanitised death
Going back, cyclical	Moving on, linear

Source: Rumble (2010).

their world view or commercial policy. Sometimes this means that natural burial becomes a contested practice between those establishing sites and those using them. Moreover, values become acutely contested when the values of subordinate groups are encompassed in the collective concerns of a larger, more inclusive, group. This is why the Arbory Trust has found that as the number of burials or reservations increases annually, they have had to get 'tougher' on permitting visitors to conduct activities based on their personally held values that conflict with those of the Trust. Benches can no longer be erected, plastic items are more thoroughly removed from graves and trees are no longer allocated to individuals under sponsorship. In some ways these gradual changes in management were inevitable as the Trust's success grew, but there will always be others for whom these rules and regulations are questionable. With its success and increased level of use the Arbory Trust has had to define its memorialization boundaries all the more firmly even though this has sometimes led to the subordination of other people's natural burial values in the process.

In terms of the oppositions of symbolic and material expressions of values described in Table 3.1 we should say that not all individuals supporting Barton Glebe or natural burial will identify with the complete list. Nevertheless, only time will tell if natural burial provision becomes more definitively aligned with particular core values or if the practice will accommodate increasingly diverse values as natural burial becomes more inclusive, while not forgetting, however, that natural burial providers are partly beholden to the pace of change in public attitudes.[119]

4

Self-gift, soil and society

So far, we have considered natural burial both as a cultural concept and social practice, and have followed its historical trajectory within the United Kingdom in alignment with ethnographic material drawn from the particular site of Barton Glebe in Cambridgeshire. In this chapter our analytical focus narrows still further, through our interview material, to show how some people seem to make sense of their own mortality and experience of bereavement through the two motifs of 'returning to nature' and of desiring to 'give something back'. These very desires were aptly captured in Pam Ayer's poem, 'Woodland Burial' in which she sought not to be laid 'in some gloomy churchyard' amid ancient bones and an overall 'dryness' but in 'leafy loam' with some 'native tree' 'affectionately' planted over her. In a most telling fashion she speaks of how something 'fine and bountiful' might be wrought from 'decay'. She also uses the widely popular notion of 'closure' as an outcome of the whole process.[1] This poem reflects a common perception of natural burial as using one's body to fertilize soil that, in turn, will nourish new life. She captures not only a sentiment of reciprocal nourishment, evident among many natural burial supporters, but also the idea that by nourishing the earth one nourishes one's spirit or soul before God or humanity. In Britain today some express the opinion that churchyards, cemeteries and crematoria have become inanimate places in which 'the dust of ancient bones has spread a dryness over all'. By sharp contrast, natural burial grounds are understood to consist of animate earth whose 'leafy loam' nourishes a multiple array of life forms. This innovative burial practice is, then, replete not only with allusions to its life-giving potential but also with a sense of dynamic reciprocal relations between humans and nature. In all of this we find expressions of symbolic opportunities for gift giving by the living in the context of death and bereavement. It seems to us that such allusion to gift giving profoundly enhances the allure of natural burial and substantiates its therapeutic benefits. And it does so by providing a creative means for the preregistered and bereaved to imagine continuity beyond death while, concurrently, affirming meaningful relations, memories and values with the living. The gift element is explicit in individual motivations for choosing natural burial when people speak of their desire to go 'back to nature; give something back; fertilize the soil; to be of use' or of going 'back into that oneness with creation'.

The appeal of gift giving is something that has also been clearly identified and used by those marketing natural burial who frequently speak of this choice as enabling a person to make a last statement about themselves as they undertake an altruistic act, even in their death. 'Let your last footprint be a green one' is an advertising slogan trade marked by an eco-coffin supplier and encapsulates a marketing tendency to associate natural burial with the notion of 'giving something back' in an ecologically sensitive manner. 'Giving back to nature' offers hope and a kind of immortality as well as promising the pleasure of woodland for future generations. Such marketed promises of gift giving can be quite explicit as these cases show.

> A green burial is a natural way to celebrate a life, a way of giving back to nature and the environment a gift for our children, grandchildren and all future generations, the gift being a memorial woodland.[2]

> As people become more aware not only of their responsibility to the environment but also of their ability to choose where their ultimate resting place will be, more and more are turning to woodland burial, where their impact on the environment is considerably less than that of cremation, and where they know they will rest in a beautiful, natural setting which their family and friends may return to with pleasure.[3]

This burial practice speaks of offering oneself to 'the landscape and generations to come' by choosing to have a natural burial, or by sponsoring a memorial tree, for a bereaved family may not only offer 'a gift to the one who has passed away, but to the landscape and to generations to come'.[4] Marketing of this sort is based upon an imagined implicit contract between the deceased, the landscape and present and future kin, all encapsulated in the notion that one may 'celebrate a life by giving new life'.[5]

To develop these references of gift giving in a more theoretical direction we suggest that natural burial reconfigures social relations between the living and the dead and their place in the world in and through the idiom of 'gifting' oneself or one's deceased relative to 'nature', or by providing 'an important gift for our children, their children, their grandchildren'.[6] Such terms invite a notion of gift giving in relation to wider social values that has, until now, only been available in the idea and practice of giving one's body for medical research. Yet, natural burial and organ or blood donation appear to be parallel phenomena that share, to some extent, the same sense of social responsibility and of making a contribution that will benefit society at large. To offer oneself as a gift in an act of 'recycling' the body after death carries a strong social as well as a biological or ecological message. Perhaps those Filipino citizens who offer their kidneys for transplantation as an 'act for the public good',[7] those who give blood in England in 'a desire to help'[8] and those who choose to have a natural burial in order to 'give something back' are all contributing something positive for the benefit of future generations. And this is evocative of our previous accounts of those engaged in achieving some form of symbolic immortality.[9] Clearly these acts are underpinned by an implicit moral imperative – in the Durkheimian sense of social worth – because of the altruistic associations inherent in them. But, the variety of meanings that may be associated with aspects of 'giving' is extensive, offering great scope for symbolic creativity, as this case of a woman's explanation of her intention to preregister at Barton Glebe.

> I think I'll most definitely have a woodland burial, I mean I am a Christian, but for me it's much more about the spirit side and the rejuvenation and the giving something back . . . It's [woodland burial] linked to charity and giving isn't it, because it's perceived as a very good thing to do, because you're not damaging the environment.

Though many might say with Grimes that death rites, across time and cultures, reflect local cosmologies articulating an understanding of destiny, indeed the very nature of human life, such a sense of an agreed cosmology may well not hold during times of significant social change and shifts in forms of belief.[10] And this may well be the case in the later twentieth and early twenty-first centuries in Britain, as in many parts of Europe and the Western world, where marked shifts in religious beliefs have occurred. Though it is beyond our intention to engage in any extensive comment on ensuing notions of secularization, evidence shows that while a majority may still self-define as Christians in census reports, that does not necessarily indicate either knowledge of, or subscription to, anything that would parallel orthodox theological beliefs concerning an afterlife. Davies and Shaw demonstrated this not only for the general public but also for churchgoing folk.[11] What we tend to find is a complex mix of ideas, often involving some longstanding Christian notions of heaven or afterlife alongside the idea of becoming reunited with their loved ones. Such anticipations are often aligned with notions of a soul or life force that leaves the body at death which may or may not resonate with formal Christian notions of a resurrection of the body. A significant minority speak of coming back in some form or other, a perspective that is extremely complex and should probably not be interpreted as some kind of formal Indian notion of reincarnation on the basis of karma and ideas of merit, but of a sense of continuity of life and the ongoing nature of family ties. It has also been found that men more than women opt for death as simply the end of life. As might be expected with an aspect of human thought that self-evidently belongs to the unknown many such ideas are frequently held in paradoxical tension.

It is not surprising then that the woman's quotation cited above embraces a variety of ideas. She speaks of being a Christian but without reference to resurrection. As with most believers her reference is to the 'spirit side'. Though one must be careful in terms of how to interpret her words, it seems that where one might have anticipated a reference to resurrection there appears the idea of 'rejuvenation', but less of oneself in an anticipated – eschatological or doctrinally defined – future, but in terms of ecology. Her concern is certainly with 'giving something back' and with 'giving' in general, a notion she links with 'charity' as a 'good thing'; its positive character lying in 'not damaging the environment'. She is making the best of available terms as she comes to grips with the innovation of natural burial. There would seem to us to be some questions begged over just what is meant by giving to future generations and by rejuvenation and the environment. Certainly, difficulties emerge if one tries to be too schematic in understanding people's comments. Older culturally received notions, such as 'charity' in this case; vie with more recent notions of 'the environment' as folk work towards a decision over the mode of their future funeral. And, to reiterate a point made in Chapter 1 and above, such thoughts now occur at a time when marketing strategies that purvey a funeral professional's own agenda utilize ideas of a moral imperative or at least of a voluntary obligation to 'give something back'. Given that the great majority of Britons are still currently cremated or receive ordinary cemetery burial this association between death rites and symbolic gestures towards a greater good can hardly be described as socially normative. So far, then, the element of reciprocity has not attained its cultural status as in, for example, Tibetan 'sky burial', where the exposed corpse is offered to the birds as a 'final act of charity.[12] That case exemplifies a cultural group's adaptation to environment, given Tibet's climate, altitude and land resources that make burial exceedingly difficult. It also reflects the way philosophical–theological ideas, in this case of departing spirit, may cohere with environmental practicalities. Traditional Indian cremation, too, uses the clear language of reciprocity but in that case the cremated body is, as it were, the last sacrificial offering the devotee offers to the deity.[13] Nevertheless, whether we are speaking of sky burial, Indian cremation, natural burial or organ donation, the fact remains that, at the very least, some symbolic reciprocal gesture occurs through the corpse seen as a gift to someone or something else.

These references to gifts and gift giving inevitably bring our theoretical attention to the early French social scientist Marcel Mauss and to those he has inspired. His seminal work *The Gift: Forms and functions of exchange in archaic societies,* portrayed gift giving as nearly always 'obligatory and interested', therefore, creating an expectation to reciprocate.[14] Such exchange helped create and sustain social contracts and social order, with a social bond being created between the giver and receiver because, as he put it, part of the giver is retained in the gift. Mauss was part of the group surrounding Emile Durkheim, the doyen of sociology–anthropology over the turn of the nineteenth and early twentieth century, its theoretical goal was to think of 'society' as a totality, rather than to think of isolated cultural items, practices or traditions as, for example, seemed to be the case with some British contemporaries such as Sir James Frazer of the famed *Golden Bough* and very many other cataloguers of human doings.[15] Consequently, Mauss was deeply interested in what 'constitutes a totality of human experience' and in how reciprocal exchange contributed to that.[16] Gift giving 'establishes and confirms a relationship between people and in this way has been described as a kind of cornerstone of society', because 'how people give and receive is a matter of what kind of relationships they imagine they make and keep with each other'.[17]

Mauss not only identified a threefold obligation that he argued, created and maintained social solidarity among people, namely, the obligation to give, to receive, to reciprocate but also a fourth obligation of giving to the gods. It is precisely this 'fourth obligation' that interests us over natural burial. This category of 'the fourth obligation' refers to any ultimate agent, cause or cluster of prime social values, upon which humans acknowledge dependence and in relation to which they understand their origins, whether as divine being, nature, the environment or humanity at large. The traditional Hindu idea already cited, of the body given in cremation as the last offering to deity, exemplifies such a case of the 'fourth obligation' and brings us to the somewhat analogous case of the human corpse in natural burial. For some of our evidence takes the form of rhetorical formulations of the body of the deceased conceived of as a gift that offers new life through its very decomposition. Such an image fosters the notion in the living that natural burial allows one to 'leave this world a better place'[18] through its 'natural', unfettered decomposition in the soil. The corpse is understood to be a fertile source for new life given as a gift in acknowledgement of the resources consumed by the former living person. The donor in natural burial practice can be the deceased or even the bereaved family while the recipient can be variously construed as the deceased's surviving kin, wider society or even the soil as a receiver of nutrients and the life it will, in turn, sustain. Throughout these ideas the 'gift' motif radically acknowledges interdependence and kinship.

In this approach we encounter natural burial as a symbolic gesture of what life should be about, rather than what it already is: accordingly, in preregistered users' allusions to gifting their bodies to the earth, nature, woodland or to future generations, what we encounter are inherently ethical statements concerning wider society and the future of humanity. Accommodating to that view, and perhaps even fostering it, natural burial is frequently advertised and spoken of as a mode of gift giving that is ethically meritorious. Certainly, site operators advertise in this way, and it is an outlook also expressed by those attracted to this funerary form. As one preregistered woman at Barton Glebe claimed, 'one is able to reconnect with values that really matter in life'. In this sense natural burial encapsulates a sense of contribution to society's values as well as being a 'gestural act' that is 'an act of atonement for a life that consumed far too much energy'.[19]

Body as waste – Body as gift

As for the corpse, there is a compelling notion that it is able to fertilize the soil to nurture new life from death in a symbiosis that resonates with a notion of creation: the corpse being 'a fertile element returning to a fertile world'.[20] Beyond our work on natural burial, Bloch and Parry have long established a link between the renewal of fertility and death rites, finding in many different societies that the 'fecundity of people, or of animals and crops, or of all three' is aligned with ritual that becomes a focus for revitalization and is *culturally conceived* to be most essential to the reproduction of social order'.[21] Relating this to natural burial, we could argue that the fertility of the corpse is literally and imaginatively given back to the soil in an act of revitalization that will ensure sustainability of nothing less than that on which society depends, planet earth itself. At a time of a heightened sense of risk over our planet's ecological future the 'irreversible artificiality of nature is . . . confirmed precisely by its conservation through ecological intervention'.[22] Working from that assumption we can see how the life crisis of death as it impacts upon an individual or group may be imaginatively subverted by using death itself as an opportunity to slow down, change the course of or even prevent planetary crisis. This natural burial quite literally epitomizes that 'death is a source of life. Every death makes available a new potentiality for life, and one creature's loss is another's gain'.[23] Another example dramatically illustrates something of this outlook for when the following man describes himself as 'worm-food' he changes the status of his body from being waste needing disposal to a gift 'helping the cycle of life'. This is how he speaks:

> . . . burial at sea is quite holistic – going back to the elements and food for fishes . . . it's not quite as easy as a woodland burial though . . . I always liked the idea of sky burial that the South American Indians used. What it is, is that it's going one step further, it's actually *feeding* the animals, and of course in American mythology, it's their spirit people that are in the form of animals so I can understand it perfectly you know. Why shouldn't a few crows have a good feed off you? Again, it's helping the cycle of life. You go in the dirt and be worm-food, what's the difference between worm-food and crow-food?

His 'holistic' conception of death, life and the demise of his physical body, demonstrates an enchantment in the world or, perhaps, its re-enchantment in the sense of being an imaginative re-appropriation of intimacy with other forms of life made possible by perceiving the body not as 'waste' but as a 'gift' bestowing life-giving properties back into the earth, allowing future generations to reap recreational benefits from a protected natural habitat.

This is a highly important theoretical part of our argument, for once the corpse is understood as a gift it assumes quite distinctive symbolic powers. One of these is that it detracts from the idea of the corpse as a commercial commodity, an idea that is abhorrent within the funeral industry, despite the fact that it is, precisely, an entity to be processed. The domain of funeral management, especially that dealing with the preparation of the corpse for burial, is replete with conventions aimed at maintaining the dignity of the dead person. The very notion of dignity becomes symbolic of identity and personhood and not of a thing or mere object. It is 'persons' who have dignity, even those dead 'persons' who are in the liminal stage of identity of leaving the realm of the living for that of the dead. Funeral directors are also situated in this somewhat ambiguous location for they deal with a 'thing' that was, and in some senses still is, a 'person'. Its enduring identity being conferred by the relationships living people still have with 'him' or 'her', reflected in visits made to 'pay their respects' to the deceased person, often at funeral directors' premises.

What is more, they are paid for their services after the fashion of a market economy, and this itself is a potentially difficult area ripe for controversy. In broad cultural terms, personal relationships operate in complex ways that often involve gift giving and sometimes that will include money as such. And yet there is a degree of reticence over 'paying for services' when they are of a personal kind. This is probably why, in a British context, the payment for some 'personal service' often includes a tip as well as the basic cost of the job done. But, it could be argued, that every 'tip' carries with it something of a non-monetary value expressing the person to person activity that has occurred. Contexts such as provision of food in a restaurant or the cutting of hair, for example, involve personal encounters that are not the same as paying for a newspaper. Within the context of the majority of funerals conducted by priests, for example, the payment for the rite is made by the funeral director and not directly by a family representative. It is as though 'money' as such seems out of place in the actual ritual arena. In comparative terms this is something that Parry has showed in great depth and for the very distinctive tradition of Indian funerary priests in which funeral fees are aligned with the sins of the deceased and mark a life of cosmic peril for the officiant.[24] While we are not, in any sense, making such a connection between that Indian system and either Christian priests or funeral directors in Britain, what we are highlighting is the subtle complexity over payment for personal service of a more intimate type.

In a somewhat similar fashion, the issue of just how much to spend on a funeral opens up questions of economic cost in relation to personal worth. What the dead person 'means to' their surviving kin is something that, in everyday life, never take an ultimate economic form. This is why, for example, the issue of kidnapping or, in contemporary terms even of piracy and hostage taking in the Indian Ocean, raises the question of how much a particular life or group of lives is 'worth'. The same issue arises over the payment of medical costs by the National Health Service in the United Kingdom when some medicine is deemed 'too expensive', if its outcome might yield only some months of life. In the public mind, especially as managed or manipulated by the media, any cost–benefit analysis of life–death issues becomes problematic. Yet, in reality, few would agree that a pill costing a million pounds would be worth administering to a sick person if it only delayed death by a week. These very broad concerns over the worth of life as set against the cost of life-related services have been included here to help set a cultural scene of market economies and personal relationships, of the cost and worth of things, that extends not only into the funeral directing business but also into the self-reflection of individuals as they ponder their death or those of their relatives.

So, according to our analysis, some natural burial users are resetting some of the values framing the funeral directing business by implicitly aligning its commodity system of market exchange with a gift-system open to fostering life values. Their motifs of 'giving something back', or 'going back to nature', all through a mode of disposal that is popularly characterized as 'simple' and involving 'no fuss', means that the work of funeral directors is serving an identifiable end endowed with high levels of value. Although beyond the scope of this study, the issues of services rendered for the preparation of the body for religious burial or cremation could also be explored. What does interest us more immediately, however, concerns the status or identity of a corpse destined for natural burial, especially in terms of its 'dignity'. We have already indicated that this notion of 'dignity' relates both to identity during life and to the funeral director's treatment of the corpse; the question that now remains is whether its destination in natural burial affects its status still further.

In response, it seems to us that natural burial does bring new factors into the identification of the corpse, especially in terms of a 'dignity' enhanced through a disavowal of conspicuous consumption and commodity exchange. For those choosing natural burial are negating or at least challenging the idea of commercial profit through their desire for 'a simple, no fuss' mode of disposal in which the deceased is symbolically 'giving something back'. Something analogous is found in the medical transfer of blood and major organs where ethical issues imply that it is only when these take the form of a gift that the dignity of neither donor nor recipient is compromised: for such donations are understood to be distinct from commodity exchange.[25] By contrast, 'the sale of body parts such as hair and fingernails have often been explained by recourse to the logic of waste. These body parts it is argued, are "abandoned" by the living, functioning body, and may thus be sold . . . The sale of waste tissue is acceptable; the sale of integral organs is not'.[26] This is probably because the organs are still animated, with the capacity to pass life-giving power to another person. By some degree of analogy, natural burial supporters see the sale and purchase of such a funeral as rather different from that of a traditional cemetery-destined funeral. For, as already intimated, the 'return to nature' effected by the burial carries with it an opportunity for the deceased to 'give something back'. This very factor adds a positive valuation to the whole process and, to some degree, reduces the criticism sometimes attracted by funeral directors as those who simply sell a service and treat death as a commodity.

Yet another aspect of the complex market-economy model of funerals, and one we find problematic, derives from Baudrillard's argument that death must be warded off 'in the interests of life as value' where 'life as positivity' sees 'life as accumulation, death as due payment'.[27] This emphasis upon the social nature of death, and the social contract that underlies it, sets death within the political economy of the Western world and leads to the argument that,[28]

> . . . the dead have just passed away and no longer have anything to exchange. The dead are residual even before dying. At the end of a lifetime of accumulation, the dead are subtracted from the total in an economic operation . . . they serve entirely as alibis for the living and to their obvious superiority over the dead. This is a flat, one-dimensional death, the end

of a biological journey, settling a credit: 'giving in one's soul', like a tyre, a container emptied of its contents. What banality![29]

By sharp contrast, our specific findings on natural burial contradict Baudrillard's general argument on death, for natural burial is felt to be empowering by some of those who engage with it precisely because the dead *do* have something of symbolic value to exchange. This is especially obvious among those who preregister for natural burial and clearly see themselves as offering their life-giving potential in order to create something of value for the living in the life forms of trees, meadows, woodlands and soil. And this is certainly the case as far as their intention and wishes are concerned, irrespective of its actual biological reality. Natural burial contradicts Baudrillard's banality. Rather than mark 'the end of a biological journey' it becomes significant, an empowering experience of *giving something back* to society or to the earth. It contributes to the living while affirming the deceased's individually held values. This highlights the fact that natural burial is a practice above and beyond any simple economic operation. A similar promise of transcending mere economic exchange created by death is offered in the recent Swedish innovation known as Promession.[30] This would seek to render the corpse into a form of compost so that bereaved relatives could utilize the deceased's nutrients in the garden as a living memorial. Here, again, a form of gift-exchange terminology is deployed to give the deceased a far from passive and negative status for the living.

Natural burial and the gift

Following that brief comment on Baudrillard the time is now right to think more clearly still about natural burial in terms of gift theory. Foundational to any such account of reciprocity is Mauss's creative study of *The Gift*, whose committed sense that 'human relationships cannot be contained wholly within usury forms of exchange', and whose challenge of the assumption that 'human relationships aim towards only utilitarian ends', marks its deeply human intention.[31] Through it we see how gift giving allows givers to consolidate or create relationships, and this is no less true through natural burial both as a notion and symbolic act of 'giving something back'. If, then, giving in general can be an empowering behaviour then to give in terms of one's core values concerning life and death is to reaffirm the meaning of one's life in a most fulsome fashion. So it is that natural burial,

> . . . can also give deep psychological satisfaction to people who feel that through their death they are supporting the collective good of humanity and often expressing their philosophy in life.[32]

Natural burial thus becomes a mode of burial that allows users, especially those who preregister, to consolidate their relationships and core values through some sense of giving. But, the question still remains as to precisely what is being given and to whom? In theoretical terms our response takes the corpse itself to be the inalienable gift of Mauss's 'fourth obligation'. It is not simply the corpse, however, that constitutes the inalienable gift but rather its anticipated and accepted decomposition and its life-giving properties. This is a body possessing a symbolic capacity of renewal. This then makes giving or going back to nature a symbolic act that acknowledges what Godelier described as 'the relationship of dependence, indebtedness, and gratitude that humans entertain with the imaginary beings'.[33] In all of this the issue of imagination, of supposition and of something desired, contributes to the actual value of a decomposed corpse but is not something that is clearly understood in popular terms. Here, however, we are in that complex domain of assumption and extrapolation over life and death whose widest framework lies in a popular sense of a cycle of life fuelled by cultural images of the seasons and whose narrow focus is found in domestic and horticultural ideas of composting and, increasingly, with local authority requirements of different kinds of waste disposal.

It is just such a combination of folk knowledge and the developing requirements of local and national authorities that creates popular ideas of 'the earth' as something that has to be sustained and whose future is far from guaranteed as hospitable to humans unless they take active responsibility in relation to it. These relatively recent life concerns over the welfare of the earth help develop those contemporary cultural values as core values as they enhance previously existing ideas of the cycles of life, the seasons and of 'nature'. So it is that at least some of the Trust's preregistered clients choose to give themselves back to their core values albeit expressed as 'giving something back' through 'returning to nature'. In the loosest of terms we might say, following Mauss's and Godelier's intentions, that they are giving themselves back to their gods. To these crucial ideas we will return in the next chapter as part of a more ideological and theological discussion of life values. For the moment we remain with the general anthropological claim that gifts:

> . . . embody the doubleness of all societies, in which there must be both sacred and profane things, both objects freely exchanged and objects preserved from exchange . . . we might say that gift practices tell conflicting narratives: on the one hand, they expound a narrative of transfer and exchange, of hierarchy, aspiration, and freedom from history; and on the other, *they retell a narrative of continuity with nature and the past, a story of human interconnectedness and humility before the transcendental*.[34]

Godelier was keen to emphasize the importance of Mauss's fourth obligation in giving to the gods or nature or 'to men in the sight of gods or nature' rather than to consider only the obligation to give, receive and reciprocate.[35] He recognized that human beings of all societies 'make gifts to beings they regard as their superiors, but this does not necessarily mean the recipient is another human being, the recipient could equally be a conceptual category such as society, God, ancestor, the clan, core values, indeed anything that is beyond monetary value.[36] In so doing Godelier emphasizes the distinction between 'alienable' gifts given in reciprocal exchange and 'inalienable' gifts offered to the Gods under Mauss's fourth obligation, gifts that can never be given in exchange or fully separated from the original giver. Davies has highlighted the way Godelier saw inalienable things as serving as an 'anchorage in time' as they tie a group to their past and root them in their sense of origin such that they 'concentrate the greatest imaginary power and, as a consequence, the greatest symbolic value', whilst also helping to 'constitute an essential part' of the identity of specific groups'.[37]

It is against such a theoretical background that it seems appropriate to view those interred at Barton Glebe as constituting an 'inalienable' gift. This is, of course, our theoretical interpretation of what people have said, and involves our assumption that a part of the deceased is, as it were, retained in the gift of their own corporeal body to the soil. They, literally become part of the soil while, symbolically, they maintain some sense of identity with that particular piece of ground: 'part of the giver is retained in the 'gift', and the giver retains some rights over it'.[38] The deceased or preregistered user gives of his or her self to something that imaginatively and symbolically transcends them. This offering could be (a) to the divine and, or, to God's creation, (b) to society and its values by sustaining the earth for future generations or repay debts to society or (c) to one's sacred origins in the sense of the soil from which human life is nourished.

Symbolic immortality and continuity

In speaking of sacred things or sacred origins we are clear that the term 'sacred' can be understood either within religious or secular narratives,[39] issues we will take further in Chapter 5 where we will also develop ideas associated with 'returning' to a source. For the moment, however, we focus only on the phrase 'to return to nature' not only, and not simply, as an expression of the passage from life to death by giving one's corporeal body as a gift to the soil, but also from life to death to life by imaging that one will sustain new life through that domain of 'nature' that will survive the demise of the corpse. To 'return to nature' is an acknowledgement of how the natural world sustains human existence, so to 'go back to nature is to become part of the earth that's sustained you', as one funeral director put it.

In this context of reciprocity Lifton's theory of symbolic immortality is germane since what is implied by those who give themselves to nature, God or future humanity is a continuity of that inalienable part of themselves beyond their corporeal body.[40] In the context of natural burial this is literally, symbolically *and* figuratively achieved through the 'natural pathway' towards symbolic immortality. The natural pathway provides a mode of transcendence to achieve symbolic immortality because the deceased is 'survived by nature',[41] with 'nature' also being a conduit for the bereaved visitors' continuing bonds with the deceased.[42] These notions are explicit not only in the narratives of the bereaved and the expectations of the preregistered but also, in some cases, also in natural burial advertising. Take for example Barbara, who is preregistered and whose husband is interred at Barton Glebe:

> . . . I mean, I'll be happy when I go if there's a nice piece of woodland there, which people will say: 'okay, so they were part and parcel of the creation of that!' Much better than having an unkempt gravestone which nobody looks after and all the letters drop off! . . . And there's a continuity about something *living* which, you know, sort of lives on through planting trees and trees carry on, which I think is a lot nicer than a piece of stone.

Here we have an explicit articulation of symbolic immortality imaginatively realized through the natural pathway identified by Lifton for whom the attainment and pursuit of symbolic immortality does not involve a denial of death but, rather, represents 'a compelling universal urge to maintain an inner sense of continuous symbolic relationship, over time and space, with the various elements of life'.[43] Immortality becomes 'man's symbolization of his ties with both his biological fellows and his history, past and future'.[44] Our argument, in effect, has been articulating this very notion, but in terms of Mauss's fourth obligation of reciprocity. Behind this alliance of concepts lies our sense of complementarity between symbolic immortality in clinical psychology and reciprocity in anthropology. Both hermeneutic terms capture something of how humans endeavour to express an infinite past and future, albeit through an essentially ineffable understanding of life and death.

Lifton's theory emerged from clinical work undertaken with survivors of Hiroshima. For these Japanese, he noted that 'the theme of eternal nature . . . is very vivid . . . and was one of the most important kinds of imagery for survivors of the atomic bomb'.[45,46] How curious then, that Japan was one of the first countries outside of Britain where one encounters 'tree burial'. Is this further evidence that natural burial practice is a prime example of Lifton's affirmation of a natural pathway to symbolic immortality and that there are specific cultural perceptions of nature that facilitate the instigation of natural burial provision in particular countries and not others? It would seem so. Indeed, some much needed comparative cultural research on natural burial is currently being pursued by Boret on tree burial in Japan (*jumokuso*).[47] He claims that this recent Japanese burial practice 'provides individuals with the prospect of ecological immortality, in which one's own death is an instrument for the regeneration of life within a cycle of nature'.[48] This prospect, Boret argues, comes from a fundamental cultural shift in Japan from 'social immortality' through its ancestral grave system, to an 'ecological immortality' in tree burial.

However, perhaps Boret's understanding of ecological immortality could be pressed further to see that the use of the corporeal body as a source of regenerating the earth is not the only connotation of ecological immortality for, as Lifton argued, it also concerns the imaginative location of self-identity within nature after one's corpse decomposes. A continuity of self is perpetuated within nature so that a 'return to nature' also marks a 'relational emplacement'.[49] The location of the deceased within nature allows bereaved visitors to understand the natural landscape as symbolically being the deceased and, in some sense, constituting part of their relationship to the dead. A key idea that emerges from this is that the natural burial ground has the capacity to materialize the inalienable nature of a relationship between the living and the dead. The very landscape may come to symbolize, and in that sense participate in that which it represents, which is nothing less than a grieving visitor's relationship with the deceased, a relationship possessing inalienable qualities. It is with that in mind that we can see how the natural landscape of Barton Glebe woodland burial ground became a place for the bereaved to 'evoke what is most precious'.[50]

Inalienable yet transformed narrative bonding

To approach burial sites and human relationships through this notion of inalienability is extremely valuable when extending the discussion to grief and to theories of grief. In particular it allows us to make some theoretical contribution to the relatively recent approaches described in terms of continuing bonds,[51] and also of the construction of narratives of the dead by the living.[52]

The continuing bonds motif has served as a major corrective as some would see it, or as a valuable complement as others might say, to the familiar and long established psychoanalytic notion of detachment from the dead as a major goal of Freud's grief work and that of his successors.[53] Their accounts of attachment and loss with a subsequent accommodation to loss through detachment of psychological energy from the now dead person was perfectly intelligible given psychoanalytical ideas of energies that drive the developmental processes of human identity. It becomes less intelligible, however, from the different theoretical approach, driven by ideas of ongoing life narratives and the role of memory in their construction. The combined explanatory power of a continuation of some kind of bonding with the dead through the construction of narratives of the self in relation to them has provided a persuasive approach to grief for increasing numbers of people. One reason for this probably lies in its immediacy of appeal to an essential lay public not versed in the professional mystique and restricted practice of psychoanalysis but familiar with active memories and dreams of the dead as well as with their roles in family stories, in anniversaries, birthdays, photographs and the like. The part played by visiting traditional graves or sites of memory also played their part in narrative bonding with the dead. The very material cultures of most households bear witness to the narrative presence of the dead in the lives of the living. But a single phrase such as 'continuing bonds' or even 'narrative' accounts of memory may be deceptive in its apparent simplicity, for human life proceeds with change being integral to its dynamism. What, in effect, happens to many people is that bonds continue but are transformed, just as narratives also change with time and hindsight.

Such transformed continuation is precisely what natural burial fosters as the site provides a medium for talking about oneself, one's views of life and death and one's relationships with family and others. The direction of this self-reflection will, inevitably, take different directions for those anticipating their own burial and for those reflecting upon their deceased kin. For both, however, the site becomes its own form of 'significant other' through which self-realization may continue or creative memorialization flourish, issues to which we return in Chapter 5. For the moment we take the case of in a bereaved widow called Kathy, who regularly visits her husband's grave at Barton Glebe:

[His] grave is still unmarked, and I find it doesn't worry me. Or rather, it's marked by all the little wild flowers I've been planting intermittently. I still go there quite a lot, but only when the weather's nice – overtly mostly just to see how the flowers are getting on, but at another level, I think, to in some way stay centred in the love [he] gave me, and to acknowledge that connectedness I still have with him . . . I still feel very rooted in [his] love, even though he is no more, and for me, I think because of the move from the home where we had lived together, his grave and the whole place became a profound symbol to me of rootedness and connectedness, and that has continued. The toad is still there; I seem to manage to disturb him each autumn when I'm planting bulbs, and he seems to survive!

Kathy's candid description of her grave visits illustrates that, 'to have roots in a place is to have a secure point from which to look out on the world'.[54] In visiting the grave to 'stay centred' on her husband's love, Kathy is creating a new 'home' for herself in the world, in which lies 'an irreplaceable centre of significance'.[55] Her relationship with her late husband brings added significance to Barton Glebe because it becomes a place fostering an ongoing relationship. The site can also provide a new arena in which the disorder, disconnectedness and homelessness associated with bereavement may be creatively addressed. This seems to be what Kathy is doing in her visits. She also reaffirms her relationship with all that is inalienable to her identity and understanding of the world through her relationship with her late husband. The place is integral to the developing narrative of their lifetime's love and, for her, it becomes part of a transformation of pre-existing bonds.

Here, Relph's articulation of the widespread recognition that 'a deep human need exists for associations with significant places' is useful, especially when aligned with the idea that significance involves a sense of personal authenticity.[56] It would seem that at least some in contemporary Britain do seek an alternative to what must appear to them as the inauthentic non-place or the placelessness associated with other customary locations of the dead. This makes the development of natural burial, at least in part, an attempt to relocate an authentic sense of relationship and, if that relationship is seen as essentially inalienable, it becomes quite understandable that a natural burial site should participate in its inalienability.

Moral, animate, soil

If we move from those reflecting upon the site as the repository of their dead kin to those anticipating it as their own burial site another dynamic of inalienability comes to the fore, one involving the land itself. Now, the idioms to 'return to nature' or to 'give something back' focus on the soil of the burial site. In a more sociological soil analysis we see it as participating in the moral quality of society as an enduring entity framing human life and bringing order to society. One way of portraying this nuanced issue is to speak of animate and inanimate soil rather than of 'moral' or 'immoral' soil, since these latter descriptions fail to capture the sense of vitality implicit in what people say.

From what people do say it would seem that cemeteries and crematoria are perceived by some today as comprised of inanimate earth whilst natural burial grounds exemplify animate earth. What is more, this cultural imagery carries with it the capacity to create the symbolic possibility of therapeutic notions of reciprocity through the death of a corporeal body. This reflects the strong theoretical world of Emile Durkheim, Robert Hertz, Marcel Mauss and to an extent of Arnold Van Gennep, whose shared notion of society as a moral community carries powerful connotations of well-being and human flourishing, and whose negative contexts could foster malaise. Theoretically speaking, that view of the social world and its constituent individuals yields 'a community of living subjects held together by an intricate gift economy – wherein each being, each life is nourished by a host of others, and then gives of its life in return'.[57] In our present context, the soil receiving human bodies seems to be understood not simply as soil or the earth beneath our feet but fertile soil that produces plant life. Soil and plants combine together in constituting soil as medium of growth, or soil as matrix of life. We do not utilize 'matrix' because of any comments in the line of a 'return to the womb', but because of soil being viewed as fertile and not as inert. Again we return to this point in Chapter 5. For the present we remain with soil fertility and especially with the outcome of that capacity.

One major expression of soil's social fertility is carried in the name often used for natural burial, namely, woodland burial. From its early period this alternative form of burial had trees as a dominant motif, and that probably contributed to its early success. Trees, particularly the oak, have strong indigenous appeal because they embody and reinforce culturally resonant symbolic notions such as longevity, British liberty,[58] and national identity,[59] as well as romanticism for nature and the English countryside. Roses,[60] as well as oak trees have historically – and continue to have – explicit English cultural motifs bound up in 'discourses of Englishness'.[61] Davies argued some time ago, that humans have long possessed intimate relationships with trees, an issue we will follow in Chapter 5.[62] Others have developed similar points on the links between physical, cultural and spiritual domains.[63] Jones and Cloke speak precisely of 'arboriculture' to emphasize the social constructions of trees as well as their dynamic materiality.[64] Trees are given the symbolic quality of displaying transgenerational continuity or longevity.[65] The Arbory Trust implicitly articulates this arboreal quality on its website when claiming that by choosing a woodland burial one is creating something for one's grandchildren to enjoy in the future. The life of trees and the lives of people are inextricably bound up because trees manifestly grow within the living memory of a person, but often grow on beyond it to bridge the temporality of the fixed landscape and the transient, fleeting landscape[66] through 'an intergenerational model of time'.[67] Perhaps this confers upon trees their powerful agency and salience in their role as memorials to the dead? Trees appear rooted and fixed in ever changing natural and man-made landscapes, and where cycles or routines of time are changing under modern living.

But the prime factor of trees and cemeteries is that trees are alive. This continues the theme of animate earth, and of earth plus its vegetative output as a single entity in the cultural images many seem to have over natural or woodland burial sites: the dead are buried into what they will become.

In addition to trees, material symbolism abounds in a natural burial ground in wild flowers, water, many species of birds, soil and even weather patterns and the apparently inanimate stones. For each category of naturally occurring thing found in or associated with natural burial gives rise to endless culturally constructed, metaphorical associations that help folk in twenty-first century Britain talk about, reflect upon, and cope with death, a subject often thought to be marginalized in increasing secular lives.[68] This difficulty may, perhaps, be one of the reasons why people try and create a positive outcome and meaning around death, especially if traditional religious resources are absent for any reason. For example, Joe Sehee, Founder and Executive Director of North America's Green Burial Council thought that green burial 'allows people to know that their final act on Earth has really contributed to a positive purpose'. The narrator in the online film from which this statement is taken then says that through green burial 'a person's death may be tied directly to environmental rebirth!'[69] What this media coverage suggests is that by purposefully giving one's self in the 'final act' of being buried in a natural burial ground, 'environmental rebirth' results. This rhetoric illustrates a general trend in mortuary rites that stress 'cyclical processes of renewal' so that eternal order is maintained despite death.[70]

One key theoretical issue arising from these attitudes to natural burial sites concerns what they may symbolize concerning the relationship between individual and society at large. Some time ago Bloch and Parry suggested that in Western cultures the individual stands in opposition to society because of an 'ideological stress' on an individual's 'unrepeatable biography'; subsequently, the death of an individual poses no challenge to society's continuity. They argued that one effect of this way of thought is to render the symbolic connection of death with fertility much weaker than in cultures or societies where the individual is understood as integral to a whole.[71] Contrary to their conclusion however, the innovation of natural burial in Britain and America reinforces a direct symbolic connection between death, fertility of the soil and its ensuing life forms. To what extent natural burial therefore constitutes a cultural shift away from the dominance of individualism is uncertain, but it could be argued that the reappearance of this symbolic coupling between death and fertility in natural burial practice is fostered by ecological movements that present a view of life as 'under permanent threat of extinction'.[72] Subsequently, an opportunity to 'give something back' to life has renewed meaning and, becomes revalued in contemporary life, an issue that we will also take up in Chapter 5.

Whose nature? What nature?

To 'return to nature' materializes a social relationship with nature, yet what 'nature' is being articulated?[73] Beck would argue that it is a 'natural blend', a product of the extent to which 'nature' has become socially internalized in post-industrial society where 'the allure of ecology' is 'a modern experience'.[74] An example Beck offers to support his thesis that nature has become socially integrated in our society is the sense in which the word 'nature' is often articulated in a context where 'the subject under discussion is the shaping of life in society and the provision of social norms'.[75] It is worthwhile reflecting upon this claim in relation to Barton Glebe and natural burial more generally, for these clearly show how 'the natural' or 'nature' is a human social projection; a wish fulfilment in the context of death rites.[76]

We have already argued that one way 'nature' gratifies human desires in the context of natural burial is through a human projection of symbolic immortality on to nature by offering the corporeal body to bring new life to the soil. This desire was expressed in the poem at the beginning of this chapter where the natural world will 'hold some part of me'. Contrary, then, to some commentators' opinions,[77] natural burial does not necessitate the oblivion of our identities. Moreover, natural burial is not, primarily, an individualistic practice but is inherently communitarian and unifying because it provides a symbolic opportunity to give to society and future life. To secure continuity and well-being, which are often threatened by death, there needs to be a correlative reinforcement in the external world of the individual concerned. Thus nature is readily appropriated to provide reinforcement. Nature becomes a utopia which promises to fulfil the desire of the poet to 'hold some part of me'. To borrow from Beck the desire for inner emotional–psychological stability and healing in confronting death is reinforced in an external projection of nature as therapy and as enduring.[78] This is achieved through a particular cultural construction of nature, the romanticism of nature, in the context of death. Possibly Romanticism endures because of an environmental crisis presented as cultural fact and a condition of advanced industrial society that encourages people to yearn for its antithesis.[79] Moreover, Beck argues that when guiding principles for the conduct of human life become obsolete, threatened or problematic, such as the gradual decline in the authority of institutionalized religion, then there is a tendency for nature to appear 'as a passageway to 'consecrated' self-evident truths; as an endangered store of unbreakable rules to be discovered, guarded and cultivated'.[80] Certainly 'nature' is a nebulous concept that permits endless identities to be constructed in relation to it. It is an elusive, relational concept readily used by humans in making meaning of life and death since people can construct a nature that suits their individual needs and life experience but always where the value of life is emphasized over and above death. In more technical terms 'nature' serves as a second or higher order idea. Rappaport utilized this philosophical sense to describe words that all members of a group could use in a sensible way until anyone was asked to furnish a sharp definition of the term, than contradictions could easily ensue.[81] It would seem that the variety of names used for this kind of rite, whether natural, green, woodland, ecological, or natural burial are coming to denote a practice that many have a sense of without that 'sense' possessing any corresponding detailed information. This is, of course, as we would expect of a cultural practice in its early period of growth.

Locating a spiritual dimension in life and death

'Nature', then, provides both a material means of articulating affinity to one's origins, as in identity, prime aspects of being, and core values, and of materializing the ineffable and inalienable, with or without God. An 'ecological framing of identity' need not be secular for it can also be another means of drawing closer to God and to God's creation, and therefore, 'an ecological framing of identity' does not necessarily produce 'its own form of secular eschatology'.[82] Rather, it can be a way of relating to secular or religious inalienable truths because 'nature' is the mode through which ontological imaginaries are processed and, depending on the individual, 'nature' can be god given, earth bound, or both. Thus those attracted to natural burial are not necessarily atheists, since the cultural practice of natural burial that utilizes nature as a rhetorical device encompasses an array of ontologies.

Natural burial fosters a holistic understanding of humanity's place in the world, irrespective of whether or not one gives credence to the notion of eschatological or retrospective fulfilments of identity as discussed above. However, because natural burial nurtures an 'intrinsic relationship between the human body and the world as a natural system within which the ongoingness of life is grounded in the successive life and death of individual animals and plants, indeed, of all things', what is symbolized and reaffirmed in this practice is the depth of our relations beyond ourselves and therefore to existence.[83] And this is where Davies's claim to 'spirituality' as the new mode with which to articulate death and dying is grounded, because what is understood as 'spiritual' by those who visit Barton Glebe is the affirmation of 'the depth and quality of life'.[84] Irrespective of individual, personal beliefs, natural burial provides an arena for this affirmation of value for the living. To 'return to nature' is not to deny death, but to affirm the value and sanctity of life and relations in spite of death.

It could be argued that contemporary Britain now has an ecological understanding as well as a mythic one, of how people are 'participants in natural life cycles . . . that what we give to nature affects what nature gives to us . . . ' an understanding that has been conferred scientifically, socially and spiritually.[85] In this sense, the innovation of natural burial captures people's imagination because it is germane to political and scientific discourses on environmental destruction. But, as we have shown, natural burial indicates more than this if we analyse the allusions made in connection to natural burial in relation to gift theory, especially gifts of the 'fourth obligation', which materialize a narrative about how particular people perceive their interconnectedness, continuity with the past and 'humility before the transcendental'.[86] By understanding natural burial's marketed allusions and preregistered users' desires to 'give something back' as a contemporary, cultural example of gift giving to 'gods' or foci of core values, then natural burial presents an opportunity for people to pursue continuity with their core values and authentic identity.

Despite post-industrial societies no longer relying upon the basic social structures of society being produced and reproduced through gift exchange, the giving of gifts though 'a subjective, personal and individual matter', remains an 'expression and the instrument of personal relationships located beyond the spheres of the market and the state'.[87] Therefore, 'giving something back' in natural burial encapsulates the inalienable relationships constituting the identity of the deceased or preregistered user, as well as affirming the ineffable qualities of life itself that stand outside of commodity exchange. Those who have chosen to 'return to nature' are giving voice to a meta-level of existence, that is, to the value of life. The value of life and all that is inalienable within people's identities is symbolically and performatively realized in 'going back to nature'.

Natural burial also gives material expression to the belief that death is necessary to life in a manner that provides hope and comfort for the bereaved and empowers the place of the dead in modern society. They do not have to be forgotten in neglected cemeteries and toppling headstones. The dead assert their value to the living by securing areas of tree cover or meadow field within which the living and the wider natural world may prosper. Natural burial imaginatively and symbolically empowers the dying, the dead and the bereaved, by perpetuating the significance of the relational, dependent and enduring aspects of life in a more-than-human living world.

By harnessing people's imaginative capabilities, natural burial – conceptually at least – is another example of humankind's creative attempt to overcome the ontological crisis and ensuing insecurities posed by death. As a newly emergent cultural phenomenon, it is more than just accountable to an environmental agenda, as is often implied in the media and marketing of eco-coffins and natural burial grounds. Rather, the practice harnesses pre-existing cultural idioms linking 'nature' with healing and renewal to offer symbolic transcendence of mortality in which death does not result in oblivion, but the propagation of new life. The dead continue 'living' in memories and the landscape, which is highly therapeutic for the bereaved in coming to terms with their grief:

> You know, it's about trees and sustainability and putting something back and having the thought that your loved one is part of that continuance you know. The land and sustaining that, you know. (A funeral director talking about the appeal of natural burial)

Here we see how natural burial is replete with ritual symbolism, upon which the bereaved, preregistered users, funeral directors and funeral celebrants among many capitalize. The success of this ritual symbolism lies in the 'transformative potential' of the symbol: 'the symbolic power of trees comes from the fact that they are good substitutes for humans . . . they both share "life" ', while rituals 'exploit the parallels and connections established by the partly shared processes of humans and non-humans in order to link dramatically the former with the latter'.[88] In the case of natural burial the deceased can 'return to nature' and symbolically obtain a form of immortality. As for trees, even when felled or thought dead, they continue to provide an environment for other living things: they can be ambiguously dead and alive.[89] Similarly, the deceased's corpse is symbolically invested with providing new sources of life from its very decomposition in a natural burial site, a notion supported and bolstered by the very use of biodegradable coffins, designed to decompose rapidly back into the soil and not inhibit rapid decomposition of the corpse. Be it a tree, the wider 'natural' landscape or a corpse, each reinforces the symbolism and metaphor of the other in being ambiguously dead or alive and a source of new life. 'Trees do not have a life, they propagate life'.[90] The same could be said of the wild flowers and the idealized role of the corpse in natural burial: they propagate or sustain life. It is this life-giving property of the corpse however, that offers emotional support to the living, either in facing their mortality or attempting to readjust to life in bereavement. It is also the life-giving potential of the corpse, through fertilizing the soil to propagate new life, which also permits human imagination to conceptualize burying a corpse in a natural burial ground as a gift that offers great therapeutic impact. The symbolic cycles of life and death that are culturally symbolized in 'nature' offer hope to the living whilst the natural symbolism encapsulated in the landscapes of natural burial grounds offers hope that death is not the end. Neither is death out of place in the order of things that bestow great comfort upon those who gather at the graveside or are contemplating making their own funeral plans as with this widow who has preregistered for a grave at Barton Glebe where her husband is already buried.

It's a comfort! The *continuity* of seeing things go on. You know, it makes *dying* just like leaves falling off a tree. It's all . . . [pause] . . . circular . . . isn't it?

The dead can continue to exist in nature; while for the bereaved, natural burial remains a material and cultural death practice that engenders emotional attachments to aspects of the natural world that have become their continuing relationship with the deceased. Grave visits, even to a natural burial ground like Barton Glebe, where graves are not visually apparent, constitute the practice or acting out of inalienable relationships. Barton Glebe *is* a memorial landscape, but memories there are not anchored in inscriptions on headstones but in and through the 'natural' world of a toad, badger, and skylark's song, bluebells and leaves falling off trees. All may foster memories. It is against that background that we now turn to explore aspects of Christian rite and practice that have sustained British traditions for so long and still do for a majority of people.

5

Spirituality, theology, self and sense of place

In this final chapter we both develop and bring to a conclusion some of the key issues raised in earlier chapters on spirituality and theology in relation to ideas of self, imagination, emotion and choice of funeral. We saw in Chapter 4 how natural burial places provide a means for self-reflection, for expressing ideas of life and death and of family relationships. Now, we continue that theme as we see how such a site, and talk about it, provides for some an ongoing expansion of self-realization and of some sense of death-transcendence through the renewal, solace and therapy accessible through 'nature'. For others, such goals are sought by quite different routes; the techno-science of cryonics promises a tiny minority a frozen state until such times as science provides deliverance from a person's cause of death or, for many millions more, the religious path of eschatology with its last things of resurrection, judgement and heavenly destinies.

Lifestyles and death-styles

Such diversity highlights the intriguing theme of the interplay of death-style and lifestyle already introduced in previous chapters. From a theoretical perspective it is easy to assume that every society possesses an obvious congruence between these, especially since many ethnographic studies tell how 'the beliefs' of this or that people on matters of human destiny come to symbolic expression in their death rites. And, doubtless, it is the case that such universes of meaning have given an integrated sense of life and death to many, not least in the long history of Christian traditions. Such extensive cultural uniformity is less easily sustainable, however, in large-scale societies possessing significant cultural diversity through social–economic, class, political, ethnic, religious and secular factors. Diversity is also fostered through commercial entrepreneurialism, artistic creativity and developments in science and engineering.

Though this means that we need to be cautious when speaking of any single lifestyle in such a mixed society as that of Great Britain, even complex societies need a degree of shared cultural practice if social life is to be feasible and chaos avoided. This is evidently the case in terms of law, taxation, education and healthcare, even though each entertains fuzzy boundaries around what certain subgroups find acceptable. In terms of funeral rites, too, there has been a broad general conformity to a pattern of rites, albeit a pattern that has changed over time through complex expressions of popular sentiment, as well as through innovatory provision identified and marketed through funeral providers as commercial entrepreneurs.

As we indicated in Chapter 1, the centuries-long dominance of Christianity, whether in its Catholic, Anglican or Free-Church forms, largely controlled funeral rites and the location of the dead, albeit in relation to local custom. Their shared assumption lay in corpse burial and in a theological affirmation of resurrection. The industrial revolution's massing of people in urban areas, along with its mechanical invention, then made cremation both desirable and practicable and, by the mid-twentieth century, normative. However, the continued availability though minority use of corpse burial alongside cremation ensured that the significant rise in immigrant groups both from traditional Islamic burial cultures and Indian-related cremation cultures possessed easy access to British funeral forms, albeit with some cultural additions. When a mortuary tradition was simply culturally impossible in the host culture, as with Zoroastrians and their long Persian and Indian tradition of body exposure for vulture consumption, then one of the existing British practices, namely, cremation, became acceptable after appropriate cultural reinterpretation.[1]

In general terms, there would seem to be some real basis for using the notion of lifestyle and death-style as a way of indicating a degree of congruence in the overall cultural practices of a group. Historically speaking, this was the case when the burial of the Christian faithful symbolically reflected the liturgical and theological language of the burial of Jesus. Their experience of Christian creeds, reminding them that Jesus has been 'crucified, dead and buried' and had, subsequently risen from the dead, would reinforce their own expectation of burial and future life. Similarly, the grave provided an alluring symbol as a place of rest or sleep until the time of resurrection, an idea that could run in parallel with notions of the soul being in some post-mortem state until the final resurrection.

Cultural framing of styles

The mid-nineteenth century advent of civic cemeteries, justified by overpopulated towns and churchyards, can be seen as distancing the dead from the church as a building and, as Jupp thinks, can also be viewed as one step in the direction of secularization.[2,3] Then, with the implementation of cremation from the 1880s, its slow growth but more rapid expansion from the 1960s,[4] several further steps became possible.[5] First, cremation created a new kind of place – the crematorium.[6] Second, it produced a potential symbolic confusion with fire replacing the earth as the immediate medium of body reception because the Christian tradition had tended to align fire with hell's destruction or the heretic's punishment, whereas the earth was the proper domain for Christian burial despite the fact that Jesus was not 'buried' in the sense of being interred but was entombed. Third, cremation generated cremated remains; such ashes constituted a new kind of symbolic substance that could, as initially it was, be placed in a container, almost as a miniature coffin, and buried.[7] As such, the language of burial remained verbally and liturgically intact even if its dynamics shifted in emotional comprehension. The planting of a rose bush over or with the cremated remains, along with a plaque or inscription, brought some kind of immediate sign of place to where the dead 'were'. But, being easily portable, cremated remains could also be removed from the crematorium and, echoing Jupp's point, be removed still further from ecclesiastical control. From the 1970s that was precisely what happened, as remains were placed in a great variety of places in ways that offer the clearest possible example of how lifestyle and death-style were given new potential for increased coherence.[8] For many, that coherence was framed by a non-religious scheme, it echoed personal or family ideas of life and death and the place of the dead in the memory and contemporary experience of the living. The ashes could be placed in a garden with a rose or some other tree or plant to mark the spot's significance, equally, they might be placed in a river, sports field, mountain or some other location, but almost certainly the 'place' would hold an attributed significance of a distinctly personal or family form.

Given that the teachings of the British churches on the afterlife had become increasingly vague during the nineteenth and twentieth centuries, and since Anglican funeral rites from the sixteenth to the later twentieth centuries remained virtually static, expressing only broad generalization, it was not surprising that individual clergy and individuals at large developed their own rough ideas or favourite images. The relative uniformity of the liturgical words and hymns used at funerals gave a sense of shared views that probably did not exist.[9] This became increasingly evident from the closing years of the twentieth century as people began to request and use their own preferred music and readings at funerals of all sorts, with people other than clergy also speaking at or even conducting funeral rites. So, while clergy continued to dominate the formal ritual event, their stage was sometimes shared by lay people and, in an increasing minority of funerals their role was entirely replaced by a civil or secular celebrants, drawn for example from the British Humanist Association or from an increasing number of other celebrants, some allied with self-established ritual celebrant groups, others simply being freelance. In all of this, the continued rise of funeral directors as a major business stratum within British society was deeply significant as those whose immediacy of contact with the bereaved allowed opportunity for outlining the increasing options for funeral form and for ritual celebrant. Even in a society where large numbers of people describe themselves in census terms as Christian, most would probably not describe themselves as active church-going Christians. Until fairly recently that distinction would make little difference when it came to funerals since the Church of England vicar or minister of some other denomination would be the obvious person to contact to conduct the ceremony. The very continuation of a duty list of clergy at crematoria for some years around the 1960s illustrated this tendency.[10]

Natural burial – An emergent spirituality?

It is against this complex pattern of change that natural burial emerged in the 1990s and, as the evidence in previous chapters suggests, it implemented attitudes that had been forming in Great Britain for some time. These included a refocusing of attention from traditionally religious afterlife concepts to more personally constructed beliefs accepted and shared by family and friends. This shift involves many factors, two of which are relevant here, one concerning beliefs and the other the networked links of people.

First, because it is difficult to know when to speak of 'beliefs' rather than of ideas or of values we follow previous work in taking a value to be an emotion-charged idea, with such values being counted as 'beliefs' when related to an individual's or group's core concepts respecting life's meaning and destiny.[11] Here, we also acknowledge that it is sometimes difficult to know when one is referring to what traditionally might be called 'religion', or to what is increasingly described as either the 'spirituality' or even the simple 'humanism' or humanity of people. In fact 'spirituality' is a good word to use to refer to the way people speak and act in relation to the core ideas that drive their lives, for it not only reflects how traditional religious traditions speak of the formation of a distinctive outlook among members but it also catches the meaning of that word when used today by those who would say they were 'not religious' but who certainly foster a sense of the depth and meaningfulness of life. One theoretical concept that shows the value of employing 'spirituality' as a generic term for just this kind of self-identity and personal worth is that of *habitus*.[12] Indeed, there is a strong family resemblance between these terms – spirituality and *habitus*. In sociological accounts of identity, for example, it has become customary to use *habitus* to describe the embodiment of values and dispositions of people within a particular group. 'Spirituality' and '*habitus*' are, then, strongly related terms with, perhaps, 'spirituality' being slightly more applicable to the world view of a person and '*habitus*' to the embodied practice of that perspective. These matters of emphasis are themselves, valuable when describing different aspects of life. One advantage of the term 'spirituality' is as a model that can be qualified in a number of ways, as in, say, Methodist spirituality or Humanist spirituality. The use of the term is also advantageous in that it affords equality to all groups. By speaking of Methodist spirituality or secular spirituality an equivalence is accorded each while also avoiding the additional problems associated with differentiation between 'religion' and some other life-orientation. This is an important consideration as this concluding chapter now seeks to integrate many of the points made throughout this study while also arguing that the emergence of natural burial as a single phenomenon presents us with a number of motives and thoughts that seem to create a cluster of concepts that may indicate a distinctive mode of spirituality. Atheism, too, can be accorded a form of spirituality in which an ethical commitment to 'fidelity to humanity and to our own duty to be human' is but one option.[13] The depth of feeling that one may have for another, or which a group may share, is as much dependent upon the widespread human capacity to possess emotions and to empathize with each other on the basis of that. Bereavement is but one arena in which emotions of grief are prompted and performed for the succour of many.

Our second major theoretical issue then concerns the group nature of habitus, its formation and performance. This pinpoints the challenge surrounding what we frequently describe as the relationship between the 'individual' and 'society'. This was highlighted in Chapter 1 as a key issue within this study precisely because there are difficulties involved when speaking of 'individual decision making' over aspects of death and funerals. Although we certainly have examples where a person seems to act as an isolated individual and others where family decision making is prominent, it is probably wise, on balance, to assume that when speaking of an 'individual' we usually refer to a person set within some network of relationships. The distinction between the 'individual' and 'society' that underlies most social science should be taken as an abstraction rather than a definitive description of how people think of themselves, their wishes and obligations.[14]

Imagining self

Moreover, the way people think of themselves in terms of their death and its entrainments involves just these issues of belief and of the 'individual and society' link. Within this complex situation the role of the imagination within human life assumes an enormous proportion as the creative source that anticipates and plans for what we and others might do in the future, for the way relationships may transpire, and for how goals be achieved and dangers avoided. As such the imagination is a means of relating contemporary emotions to anticipated emotional states. Given that most people seek to survive and, if possible, to flourish rather than perish, many prefer to imagine states of pleasure rather than pain and contexts that enhance relationships and environments rather than deplete them. Imagination bears close relationships with memory and can be schooled by its lessons from the past as plans are made for the future. One of the key features of the major world religions, as well as of local traditions that seek to explain human life and destiny, has been to engender myths and religious doctrines that portray the wider framework of existence, including pictures of the afterlife. While this is not the place to explore the rationale of such depictions, it is worth noting that from a non-theological perspective those images are frequently embedded in some account of the moral nature of human social life with rewards and punishments received in the afterlife depending upon one's performance on earth.[15] The theological accounts of medieval Christianity furnished a panoramic grand narrative of post-mortality where purgatory, hell and heaven all had their parts to play as did those earth-focused church rites that were believed to foster the soul's after-death welfare. Many of these beliefs still exist in modified forms across the globe especially where conservatively traditional forms of religion obtain.

However, for increasing numbers of Britons belief in anything like a cleansing and preparatory purgatory, or a punishing hell, is out of the question. These are ideological and emotional states that many now find difficult to imagine. In the absence of a hierarchical church to which large numbers voluntarily submit themselves, as is now the case in Great Britain, individuals are unlikely to accept or be attracted to beliefs that involve punishment for sins. This is evident in the broad liberalism of Anglicanism and most Protestant denominations, and also relates to the demise of Roman Catholic authority over its membership on issues such as birth control. Where strong affirmation of beliefs does exist in the United Kingdom, as in some Evangelical and Charismatic groups, group members are attracted to teachings that offer a degree of joy aligned with a certainty of salvation and heaven and of the current immediacy of a divine presence.[16] While such groups do affirm the reality of hell, and do so in ways that numerous other churches do not, they often affirm it for unbelievers and not for themselves. Much has been made of how Hell beliefs declined in the nineteenth century in Great Britain and virtually ceased after the First World War's own hell of the trenches. In some respects, much the same could probably be said about the decline of beliefs in anything like a traditional 'heaven' in the twentieth century. Whatever might be the case in a conservatively influenced United States, in Britain, as in much of western and northern Europe, a marked agnosticism merges with a secular irrelevance as far as these things are concerned. The Christian grand narrative of the afterlife has lost its grandeur for what is probably a majority of the population. Certainly in terms of afterlife beliefs, we know that the dogmatically important Christian idea of the resurrection of the body plays a small minority role even for churchgoers. If people believe in an afterlife it is as a soul that 'goes on'. In demographic terms it is also the case that the difference between men and women is great, with fewer men believing in afterlife motifs than do women.[17]

While involving complex issues, beliefs are certainly intimately aligned with imagination and with the emotions they trigger and the moods they foster. Though often taught as doctrinal facts and accepted as such, beliefs are powerful only when they capture the imagination, are pervaded by moods rooted in emotions. Furthermore, the cultural or political power wielded by doctrinal-teaching agencies such as churches is highly significant in terms of the plausibility of religious ideas to a population. People have and do accept beliefs that to others, or to themselves in different contexts, appear silly, for the power of community allegiance over individual belief is dramatically strong. Here it is worth noting that while one of points of the idea of secularization lies in the decline of such power within the public domain, the trickle-down effect into the private domain should not be ignored. For whatever reasons, some religious commentators advocate the public–private divide over religious issues and secularization, but it is not a persuasive stance. It is, certainly, the case in the United Kingdom that there are strong groups of conservative religious believers of all religions who maintain firm and clear religious teachings and ethical practices within their own 'communities' or religious groups, and who sometimes see it their duty to seek to make their views evident also within the public domain, but the majority population, in all its varied complexity, does not share their ongoing religious grand narrative, or may share it to a degree but alongside their own reinterpretation of it. This is especially apparent over a festivity such as Christmas, where a clear Christian idea coexists alongside family and commercial holidaying. The grand narrative of divine incarnation, so clearly expressed in Christmas carols, is easily transformed into emotional motifs of family care, togetherness and childhood all sustained by extensive commercial and media-based ventures. The diverse extent of so much readily available symbolism offers scope for many imaginations to gain the emotional satisfaction they desire. Moreover, many idiosyncratic imaginations nest within the branches of the grand narrative of nature or ecology that attracts them. And it is to such idiosyncratic nesting within a wider ideological and emotional resource that we now turn when seeking to understand natural burial. Here the issue of precise context is important in that many sites expressly advertise their green credentials and are, in effect the new ritualized symbolism of an ecological ideology. While Barton Glebe woodland burial site was especially established under the aegis of the Church of England and was consecrated as such, it is first and foremost a woodland burial site for all faiths and none to use.

How to talk: Grand and partial narratives

To speak of a grand narrative of nature is to suggest that many concerns over recent decades have tended to coalesce in an overarching concern not simply with 'nature', itself a fully culture-framed concept, but with the survival of the natural world as an ongoing habitation for humanity. Many became familiar with the Gaia hypothesis and later with more substantial Gaia theory from the 1970s, especially as popular accounts of depletion in the ozone layer that helps protect us from ultraviolet light combined with such things as the destruction of South American rain forests and of numerous animals, insect and plant species. The underlying motif of survival reflected emotions of fear and anxiety. Within the European Union, and down to the level of local authorities, issues of conservation increased with additional matters of waste disposal hitting home at the domestic level, and this is of particular importance because, when people are asked to place empty bottles in one container, paper and plastics in others and are much encouraged to compost organic waste material on a daily and weekly basis, we begin to see a form of ecological ethics being appropriated as much through pragmatism as through some supernatural or governmental edict. Under such circumstances these pragmatic actions fashion a way of life; we might even say they help create habitus and foster forms of spirituality. Here, if we might express it in this way, we are dealing with a form of trickle-up effect as mundane activities pervade notions of identity and destiny.

While it is not easy to talk about identity and destiny in a few paragraphs what we can say is that, in Britain, many have tended to hold broad ideas of a soul or some kind of life force that continues after the death of the material body, and though philosophers and theologians often organize such ideas by means of classical and medieval thought they tend to exist as clusters of idiosyncratic notions within an individual's thinking. This configuration of 'self' involves, at least for a minority of people, the possibility of coming back after death in some personal form or other, an idea that is not at all necessarily linked to Indian notions of transmigration on the basis of ideas of karma, but have a thought-life of their own that may well be allied with ideas of an ongoing family identity. These are speculative issues. What we do know is that many, including some churchgoing Christians, do not think of their personal destiny in terms of the formal teachings of resurrection, but much more in terms of a soul of some kind. The idea of a resurrection at some future 'time', perhaps after a period of 'sleep' or 'rest' in the grave, seems to hold but little appeal for many contemporary Christians who, if anything, are much more likely to think of themselves as moving on into a much more immediate afterlife context with God.[18] Even if Christians adhere strongly to the belief in the resurrection of Jesus that does not, necessarily, feed immediately into a belief about their own destiny of resurrection as theologians would often like to think. People are perfectly able to combine a belief that something happened to Jesus and that something different will happen to themselves.

The significance of these various points is that they allow us to paint a backcloth for the issue of the imagined self in natural burial. Here, however, we need to be rather cautious as we approach the ways in which people think about themselves in terms of their identity and destiny. Philosophers, for example, are often keen to make the point that we cannot imagine our own death and, while that may be technically true in the sense that we do not possess the capacity to imagine our non-existence, it is not a true reflection of how some people at least speak, think and live.[19] Most are not philosophers who find ease or even emotional repose in the power of a logical argument on the incapacity of existing entities to understand non-existence.

As earlier chapters have made clear, some people speak of their own death and post-mortem future in rather direct terms of sense perception, they also use similar language when speaking of their dead relatives. They speak of being part of the natural burial site, of being in a beautiful place, or of possessing a good view. They refer to birdlife and birdsong, to peace and to quiet and of a location that is like a park, or garden, or garden-centre that others may visit and enjoy. In relation to Barton Glebe, one daughter spoke of her father, who was a local farmer and who enjoyed hunting and shooting, as being glad that he could be buried in this site facing in the direction of some of these key activities of his. Indeed, she tells how he used to look in a particular direction from his bedroom window when still alive and she is so pleased that she was given a degree of freedom as to which way he could face when buried. She makes the point that had he been buried in a churchyard he would have had to face east, as is the Christian custom in Britain, and that 'wouldn't have suited him at all'. She went on to say how appropriate it was that his grave lies in the area designated by the name 'clover' since 'he used to plant clover'. This particular example shows how a person's identity in life is extended to frame and give some significance to his grave and, we are to assume, also to his death. Some familiar rather than alien themes are identified in the burial. Another woman, a middle aged nurse, speaks of having been to Barton Glebe, liking it, and taking her mother to see it. As a result they have both signed up to be buried there and she speaks with a sense of calm acceptance not only of the fact that they will both be there 'together', but that some of her friends, too, have signed up for the site and they will 'all be there together'. Here we have an imaged post-mortem context of friends and family being together in this place. She certainly does not give the impression of some joint awareness of the group in their death, but she does speak in the present in a way that makes some sense of her current identity and which does not separate it from her sense of death. Life is not senseless and death will not be senseless. What is interesting in this case is that it is the broad sense of a beautiful place, and one without any particular ideological constraint, that allows freedom of thought to imagine it as a context of friendship. To invoke the image of alien anthropologists working at Barton Glebe one might imagine them reporting that the British believe they can see, hear and feel when or after they are dead. While it would be easy to respond immediately and say 'and of course they do not believe that', the issue is an interesting one for it seems that in our imagination our anticipated corpse is partially animated. This reflects the fact that the imagination and its allied emotions comprise a dynamic complex, one that has allowed religious traditions to assert and teach afterlife beliefs with which people have been able to identify themselves, their thoughts and feelings. The pleasures of paradise, the pains of hell, the many experiences of intermediate transitory domains in Indian traditions, the domains of ancestors and the shady gloom of many ancient and local traditions, all reflect emotional states that are given names in these traditions. However, human inventiveness does not, of course, stop there. The US Company, aptly named Celestis, provides the opportunity for cremated remains to be sent into space by rocket. Cutting interpreted these post-cremation services as offering 'an afterlife journey narrative' that permits transcendence by drawing upon a quintessentially American cultural imaginary of technoscience that is 'technophilic, commercialised, and inspired by an optimistic frontier spirit of exploration'.[20] If that US cultural image of technoscience reflects one pole of hope fostered in the face of death then natural burial reflects its opposite pole and, indeed, brings out one feature of the 'natural' in 'natural burial', that is, an act that is relatively unprocessed and free from technological additions.

In-life narratives of afterlife

So it is that, in the many named phenomenon of natural, ecological, green or woodland burial, new opportunities have come to exist for imagining the self in its death and destiny. As previous chapters have shown, the human body's future locale, whether as a corpse or as cremated remains, furnishes opportunity for current self-reflection and for the creation of a narrative-in-life that will make some sense of a narrative-in-death. At this early stage of natural burial in the United Kingdom one of its key features lies in the openness and opportunity for creative in-life narratives that embrace the significance of one's death. While the choice of terminology for the practice offers something of a suggestive theme, some Britons are ever-ready to create their own variation on it. In Chapter 1 we sketched the possibility of 'ecological' nomenclature implicating scientific ideas; 'green' references indicating political activism; with 'natural' burial suggesting some distance from commercialism but alliance with the organic world, and with 'woodland' themes echoing British landscape traditions. We have found elements of all of these possibilities in the way people speak, sometimes deploying one or more within their single narrative.

The very variety of ideas embedded in these motifs is one reason why natural burial is potentially appealing to an increasing number of people. Just as Chapter 4 drew attention to the use of 'woodland burial' as an alternative name for 'natural burial', bringing with it the additional qualifier of trees and their cultural capital so it is that the phrase, 'green burial', carries its own potential symbolism in terms of British cultural classification of colour where 'green' voices connotations both of life and safety.[21] To the long established 'green shoots' of Spring, bespeaking new life in the seasons or to green traffic lights announcing that it is safe to cross roads or drive ahead have been added the idea of being 'green' in the sense of being ecologically responsible. It is as though the 'green shoots' and the safe colour green combine in this ethical attitude towards the world. Green also has the advantage of an added significance through the familiarity of often being paired with red, a colour often understood to demarcate anger or danger. And, certainly, green contrasts with black which is the prime British colour for death.[22]

It would seem that while both green and red are dynamic indicators referring to processes of change, black marks a more static state. A significant minority of funerals in Britain, not least natural burials, now avoid what had come to be a firmly entrenched repertoire of 'black' as a colour of mourning, opting instead for joyous or celebratory colours, often including decorations on coffins of various kinds. Indeed, once flowers are used in any ceremonial event colour becomes an inevitable concomitant since black, and even dark, flowers are very rare in cultivation let alone in the natural state. Certainly, colour symbolism remains important as the emotional framing of funerals changes and as they express something of the narrative of the life of the deceased. The image of 'celebration of life' seems to have become an increasingly popular designation, not only of the memorial ceremonies that accompany more famous lives but also of the actual funerals of more ordinary people.

As Chapter 4 also made clear, narrative has also been very significant for grief theory at the interpersonal level just as it has been much debated for meta-narratives or overarching understandings that underpin a society's sense of itself. In this study we have drawn attention not only to the in-life narratives that some develop in relation to natural burial but also to the power of natural burial sites as a new canvass on which the imagination may work its ongoing self-narrative. This new opportunity offers a degree of imaginative creativity free from the cultural constraints associated with churchyards, civic cemeteries, or crematoria: an opportunity in which lifestyle may now be extended to embrace a death-style as Chapter 3 made abundantly clear.

To speak of a freedom of choice is to summarize a variety of factors whose collective influence is likely to affect the popularity of natural burial in the coming decades. For such a freedom reflects a degree of cultural openness that is matched and catalysed by the commercial opportunities provided by astute funeral services, as well as by the very notion of 'choice' that has become a watchword of British Government in respect of healthcare and educational services. To this may be added the ritual-religious freedom to choose between traditional clergy, civil, secular, or family members to conduct funeral rites. In other words, natural burial has emerged in a social world of ritual opportunity. This is an important point because the British have, in fact, experienced a real freedom of choice over funerary matters when compared, for example, with Dutch or Swedish laws governing the use of cremated remains that have been much more restrictive than in Britain. Then, in Finland for example, the great majority of funeral rites are still controlled by the state Lutheran Church and its clergy, which limits to a great degree the options available to people in terms of form of funeral rite.

What is interesting and important for the Barton Glebe site is that it was created under the auspices of the Church of England to be a woodland burial site, though the form of services framing burial there is left largely open to the users concerned. This context and openness raises the interesting question of the form that theological narratives should or might take in association with natural burial, especially in relation to the decline of sharply defined Christian grand narratives in the population at large. We have already seen how the cyclical processes of life and death in the natural world, alongside the imaginative potential of the corpse to propagate new life, possess an enhanced resonance in the context of natural burial practice. This raises the question of how Christian theology may maintain or develop a deeper resonance in the spiritual lives of the living who attend a funeral or graveside in a natural burial ground.

Adam, Jesus, graves and theology

From a traditional theological perspective, Christianity sees any earth-grave as holding at least a two-fold yet integrated significance, one concerning human death and the other Christ's resurrection. The first sees the grave as marking a return of humanity whence they came echoing one of the Genesis myths of creation that speaks of the first man being made from the dust of the ground and returning to dust after death.[23] That account goes on to speak not only of that ground becoming cursed through human disobedience of divine commandment but also of death as an outcome of that disobedience, a death through which mankind returns to its native dust. The cycle of creation from dust, disobedience to divine command with an ensuing death and return to dust is often depicted as the creation and 'Fall' of humanity. The biblical idiom of humans being dust, being taken from dust and returning to dust became culturally embedded in the phrase, 'earth to earth, ashes to ashes, dust to dust' as used for centuries in the Church of England's funeral rites.[24] There seems to be a strong negative realism underlying these words. The dust is the dust of death, it reverses the symbolism of the mist-moistened dust from which God created humanity: humanity now dies, bodies pass into the very earth that has become cursed through human disobedience. But, and this is manifoldly significant, Christian liturgical utterances over the grave do not end with 'dust to dust', but with some combination of words that move on from 'dust to dust' to an affirmation of belief that the body is buried and will become dust but only in a 'sure and certain hope of the resurrection to eternal life through our Lord Jesus Christ'.

This overall theme of dust transcended through resurrection heralds the second feature of the earth-grave, as the place from which Christ was resurrected. We have already alluded to the biblical texts and their account of the 'burial' of Jesus as his being placed in a tomb, as was part of Jewish custom of the day. He was entombed and not in any sense interred.[25] Yet, the interment sense of 'burial', the idea of being buried in the earth, came to dominate in developing Christianity, especially in Europe and in this transformation we already have an example of an imaginary replacement of tomb by earth-grave. What then of natural burial? Into what kind of earth are the dead placed? This will depend to a considerable degree upon that imaginative outlook of the individuals concerned. It could, of course be regarded in the same way as the earth of a churchyard or cemetery as the sleeping place of the dead until the day of the final resurrection. In that sense the earth-grave is hallmarked by the resurrection of Christ. Indeed, the consecration of traditional burial sites or a priest's blessing of an individual grave in non-consecrated sites, expresses this 'hallmark' and, in a sense, this is the hallmark of a Christian grave and the fact that Barton Glebe is one of those very rare UK woodland burial sites that has been formally consecrated makes this an easy option. But this perspective does not seem to typify the outlook of many of those dealt with in this particular study, at least in terms of what they said when alluding to their grave, often with some form of dynamic rather than some static mode of being. It must be said that the consecrated nature of the site did carry some importance in terms of the legal future and security of the geographical space.

Returning to earth

At its most pragmatic, the natural grave can be depicted in terms of a return to our origin, but a return devoid of both the moral judgement and future salvation theme inherent in the Adam-Christ schema. Beth, a woman whose mother and sister are buried at Barton Glebe spoke in this way of natural burial.

> I think it's a lovely idea, I really do. Well, it's a sort of dust to dust, ashes to ashes concept isn't it? As I say, it's part of life! People are just part of the whole process of living and dying and it's better than a cemetery really with all those stone memorials dotted about the place. So no, I like the idea very much. It's been a positive experience for me, but just because I like the concept of a woodland burial site: it's not industrialised as I said about crematoria in a way. It just seems natural. A natural and fitting end to someone's life. You just go back to where we've come from . . . it just seems very appropriate and fitting to me, and not egotistical at all.[26]

Beth's comments set death and life into a single process as a 'part of life' making woodland burial 'a natural and fitting end to someone's life'. She contrasts this process with the industrialized scheme of cremation and with the stone memorials of cemeteries, the latter seeming to be an intrusion into or an imposition upon what is natural. This approach reflects the theme of simplicity and of having 'no fuss' as discussed in previous chapters, and it is integral to our emphasis on the notion of 'natural' in 'natural burial'. Steven, whose wife is buried at Barton Glebe, said of woodland burial that he liked the idea that it really is dust-to-dust. Dust returns to dust and that is it.

The motif of a 'return' of the dead body, as conceptualized by the living in anticipation of their own corpse, does not stand alone as a cultural image, but could certainly be explored at length in terms of the image or 'principle of return', as in cultural ideas of a 'return to the country of origin', one particularly common in the Pacific and Southeast Asia.[27] It is also widespread in many traditional myths of journey and homecoming.[28] There is also a sense in which the Freudian understanding of the death principle, of *thanatos,* is but one intellectualized version of the same general idea with the added notion that Freud saw it as a return to the very earth itself.[29]

As to the site of return, Barton Glebe, we might add the fact that some spoke of it as containing vestiges of the deceased who chose to be buried 'right there at the beginning' when the site was first established, almost implying that they are the original owners. This is an interesting reference because it provides something of a focus of human significance within the essential natural domain of the site. It may also reflect the theme in the history of religions of how the Christian dead came to be buried in association with martyrs as the famous dead. In other words, it is not unusual for people to speak of burial places in terms of some kind of relationship with its founding bodies. One further conceptual issue that this touches upon is that of time and the way in which worth-laden, inalienable, symbols belong more to a world outside of ordinary time while much ordinary activity, not least of commercial exchange, lie squarely in the market place where 'time is money'.[30]

Fertile soil: Transitive decay

Another perspective on the dust to dust theme views the 'earth' that returns to the earth not as the sinful son or daughter of Adam and Eve but as the natural human body that had once been formed by earthly, natural processes, and that now continues those processes through its death.[31] Here the earth that receives the body is not barren earth that simply provides a resting place until the resurrection but is fertile in the more directly obvious sense of producing and sustaining plant and animal life. The soil constitutes a medium of growth. It is the matrix of life, though here it might be wise to avoid thinking of 'matrix' in the sense of 'return to the womb'. The key issue is that the soil receiving the corpse is not inert but, as part of an entire site, is deemed as fertile: it is certainly not cursed. What is anticipated is that the corpse will decay and in some way contribute to the soil's fertility and ongoing capacity to foster life. This perspective on decay presents a very positive imaginative possibility for those anticipating their burial or who ponder the death of their kin, for it is decay into fruitful generation of life and, as such, it is a transitive decay and not what we might call the intransitive decay of en-coffined rotting flesh. Previous research, has given some indication of how those who worried or were anxious were so because of their imaginative thought of decay as rotting.[32] The very expression of being 'eaten by worms', for example, carries largely negative connotations in the public mind because of the idea of decay, which is largely aligned with traditional cemetery burial. In natural burial, by contrast, decay seems, by and large, to carry only positive significance, for it is only through the decay of the corpse that the potential to be nourishment for trees and wildflowers becomes possible. So it seems that it is possible for decay to carry both positive and negative values depending upon context. In symbolic terms, this is not far removed from the traditional Christian interpretation of the Genesis myth depicting death as decay into dust as opposed to the early Christian idea of the 'death' of a seed that is transformed into the new life of a plant.[33]

In theological terms, this view of the earth and soil speaks more of notions of creation than of 'Fall'. The echo here is of that part of the Genesis myth that speaks of God deeming all that he had as being not only 'good' but 'very good'.[34] While this, doubtless, is an expression of a British pastoral and romantic ideal it is, nevertheless, of real appeal to many.[35] It is a theme that could be developed through theologies of nature, of the development of life and of the way society itself is dependent upon the earth itself. 'Life' becomes a key feature in this approach. Life is ongoing, it is dynamic, it progresses; life is not a static notion, nor is it 'on hold' until some future resurrection. In fact, the dominance of the motif of life becomes the frame for death, the corpse, the funeral and for revisiting the grave. And it is here that the natural burial site itself becomes a multivocal symbol of 'life'. We have noted earlier in this book how the 'woodland' element of woodland burial, namely, trees, plays an obviously important part in constituting the larger environment, but that within this macro-environment we find that its subsets of grasses, other perennial and annual plants, as well as insects, other animals and birds, all play deeply significant parts in constituting the living environment. 'Life', as it were, exists in and through the multitude of forms of life.

'Life', as an abstract notion is, itself, a fundamental theological idea. In systematic theology, for example, it is the Holy Spirit, the third person of the Holy Trinity of divine being, who is described in the later form of the Nicene Creed as 'The Lord the giver of life'. For, in Christian thinking, God is not only the ultimate source of all being but also of the form of life that has been brought into existence on earth. The orthodox Christian idea of the creation is that God brings into existence what had not existed before, the technical language is that God creates 'out of nothing', and that the divine will and power continues to exert itself despite any and all hindrances that beset it, including human disobedience and malevolence.[36]

Life, death and gift in natural burial

Just how Christian theologians might wish to develop these ideas in relation to natural burial now becomes an interesting question. One obvious direction is to integrate the notion of life with that of gift within the context of natural burial, as follows naturally from our extensive discussion of gift theory in Chapter 4. At the core of any such integration lies a person's attitude to life, an attitude created from the dynamic fusion of imagination and emotion within the pool of potential orientations to the world available in a person's culture. From a Christian theological perspective, 'life' holds primacy of place. Not only is life integral to the divine being but also to its expression in creation. God creates because the divine nature is 'lively' and reveals its life-fullness in acts of creation. God, for example, breathes into Adam's nostrils the breath of life.[37] That liveliness continues to express itself in terms of salvation, or the quality of a self-conscious and God-related moral life that emerges despite and against all the negative constraints of human experience. In mythical-doctrinal terms, salvation brings new life from sin and evil. In a kind of symbolic parallel natural burial seems to be spoken of by some as initiating some form of salvation from negative elements accrued over a lifetime, at least in the sense of a person's negative impact upon the planet.[38] Within Christian theology this process of salvation is focused in Jesus and especially in the belief that his morally perfect life was voluntarily given or sacrificed in order that a new quality of life might become available for believers. Here the words 'given' and 'sacrificed' are deeply embedded in the theological tradition which speaks of God 'giving' Jesus as his 'son' as a sacrifice for sin. This idea was, itself, forged from the ancient Jewish cultural context of temple ritual and animal-blood sacrifice for sin. Indeed, much is made in the Jewish tradition of 'life' being in the blood and the symbolism of outpoured blood marking outpoured life is fairly self-evident.[39] Through a Christian transformation this rationale led to the great ritual event of the Mass or Eucharist in which the body and blood of Jesus are symbolically represented in bread and wine and ritually taken by believers.[40] This train of thought has also fostered a spectrum of ideas from martyrdom and self-sacrifice to acts of selflessness and charity. The underlying motive for all of these has tended to be a sense of a responsive love to God for the divine love revealed in salvation. The theological symbolism encompassing these many ideas is as rich as might be expected from two millennia of imaginative engagement with the emotions of belief.

One element of this symbolism has depicted the cross, as the site of Christ's self-sacrifice, as the tree of life which shares in a widespread cultural symbolism of the tree as a central focus of life.[41] Iconographically, that tree of the cross is sometimes portrayed as rooted in and growing from the very Garden of Eden where Adam fell from divine grace. This is signalled by a skull of the first Adam lying at the foot of the cross of Jesus as the 'second Adam'. This essential grammar of discourse of gift and sacrifice, and of sin and salvation, especially as extended into the idea of Christ's resurrection as the final vindication of his conquest of evil and of death takes one form when Jesus is described as the 'second Adam'.[42]

This sacrifice-resurrection motif also finds an easy symbolic consonance in the context of churchyards and cemeteries where memorials in the forms of crosses and the like offer supporting significance. It can, of course, also be related to burial in natural sites through the liturgical form of service used but, given the broad outlook on life that many of those choosing natural burial seem to express, this theological pattern carries a degree of symbolic inappropriateness within it.

In terms of Christian theology, the natural burial site is more of a garden than a graveyard, and in being a 'garden', is easily aligned with the ancient notion of Paradise, itself a cultivated and idealized garden.[43] Indeed, one of the two creation myths in the Book of Genesis typifies the Garden of Eden as a place where God made every tree that was pleasant to the sight and good for food.[44] And along with these aesthetic and utilitarian trees the Lord God also set the tree of life and the tree of the knowledge of good and evil: it would be this latter ethical tree that became associated with human disobedience and Adam and Eve's expulsion from Eden, for the deity was concerned that in their disobedient mode they might also now partake of the tree of life and 'live for ever'.[45] The interesting fact that this foundational theological myth of life and death is so extensively tree related, along with numerous other tree and plant-aligned symbols in the Bible, provides attractive opportunities and challenges for theological discourse related to woodland burial.

But theological language and its liturgical use is no easy task, its pitfalls are as great as are its opportunities. For, as we have indicated, in Christian theological myth humanity was expelled from Paradise, in the form of the Garden of Eden, because of disobedience to God and yet, paradoxically, because a knowledge of good and evil had been achieved. The identification of Jesus Christ as 'the Second Adam', whose cross as the tree of life gained what the first Adam lost does offer some creative opportunity for liturgical development. And yet there is something about these natural burial or woodland burial sites that seems to render the garden or even the Paradise factor redundant. It is, probably, as we have intimated in previous chapters, that those seeking this form of burial find a deeper affinity with their site through British cultural ideas of nature and romanticized landscape than with notions of Eden – Paradise. For a few, however, there is a distinctive Christian attraction deriving from the more recent interest in Celtic Christianity with its own form of nature-relatedness. Still, in this context it is interesting to observe that while Christian ideas of heaven have, following earliest Christian discourse, focused more on a heavenly city than on a heavenly garden, pride of place is, nevertheless, given to the 'tree of life' which now makes its appearance in the midst of the heavenly thoroughfare. Not only does it bear fruit every month but its leaves, too, are powerful and exist 'for the healing of the nations'.[46,47]

Gift and life

If Christian theologians wished to engage in some direct way with natural burial it would seem that there is some creative work to be done given the constraints and opportunities the tradition brings to the context. Integral to the resources available, however, is the theme of the site as a place of creative life and not of death. Aspects of the theology of ongoing creation rather than of negative features of the Fall would seem in place. So, too, are ideas of gift and, with it of thanksgiving for the life of the dead and of what they have contributed to others and to society, and of what they wished to continue to contribute by being part of the natural burial space as a place of life. Here, perhaps, ideas such as that of Christian theologian, Albert Schweitzer might be valuable. Though not always regarded as the most orthodox of theologians, Schweitzer was humane and deeply thoughtful. His theology of 'reverence for life' dawned on him as a kind of revelation as he sought to try and make sense of Christian ethics given the ravages two apparently Christian cultures had exacted on each other in the First World War. Life was a gift, not possessed by right, but to be received 'bit by bit' and day by day.[48] There was a kind of amazement in the perception that 'life' runs through so many aspects of the world. In our world, given our knowledge of genetics and of the complex interplay of ecological systems, the shared nature of life is even more apparent as various versions of the Gaia hypothesis of James Lovelock and others indicate.[49] 'Life' is more complex a notion than has ever been grasped before, especially as we learn how numerous systems interact with each other whether within an organism, between organisms, or between all of these and their wider environments.

Whatever 'life' is as an animating force, and science has much still to do to elucidate this for different levels of organization of matter, the way it is understood at the cultural level has, for ages, been driven by religious ideas such as that of a soul or spirit.[50] Often deemed mysterious yet easily symbolized in air, breath and wind, the life-force offers an immediacy of symbolism for both birth with its animation of the foetus, and for death with its cessation of animation. Some form of body–soul dualism has frequently been invoked as a theory of vitality–mortality as in Christianity with its own complex theologies of body, spirit and resurrection. But, issues of life and death are far more complex than any simple dualism allows, as is recognized in an indirect way within Christianity's various notions of the Communion of Saints that seeks to express some bond between the living and the dead who already experience some form of afterlife while awaiting their final beatitude. Or, again, the long established use of placing relics of Christian martyrs within the altars that served as focal points for the celebration of the Eucharist has reinforced this complexity.

Contemporary thought, too, brings its own ideas to bear on the vitality–mortality scheme, not least in the sense of human beings sharing life with other species, with the environment they generate, and with that future environment that human descendents will inherit as their life-platform. In some respects, attitudes to the natural environment as an inalienable inheritance for others is slightly analogous to the ancient Jewish notion of one's inalienable identity subsisting in the generations of kin yet to come. Salvation for Abraham, for example, might be said to lie in the divine promise that his descendents would be countless, a numerical promise complemented by the additional Jewish motif of a promised land for future generations.[51] Whether in ancient Judaism or in a contemporary secular world some form of continuity of identity seems, for many people at least, integral to a fulfilled life. Even in theories of grief we have witnessed a considerable emphasis on the continuing bonds between the dead and the living, in contrast to the previous psychoanalytic emphasis on the role of detachment from the lost object of affection. This not only recognizes the place of the dead as generated through the imaginative vitality of their descendents but also hints at the prospective view a person may have of their own influence on their own future descendents through their practical acts of visiting burial sites.

Giving and animacy

Many of those who have spoken of such an involved continuity of self through place have often done so through the language of gift and gift giving as previous chapters showed. Here we do not intend repeating what has already been said about gift theory except for two further points. One brings the insight of some linguists and theologians to the anthropological work of Mauss, Godelier and others already considered, while the second seeks to create a link between the ideas of gift and of vitality.

The first contribution, then, comes from an application from linguistics and its discussion of the function of the verb 'to give'. This we take from an analysis of 'to give' that extends the very familiar idea of a transitive or 'two-place verb' in which a subject is engaged with an object, for example, Mary plants seeds, to the less familiar notion of what have been called ditransitive or 'three-place verbs', verbs that not only involve a subject and an object but a subject, a direct object and an indirect object.[52] 'To give' is reckoned to be such a ditransitive verb in many of its usages. So, for example, 'I give you this message' involves myself as subject, 'you' as the direct object and 'this message' as the indirect object. The Finnish systematic theologian Risto Saarinen emphasizes the recognized fact that one feature of 'to give' as a ditransitive verb lies in the notion of 'animacy' in the direct object. In other words it is assumed that there is a degree of agency in the recipient of the act of giving. In terms of the indirect object there need be no animacy. If

'John gives Mary a book' there is an obvious animate subject 'John' and object 'Mary', but the book is not animate. In addition to this concept of animacy, Saarinen also draws attention to the notions of 'causitivity' and to the 'volitionality' inherent in the act of the subject. 'John' is intending to give, he wills to give and so on.

Our reason for stressing these constructions is that they help us understand one key issue inherent in what people have said about 'giving something back' when speaking about their funeral at Barton Glebe. The factors involved in this process are the donor, his or her future corpse, the site itself, and future kin in their relation with the site. We have already considered these in previous chapters but now we need to focus once more both on the corpse and on the burial site, while also placing an emphasis on the 'animacy' of both. Indeed, the major reason why Saarinen's discussion on quite different theological matters caught our attention was precisely because of his reference to 'animacy' and to the fact that we had already used the notion of 'animate-soil' in Chapter 4 as a way of thinking about this natural burial site as opposed to cemetery ground. What we would suggest for our material is that a person seems to speak of their future corpse as something that can be appropriately received by the animate earth. This implies that there is something animate-compatible about the corpse itself, if not that the corpse is 'animate' in some way. It would be easy in the context of natural burial to think of many cases where, following Saarinen's point, the animacy factor applies to the direct object – the burial site. But there would also seem to be a case for seeing the natural burial context as an example of what some linguists see as a 'four-place verbal construction in which a tritransitive verb is employed'.[53] For example, Tom gives his body to the site for his daughter Mary's future good: in linguistic convention 'Mary' is the beneficiary of the action. But in the natural burial case the particular interest falls upon the animacy of the direct object of the act of giving, namely, the grave or burial site.

It is this notion of animacy in the site as the recipient of the corpse-gift that provides the link with the theme of life or vitality mentioned above. To see the gift-act in terms of a living person engaging in a volitional decision to give what will be his/her corpse to the soil for the benefit of future generations or of his/her surviving kin is to see something of an imaginative world of dynamic factors: life not death is the ultimate environment; vitality not mortality is the dominant frame. Here 'life' is understood not in some form of soul that has departed the now defunct body, but as the very body-as-corpse. What is more, it is here that the expression 'give back' takes on an added significance. Although we have, so far, been using this expression 'give back' in a taken for granted sense it is now time to see a potentially additional element in it, namely, a recognition of the animacy of the vitality driven world from which the individual gained his body in the first place and to which a person now anticipates an act of return. One is not giving one's self to some inert medium but to a lively medium, to the earth as a living entity. While people do not speak of this as though to personify the earth, nor are they the kind of people who might easily be popularly and loosely identified as 'new age' or the like, they do indicate a sense of engagement with it.

At one level it would be easy to read this 'return gift' motif in simple terms of Mauss's threefold act of giving, receiving and giving back. On that basis a person would receive 'life' from the earth or the world, hold it for a lifetime, and then gives it back at death. If we did take that option we might decide to see what Mauss called 'the force' he thought was inherent within a gift to be the very factor of vitality itself. But it is probably wiser to think of this act less as a return gift than as an act of the 'fourth obligation' with its sense of something serving as a communication with the core values and identity of a person and, indeed, of a society.[54] In this sense 'giving something back' is less analogous with ordinary gift giving than with, for example, the familiar language of military deaths in the twentieth century world wars with their language of giving one's life for the Fatherland. Indeed, the shared focus on both death and on an anticipated death makes this all the more evident so that, in terms of the fourth obligation, we may still retain the theme of vitality but now see it as an 'idea' pervaded by 'emotion' and framed or qualified by the cultural notion of serving the public good. As such, this act of giving back comes to be not only a value, in the terms outlined in Chapter 1 and earlier in this final chapter, but also as a belief, given that it involves issues of destiny. On this reading, too, we may retain the notion of 'force', but now understood as the force of sentiment that pervades the way one generation views its successors and find a degree of purpose for its own life through the lives that are to follow on. In this context it is easy to see the natural burial site as comprising some form of intergenerational legacy.

There is a sense in which this approach to the return gift of one's body creates a difficult category for some traditional Christian theologies. Whereas it came to be relatively easy to view the soldiers in the world wars as engaged in self-sacrifice and, indeed, to use the sacrificial death of Christ for the sake of others as a model for that, the same does not apply to natural burial people.[55] What is the case is that both kinds of death fall into the category of not wanting a death to 'be in vain'. The human desire to ascribe some moral–social meaning to as many deaths as possible seems to continue in natural burial and to find possibilities in it that do not appear so easily in traditional forms of burial or, indeed, of cremation.

Another problem for traditional Christianity lies in the belief that became liturgically familiar in the words 'the Lord gives and the Lord takes away, blessed be the name of the Lord'.[56] This ancient Jewish idea became deep seated within Christianity in a sense that complemented the doctrine mentioned above, which described the Holy Spirit as the Lord and giver of life. In Trinitarian terms, most Christians would, probably, associate the funeral text of the Lord giving and taking away with 'God' as a totality or, perhaps, more specifically with God 'the Father' rather than with the Holy Spirit or with Jesus as the divine Son. These are issues of the interplay between systematic theology and lay beliefs and cannot be explored further here. What should be said is that God as the giver of life is not only a deeply influential concept in Christian doctrine, especially in doctrines of Creation and of Salvation, but also a belief that serves as a backcloth for ideas of suicide, including contemporary ideas of assisted suicide. Indeed, the very expression 'to take one's own life' as a description of suicide is extraordinarily telling as far as our discussion is concerned. Though we cannot pursue these issues here it needs to be noted that these issues of 'taking life' and of this study's motif of 'giving back' one's body, bear potentially strong cultural connections during a period of social change that could easily be analysed in terms of secularization. What seems to be happening is that traditional Christian ideas of the divine source of and responsibility for life are being replaced by a complicated interplay of a more self-directed sense of life-worth and a socially available means of engaging with it that is allied with ideas of nature, of the world's survival and with ideas of family and the future relationship of family members with the place of burial.

Whether in religious or secular terms, this meaning-frame of nature receiving back the dead, offers a complementary and positive basis for a variety of other funeral related concepts such as the giving of thanks for the life now ended. But, and this is a telling point, the whole issue of a life 'having ended' becomes poignant here, for there is a sense in which life continues, albeit in an imagined organic contribution to the earth itself. This apparent paradox is not unique to natural burial for in many world religious traditions one has to ask the question when someone dies as to just who or what is dead? Various ideas of the soul passing to another domain and the like raise the question as to whether the dead die at all? In an obvious sense they do, for that is precisely what grief marks in society after society; but in a less obvious way there are many teachings that indicate an ongoing identity.[57] Against that background it is not so difficult to see the point of a person understanding their current identity as living persons in terms of a time when they will be dead but also not dead.

Conclusion

Social scientific studies often find a problem over predicting the future. The inventiveness of individuals and the curious turns that societies sometime take frequently leave social theorists stranded on misplaced hypotheses. So it is with caution that we ponder funerals and the forthcoming decades. The fact that so many natural burial sites have been established within 20 years of the first one at Carlisle, and the fact that a sizable minority of people are already buried in these, make it likely that this practice will thrive as relatives of those already dead will choose to be buried in these sites with which they now have a kinship connection. One fostering factor lies in the possibility that the cremation option will attract an increasingly negative view as vague worries over air pollution grow, despite all that crematoria may do to establish their green credentials. At the time of writing there does seem to be an increasing polarization of death-ways in Britain with the key factor involving the degree of professional and technological control of the corpse.

Natural burial seems to be a development of cemetery burial, which was itself a development from churchyard burial. The degree of decreased control of the corpse that this has involved can, as we have already indicated, be read as a decrease in religious institutional control. The geographical move away from the church in the nineteenth-century civic cemetery development is extended when burials now occur in farmers' fields or the woodlands of private companies. But, in saying this, we immediately meet the fact that Barton Glebe was a Church of England initiative, with one of its intentions being that people need not 'leave the church' as it were to find a place in this innovatory practice. Typical of the 'charitable assumption' often used to describe the Church of England when at its best in pastoral relations with people, the Arbory Trust does not require a Church of England, or even a formal Christian funeral in ceremonies at the site. All that is required is that things be done respectfully, or one might say in a typically Anglican fashion, decently and in order.

Two other forms of corpse disposal are very recent and each makes claims for ecological friendliness but, unlike natural burial, each involves what many would regard as complex technology that speedily in one case and more slowly in the other reduces the body to its elements.[58] The first of these, 'Promession', is much advertised on the internet as a viable market development.[59] It involves freezing the body in liquid nitrogen prior to dehydrating it, freeze drying the remains, shaking these to small pieces that are then interred in a biodegradable container some 30–50 centimetres with an expectation of full decomposition in 6–18 months. This is widely advertised as a clearly eco-friendly form of corpse treatment. The Promessa website even speaks of the possibility of planting a bush or tree over the burial site of the treated remains.[60]

The other method, Resomation, involves a dissolving of the body under high pressure in an alkaline chemical solution. Its proponents suggest that the remaining aqueous solution could be used as a fertilizer or, alternatively, be placed in the sewerage system in a normal way of disposal of materials.

The remaining ash-like remains can be treated much as with the outcome of cremation. Both of these methods involve an engineering technology and, in Resomation, a rapid transformation of the body into its elements. In their use of technological or engineering features they both resemble cremation but their major claim to difference from the technology of cremation is that they are ecologically less harmful.

In considering the possibilities of wide acceptance of Promession and Resomation there is one question that arises from our work on natural burial, namely, the imaging of the self in relation to each of these. We have seen how numerous people approach natural burial as a means of reflecting upon themselves and their identity, as they imagine themselves and their relation to others in the future in and through the burial site, and we wonder whether these other methods allow for such an imagination of the self. While this is not to say that they and their kin do not have other means of relating to each other after death, the site seems a fairly central one. The very medium of a site, with all its plant and animal activity, conduces to its nature as an animate site that allows for a sense of participation its present and future life form. So, the question for both Resomation and Promession is whether they can provide a medium for the imagined future self? The likelihood is that they do not, at least for the kind of people currently opting for natural burial. The problem is likely to lie with the technological processes that intervene between the recently dead corpse and the out-coming powders and liquids. Still, having said that, we know that the ashes of cremation have allowed many people to imagine their future in terms of being deposited in a place of choice and the same might be true for the residues of Resomation, where the active processing of the corpse resembles both the processing of cremation and, for example, the freeze drying of the corpse as mentioned at the beginning of this chapter for the niche market of cryonics.

What is obvious is that while cremation slowly transformed traditional British funerals from the 1880s to the 1990s the new option of natural burial has made relatively rapid progress over the last two decades. The additional options, as they may be sanctioned by law and admitted into public validation, simply develop the spectrum of death options. In so doing they will certainly offer scholars of the early and mid-twenty-first century a dramatic means of assessing changing patterns of individual and group identity as commercial, religious and secular groups make their respective claims on people. For the moment, however, it is evident that people of many ideological persuasions find a depth of human significance in and through the site of burial that is, at the same time, the site of natural fecundity. Although we have already alluded to anthropological work on the symbolic interplay of death and fertility, this Conclusion also emphasizes the way that dynamic linkage generates a form of spirituality that brings significance to death and to the site of burial as far as descendents are concerned. Human beings derive some real benefit from each other when they share in ritual activity at times of emotional fluctuation allied with life and social crises, and this applies not only to traditional religious rites but also to more secular ritual innovation.

In sum, the innovation that began in Carlisle in 1993 and now widely known as natural burial need not be identified as specifically religious or specifically secular. What that shift inaugurated, however, was the growth in provision of natural burial sites that seem to have become a refuge for the bereaved and for those contemplating their own mortality, and that has been feasible as such sites have made their appeal to people's physical, emotional and spiritual needs. In particular, the natural burial site is perceived as safe, nurturing and peaceful and, as such, particularly appropriate as a place to think, ponder and feel one's way through the difficult situations occasioned by personal bereavement and its ensuing grief. Concurrently, the dead are perceived not in a negative fashion as rotting corpses but much more positively in terms of their life-giving potential. This suggests that natural burial is an innovation within British mortuary practices, one that provides an empowering alternative to crematoria, cemeteries, churchyards and informal memorials. Natural burial grounds are 'good to think', gaining their significance as a means by which self-understanding of a cycle of life and death may be achieved. Life and death attain some final and satisfactory meaning as personal and family narratives are materialized through the topography of a place and the funeral and visiting rites that occur there. That kind of embedded understanding begins to constitute a form of core spirituality that may either be an end in itself or open to a variety of personal qualifiers in more religious or more secular terms. Notably, however, the potential redundancy of the religious–secular distinction itself marks a shift in spirituality that characterizes transformations in self understanding during the later twentieth and early twenty-first century for a significant group of people.

Notes

Chapter 1

1 This project ran largely concurrently with Sheffield University's social survey of natural burial grounds, which involved mapping the UK natural burial sites. See Clayden et al. (2010a, 2010b), Powell et al. (2011) and *Natural Burial Project,* www.naturalburialresearchproject.group.shef.ac.uk/index.html [retrieved 17/08/11].

2 Davies (1995).

3 Davies et al. (1991). Contributed to the Archbishops' Commission on Rural Areas.

4 Davies and Shaw (1995). Dr Julie Rugg of York University invited this as a research project.

5 Davies (1995, 1996, 1997b, 2002, 2005a, 2005b, 2006a, 2006b, 2008b), Davies and Guest (1999) and Davies and Mates (2005).

6 Rumble (2010).

7 Full interview material appears in Rumble (2010).

8 Thomas (2011). The film was produced in 2011, funded by Durham University's Centre for Death and Life Studies and Wolfson Institute.

9 Davies (2002: 113–18).

10 Davies (1984).

11 Davies (2011: 240–4).

12 Davies (1997a).

13 This is to follow Durkheim's sociological sense of 'moral' as social (1964 [1893]: 228). Such a moral world includes laws, rules, and commandments but goes far beyond the everyday sense of 'morality'. See Durkheim (1971 [1915]: 47) for 'religion' as a 'moral community'.

14 Goldschmidt (1990: 113–20) offers creative possibilities for analysing human life as a career pursued through a life cycle.

15 Davies (2008b).

16 Davies (2011) furnishes an extensive account of identity, reciprocity and emotion in religion.

17 Bachelor (2004), Francis et al. (2005) and Hockey et al. (2010).

18 Prideaux (2005: 2).

19 Ibid., 119.

20 Ibid., 116.

21 Ibid., 119.

Chapter 2

1 Powell et al. (2011).

2 See Rumble (2010).

3 For further details, visit www.arborytrust.org.

4 Clayden (2004), Harris (2007), Rumble (2010) and West (2010).

5 Consecration involves a legal change of status of a site through a formal act of a legitimate ecclesiastical authority, in this case, the Church of England. Dedication through prayer is quite different and legally less consequentially significant.

6 See the following webpage, 'Ireland's first eco-friendly graveyard opens', *The Irish World*, www.theirishworld.com/article.asp?SubSection_Id=2&Article_Id=16017 [retrieved 18/08/11].

7 One needs only to refer to their project's website and download a copy of the database to appreciate the diversity of natural burial provision. Available to view online at www.naturalburialresearchproject.group.shef.ac.uk/database.html [retrieved 15/07/10].

8 Source: Reproduced with permission of A. Clayden, J. Hockey and T. Green, from *Back to Nature? The Cultural, Social and Emotional Implications of Natural Burial. ESRC Funded Research Project*, www.naturalburialresearch-project.group.shef.ac.uk/sites.html [retrieved 23/06/10].

9 Clayden (2004: 74).

10 Compared to the figure of 207 quoted by Sheffield University researchers in personal correspondence dated 02/08/10.

11 Calculated using the NDC's database in February 2010. This figure was given in personal correspondence, however, Clayden et al. (2010b: 120) alternatively claim 56 per cent.

12 See www.naturalburialresearchproject.group.shef.ac.uk/index.html [retrieved 18/04/10]. From unpublished research by Clayden, A. Hockey, J. and T. Green (2010) *Back to Nature? The Cultural, Social and Emotional Implications of Natural Burial.*

13 Clayden (2004: 75).

14 For a distribution map of 'natural burial preserves' in America; see http://naturalburial.coop/USA/ [retrieved 23/07/11]. One of America's 'conservation' burial grounds is also the nation's first national pagan burial ground, founded in 1995 and known as Circle Cemetery. It is located within 200 acres of nature preserve called Circle Sanctuary. For further information, see www.circlesanctuary.org/cemetery/ [retrieved 30/06/10].

15 Harris (2007: 177).

16 See Boret's (2011) doctoral research in which he undertook anthropological fieldwork at a Japanese tree burial cemetery.

17 Tremlett (2007: 30).

18 New Zealand has three natural burial sites with a further one soon to open in Palmerston North. The three existing sites are located in Wellington (Makara), New Plymouth (Awanui) and Motueka. For further information, see *Natural Burial*, www.naturalburials.co.nz [retrieved 15/09/11].

19 Australia has limited natural burial provision located in Victoria (Lilydale Memorial Park), Lismore (Bushland Cemetery at Lismore Memorial Gardens run by Lismore City Council), and Kingston, Tasmania. The Metropolitan Cemeteries Board (MCB) in Western Australia has also established natural burial areas at Freemantle Cemetery and Rockingham Regional Memorial Park.

20 See advocacy by Mike Salisbury: the current president of the natural burial cooperative in Toronto and *Natural Burial in Canada*; www.naturalburial.coop/canada/ [retrieved 06/08/11].

21 There are five natural burial grounds in the Netherlands of which three have opened in the last two years. Four are privately owned mature woodland sites while the fifth is owned independently by a farmer. See Klaassens and Groote (2010) for case studies. The Dutch Architecture Fund sponsored Volimer and Partners, based in Utrecht, to conduct a feasibility study of various landscape designs, with results published in 2011 as *Landscape as Legacy*.

22 Germany has a significant number of 'natural burial sites', but these *Friedwald* sites are for cremated remains, since legislation for the control of ashes is strict. The first opened in 2001 near Kassel, run by a private company. By 2011 there were some 37 such sites across Germany. See www.friedwald.de/Startseite.AxCMS?ActiveID=3861. Nicole Sachmerda-Schulz, a doctoral student of Leipzig is currently researching this form of burial in Germany.

23 See *Capsula Mundi*. Two Italian designers have created a biodegradable egg-shaped coffin that is interred with a tree above. The idea is that this will facilitate the propagation of memorial forests in places of burial, www.capsulamundi.it/ [retrieved 06/08/10].

24 Joyce (2009: 529).

25 Harris (2007: 165).

26 Ibid., 3.

27 Ashwood (2009).

28 In an unpublished paper Parsons (2010) highlights that although embalming took place in Britain during the eighteenth century it was largely restricted to nobility and set apart from the services of the undertaker. Parsons attributes a historical shift, the relocation of the dead resting at home to funeral parlours, as largely influencing the significant uptake of commercial embalming in this country from the late 1950s: 'The growth of embalming stems from a period when greater responsibility for the body was being acquired by funeral directors. While custody did not automatically mean embalming would be carried out, the supply of embalming was in the interests of the funeral director in contrast to the service being demanded by the bereaved' (Ibid., 5). Presently however, there are no accurate figures for embalming conducted in the United Kingdom (2010: 8). The British Institute of Embalmers (BIE, launched in 1927) does not carry out a survey, although it has tried to do this in the past. What is known however is that embalming faces challenges because of 'concerns about the environmental consequences of burying or cremating embalmed bodies, and also the threat of the withdrawal of formaldehyde by the EC' (Parsons 2010: 8). See also West (2010: 23–6).

29 Rumble (2010).

30 Clayden et al. (2010b: 135).

31 From an interview in *Green Burial – KQED QUEST* (view from 09.18 minutes) YouTube, www.youtube.com/watch?v=gTzQ0GOelHk&feature=player_embedded [retrieved 02/03/10].

32 See Worpole (2003b: 193).

33 This view is maintained by an alternative burial provider, Perpetua's Garden: Cemeteries for the 21st century, in a blog entry called *Denying Death in Green Burials?* (10 December 2009), http://perpetuasgarden.org/green-burial/integrating-death-in-green-burial/ (retrieved 02/03/10).

34 Rugg (2000).

35 Klaassens and Groote (2010: 3).

36 Tarlow (2000: 224–5).

37 Powell et al. (2011: 4)

38 Historical examples include monastic 'healing' herb gardens from the eleventh century onwards, Greek and Roman spas, public parks and gardens, as well as healing gardens attached to hospitals and hospices. Worpole claims that: 'The spiritual or "healing" properties of landscape have, in recent times, begun to be reabsorbed into the vocabulary of civic culture' (2003b: 58) and we would also extend that to the resurgence of popularity for allotments and city farms as a focus for social cohesion projects with asylum seekers, young offenders, and those with mental or physical disabilities, amongst many other targeted groups. Cf. Rubino (2007) for example.

39 Worpole (2003b: 57–8); Tarlow (2000).

40 Slater and Peillon (2009: 95) and Slater (2007).

41 Park (1994) and Schantz (2008).

42 Constantine (1981).

43 Tarlow (2000: 218).

44 Gesler (1993, 1996, 1998) and Williams (2007: 1–12).

45 Worpole (2003b: 77).

46 Rugg (2000: 272).

47 See Hobsbawn and Ranger (2005 [1983]) for this concept.

48 Arbory Trust Newsletter (July 2008).

49 Goody (1994 [1993]: 292).

50 Ibid., 312.

51 Arbory Trust (July 2008).

52 Cowling (2010: 24).

53 Weller (1999: 4).

54 Schama (1996: 15).

55 See Relph (1976).

56 Porteous (1996: 102).

57 Worpole (2003b: 194).

58 Porteous (1996: 102).

59 Slater (2007: 239).

60 Pine II and Gilmore (1998).

61 Ibid., 299.

62 *Woodland Burial Parks Group*, www.woodlandburialparks.co.uk/ [retrieved 28/01/10]. See also Sanders (2009) for a discussion of commodifying funerals as 'events' and 'amusement'.

63 See Dickens (2004: 138+).

64 See Zukin (1991).

65 Worpole (2003b: 191).

66 Francis et al. (2005: 137).

67 See Bailey (2010).

68 Davies (2005c: 145).

69 Ibid.

70 Ibid.

71 Jones (2000: 77).

72 Ibid., 79.

73 Davies (2005c: 145).

74 Schantz (2008: 72).

75 Ibid.

76 Ibid., 73.

77 See Speyer (2006).

78 For a detailed discussion on the cultural symbolism of trees, cf. Bloch (1998), Eliade (1985: 7–8), Davies (1988), Jones and Cloke (2002), Palmer and Palmer (1997: 76–82), Rival (1998).

79 Macnaghten (2004: 234).

80 Nisbet et al. (2009) and Mayer et al. (2009), for example, utilize a 'connectedness to nature' and 'nature relatedness' scale as relevant measures, though they ignore the sociocultural factors that influence emotions and behaviour or our capacity to engage with 'nature', making their results interesting but somewhat limited in application.

81 West (2010: 56–7).

82 Milligan (2007: 261–5).

83 Churchyards, however, are much more ambiguous because they are also aligned with life. For example, wedding photographs outside the church.

84 Worpole (2003b).

85 Cf. Howarth (2000: 134) who argues more widely that the boundary between life and death is becoming 'dismantled' in contemporary Western Society because of ever greater diversification in how people deal with their grief and try to maintain continuity with the dead.

86 Francis et al. (2005: 41).

87 Davies (2005a: 126).

88 Cf. the notion of 'ambiguous place attachment' in Watkins et al. (2010: 371).

89 A concerted effort has been made to preserve and/or enhance wildlife and habitat diversity in churchyards in the Living Churchyard and Cemetery Project. Originally a project for Anglican rural parishes, this project is driven by appreciation for the environmental significance of churchyards 'retaining or restating a link between the sacred and the natural' (Palmer and Palmer 1997: 83). There are parallels between the ecological value perceived in the Living Churchyard project and natural burial: both ancient churchyards and natural burial sites are seen as opportunities to retain biodiversity, perhaps more so in ancient churchyards because of lichens and butterflies flourishing in the absence of insecticides and pesticides (Worpole 2003b: 75). However, the key difference between ecological projects vested in churchyards and natural burial grounds is that of intentionality. In many cases natural burial grounds were intentionally created for perceived ecological benefit and all were created to mimic the 'natural' to varying extents, whereas churchyards have become natural places deemed ecologically valuable through neglect.

90 See Gesler (1993, 2005), Jones (2005), Morris and Thomas (2005) and Williams (2007).

91 By comparison, the adoption of natural burial in America (see Harris 2007) melds with American wilderness constructions of landscape, as opposed to the 'tamed nature' more commonly envisaged in English landscapes (Porteous 1996: 104). Therefore, it would be interesting to learn to what extent and how, bereaved Americans found their natural burial landscapes therapeutic.

92 See Milligan (2007: 261–2) regarding the capacity of 'nature' to restore and provide reflection and diversion.

93 See Conradson (2007).

94 *Denying Death in Green Burials?* (10 December 2009), *Perpetua's Garden: Cemeteries for the 21st Century*, http://perpetuasgarden.org/green-burial/integrating-death-in-green-burial/ [retrieved 02/03/11].

95 Conradson (2007: 36).

96 Woodburn (1982: 191).

97 Cf. Slater and Peillon (2009: 99) regarding similar nature–society relations in the context of domestic gardens in which one has 'gardening labor processes' in opposition to nature's growth.

98 Notice he is using active verbs in relation to cemetery visiting that reinforces the comments made by visitors and users of Barton Glebe that in a cemetery one goes a with purpose to *do* something – usually out of a sense of duty – whereas a visit to a natural burial ground inspires less a sense of duty, rather an opportunity for meditation whilst going for a walk.

99 For examples in municipal cemeteries, see Clegg (1989) and Francis et al. (2005: 56).

100 Bradbury argues that for contemporary Britons the rite of reincorporation is most likely to be the private interment or scattering of ashes where 'the remains of the deceased are "let go" into the domain of the dead' (1999: 139). This is because cremation is the most commonly utilized mode of disposal at present in the United Kingdom.

101 Hertz (1960: 81–2).

102 Such behaviour has also been observed in Dutch natural burial grounds. See Klaassens and Groote (2010).

103 Davies (2005c: 146).

104 Powell et al. (2011: 2).

105 Clayden et al. (2010b).

Chapter 3

1 As in the polythetic form of classification whose members have no single feature in common: in the monothetic form, by contrast, a single element, defines a phenomenon (Needham 1979: 64–7).

2 See Powell et al. (2011: 2).

3 See, respectively, www.naturaldeath.org.uk/ [retrieved 16/02/11]; www.good-funeralguide.co.uk [retrieved 16/02/11]; www.gravematters.us/ [retrieved 02/03/11]; www.alternativefuneralmonitor.com/2009/03/sustainable-cemetery-management.html and www.beatree.com [retrieved 16/02/11].

4 For example, The American 'Natural Burial Company' and also 'Natural Burial in the United Kingdom'.

5 Powell et al. (2011: 2).

6 See Davies (2005a, 2006b).

7 See C. Beal: www.alternativefuneralmonitor.com/2009/03/sustainable-cemetery-management.html and www.beatree.com [retrieved 16/02/11].

8 See www.somersetwillow.co.uk/ [retrieved 03/03/11].

9 King (2009).

10 Clayden et al. (2010a: 149).

11 See www.greenfuse.co.uk/ and http://freespace.virgin.net/heaven.earth/ [both retrieved 14/08/11] who describe their business as the only 'Design your Life and Death Shop' in the United Kingdom.

12 For example, Welfare State International (see www.deadgoodguides.com/pages/publications.html [retrieved 13/08/11]) who published the *Dead Good Funeral Guide* and create imaginative, secular rites of passage ceremonies.

13 Owen Jones (2008: 153).

14 See West (2010: 203–63) who provides extensive advice on how to market natural burial and suggests 15 promotional messages to convey in advertising, most of them espousing environmental values.

15 These merits are complex and difficult to ascertain because pro-environmental behaviour and values fall between *impact* and *intent*: 'people may act in ways that are proenvironmental in intent but that in fact have little or no positive environmental impact' (Stern 2000: 415).

16 For a review of the often conflicting constructions of value encapsulated in the term 'biodiversity' see Cooper (2000).

17 Clayden (2004: 70).

18 See Hofmeister (2009).

19 See Green (2003).

20 For example, see www.woodlandburialparks.co.uk/Our-Surroundings.ice [retrieved 21/01/10].

21 See Owen Jones (2008), Speyer (2006) and West (2005, 2008, 2010).

22 See Chamberlain (2005) and Morrow (2005).

23 Eco Coffins Ltd.

24 West (2008: 104).

25 For discussions on the 'green' merits of various disposal modes cf. Cowling (2009), Joyce (2009), Owen Jones (2008), Thompson (2002) and West (2008, 2010).

26 Ecocoffins®, www.ecocoffins.com/ [retrieved 22/01/10].

27 Native Woodland natural burial sites http://www.nativewoodland.eu/index.php?page=slideshow-guide [retrieved 22/01/10].

28 Green Fuse help sheet 4, *10 Tips for a Green Funeral: Make Your Final Statement for a More Sustainable World by Choosing a Green Funeral*, www.greenfuse.co.uk/pdfs/4-ten-tips-for-a-green-funeral.pdf [retrieved 22/01/10].

29 Joyce (2009).

30 www.naturalburial.coop/about-natural-burial/incineration-cremation/ [retrieved 22/01/10] and www.naturalburial.coop/about-natural-burial/conventional-burial/ [retrieved 22/01/10].

31 www.naturalburial.coop/ [retrieved 22/01/10].

32 Davies (2006b: 240).

33 Stern (2000: 415).

34 Veldman (1994: 5).

35 Walter and Gittings (2010: 168).

36 Veldman (1994: 3).

37 Beck (1995: 39).

38 See Tarlow (2000).

39 Lowenthal (1985: 175).

40 See *About Woodland Burials* where this natural burial provider has juxtaposed a photograph of a neglected, overgrown cemetery with an image of a natural burial ground of long grass and maturing trees with the caption 'If only the Victorians had thought of Woodland Burials! . . . Which of these places would you choose as your final resting place?' www.woodlandburials.co.uk/about.html [retrieved 11/08/11].

41 Tarlow (1999: 136–7).

42 See Clayden et al. (2010a).

43 Walter and Gittings (2010: 177).

44 Rumble (2010).

45 Jupp (1993: 190) citing Woodburn (1982: 206).

46 Jupp (1993: 190).

47 The irony here of course is that cardboard originates from wood pulp.

48 See Dickens (2004: 110).

49 See Vandendorpe (2000: 29).

50 See Freud (1922: 54).

51 Davies (2002: 59ff.) explored this theme of obligation and unobligedness when engaging with Ortner's (1978) study of Sherpa life and, more fully elsewhere in terms of hope and 'otherness' in religion (Davies 2002a: 172–6).

52 Beck (1995: 53).

53 We should stress that this is not unique to natural burial, Vandendorpe (2000) argues that the mixing of cremated remains with soil or water permits spiritual rebirth of life from death and survival.

54 Van Gennep (1960) and Turner (1967).

55 Prendergast et al. (2006: 895).

56 Davis (1979: 99), citing Williams (1974).

57 Berberich (2006: 207) argues: 'the English countryside has been used as the most effective evocation of Englishness: in times of war and peace alike it has been used, by the English as well as by foreigners, to express both nostalgia and hope, a sense of belonging, a yearning for home. The English landscape was held up to the soldiers of both world wars as "what they were fighting for" '.

58 King (2009: 86).

59 Lifton (1974, 1976).

60 Vigilant et al. (2003: 173).

61 Ibid.

62 Vigilant (2009: 924).

63 Ibid., 925.

64 Lifton (1974: 685). Reservation with Lifton's work lies with his assumption that there is a 'universal urge' to secure symbolic immortality. Such a generalization is typical of the human cognitive sciences preoccupied with elucidating universals in cognitive behaviour, whilst the death denial concept to which symbolic immortality is aligned, maybe little more than academic 'failure to recognize and acknowledge new (or previously marginalized) ways of making sense of mortality.' (Howarth 2007: 265). Much the same can be said of Ernest Becker's influential yet dated psychoanalytically rooted study *The Denial of Death* (Free Press, 1973).

65 Lifton (1974: 685).

66 Vigilant (2009: 925) and Lifton (1974).

67 Vigilant et al. (2003: 173).

68 Vigilant (2009: 926).

69 Colny Wood Burial Park. See http://greenfinder.co.uk/companies/eco-funerals-green-burials [retrieved 23/08/10].

70 Living Memory Olney Green Burial, www.olneygreenburial.co.uk/natural_living_memory.asp [retrieved 19/01/10].

71 West (2008: 108).

72 In sociological literature, social fragmentation is stipulated to have begun in earnest during the twentieth century. Western populations, it is often assumed, are highly geographically and socially mobile because kinship patterns changed dramatically in the twentieth century with the rise of single-parent and second-family households (Howarth 2007: 230). However, I am not convinced by these generalizations as there are trends in developing countries for individuals to live abroad in more affluent countries in order to send remittances home for example, complicating the generalisation that western cultures are more geographically mobile. The quantifier 'western populations' is too vague to be of any substantive use in our opinion.

73 By way of cultural comparison Tremlett (2007) argues that because Taiwanese 'tree burial' has an absence of social markers because there are no headstones, that this burial mode is indicative of atomization and mobility in contemporary Taiwanese society.

74 Jupp (1993: 185).

75 Rival (1998: 9).

76 Jupp (1993: 184).

77 Howarth (2007: 228).

78 Clayden's unpublished presentation 'Distribution and Diversity' given at the First National UK Natural Burial Conference, held in Sheffield on 25 March 2010 at the University of Sheffield's Department of Landscape. See www.natural-burialresearchproject.group.shef.ac.uk/conference.html [retrieved 22/08/11].

79 See Creswell (2004: 97).

80 See Dickens (2004: 100ff.) for a discussion of environmental values and anti-commodification. He lists farmers' markets, locally created money systems, and LETS schemes as pathways of resistance to commodities and consumerism. The perspective of some natural burial users would suggest that this practice might also be included.

81 Weber ([1904–5] 1930: 155–83).

82 Prothero (2001: 209).

83 Cutting (2009: 367), citing Prothero (2001: 209–11).

84 See Dickens (2004: 123ff.).

85 See Bourdieu (2004 [1979]).

86 Davies (2008b: 24–6) explores the theological-liturgical signification of coffins and introduces the notion of 'full' and 'half-symbols' in his discussion.

87 West (2010: 26–7).

88 'Natural Woven Products: Environmentally Friendly Woven Coffins', www.naturalwovencoffins.co.uk/ [retrieved 25/01/10].

89 www.bellacouche.com/ [retrieved 25/01/10].

90 Cf. Bourdieu (2004 [1979]).

91 Joyce (2009: 528).

92 For example, Kearl (2009: 877–8) claims 'affluent Americans were more likely to choose less expensive funerary options . . . than those of the working class'.

93 Dickens (2004: 143), Bourdieu (2004 [1979]) and Illouz (2009).

94 Davies (2005a) and Green (2008).

95 For example, see Qureshi (2007).

96 Connolly and Prothero (2008: 117) and Dickens (2004).

97 Owen Jones (2008: 156).

98 Howes (2005: 290).

99 See Pine II and Gilmore (1998).

100 Howes (2005).

101 Habgood (2002: 141).

102 Howes (2005: 298).

103 Of those interviewed in Rumble's (2010) study at Barton Glebe, the faiths represented were Anglican (including First-, Second- and Third-order Franciscans), Catholic, Pentecostal, Baptist, Methodist, Salvation Army, Quaker, Unitarian, 'Pagan', Humanist and Atheist.

104 Davies (2008b: 26).

105 Owen Jones (2008: 153).

106 Ibid., 156; Rumble (2010).

107 Especially, Rumble (2010).

108 Jupp (1993: 179).

109 Cowling (2010: 29).

110 Clayden and Dixon (2007: 241).

111 Davies (2005a, 2006a, 2006b, 2008b).

112 Giddens (1995 [1991]: 82, 85).

113 West (2010: 66) asserts that: 'the burial of pets is a potential marketing niche for natural burial sites' and mentions a site in Cornwall that already offers such a service. See also Jamieson (2010). Limited natural burial grounds and pet cemeteries offer this option, which Rosie would have chosen had she known about it.

114 Giddens (1995 [1991]: 85–6).

115 See Davies (2005a).

116 Worpole (2003b).

117 Prothero (2001: 98).

118 See Veldman (1994).

119 Cowling (2010: 26).

Chapter 4

1 Ayers (2006).

2 Olney Green Burial website *Why a Green Burial*, www.olneygreenburial. co.uk/natural_why_green_burial.asp [retrieved 22/07/09].

3 The Arbory Trust's homepage, http://arborytrust.org/ [retrieved 22/07/09].

4 *A Tree as a Living Memorial*, www.nrbgrounds.co.uk/memorials/trees.html [retrieved 06/05/10].

5 *Why Green Burial?* www.swansea.gov.uk/index.cfm?articleid=924 [retrieved 06/05/10]. Further research should ask what sentiments or emotions are encapsulated in this advertising appeal to 'celebrate'.

6 For example, the natural burial site is also a nature reserve or a re-forested area. Quote from *Sun Rising Natural Burial Ground*, www.midlandsgreen-pages.co.uk/companies/woodland-burials/sun-rising-natural-burial-ground/ [retrieved 06/05/10].

7 Shimanozo (2008: 35).

8 Titmuss (1973 [1970]: 256).

9 Lifton (1974, 1976).

10 Grimes (2000: 251).

11 Davies and Shaw (1995: 86–101) and Davies, D. J. (1996: 17–29).

12 Mimms (1999: 136).

13 Parry (1994). See Davies (2002b: 86 [1997a].

14 Maus (1974 [1954]: 1).

15 See James (1998) and Karsenti (1998) for Durkheim's influence on Mauss.

16 Sykes (2005: 3).

17 Sykes (2005: 1, 59).

18 West (2008: 108).

19 Cowling (2010: 27).

20 Davies (2008b: 119–20).

21 Bloch and Parry (1982: 7). Original emphasis.

22 Beck (1995: 37).

23 Bloch and Parry (1982: 8).See also Primavesi (2003).

24 Parry (1994).

25 Mitchell (2004: 123–4).

26 Mitchell (2001: 124).

27 Baudrillard (1993: 147).

28 We are critical of the lack of empirical evidence used to illustrate his argument and his uncritical use of terms such as 'Western', 'traditional' and 'primitives'. His abstracted generalizations tend to nullify the effects of socio-cultural and historical particularities. His argument would be compelling if he could show how the reality he presents operates despite geographical, historical and cultural differences.

29 Baudrillard (1993: 164).

30 See the company's UK website at www.promessa.org.uk/index.php [retrieved 12/04/11].

31 Sykes (2005: 3).

32 West (2010: xviii).

33 Godelier (1999: 175).

34 Osteen (2002b: 9–10). Our emphasis.

35 Mauss (1974: 12) and Godelier (1999: 13).

36 Godelier (1999: 13).

37 Davies (2002a: 13), citing Godelier (1999: 32–3, 120).

38 Davies (2002: 196).

39 Osteen (2002a: 241).

40 Lifton (1974, 1976). Also see Kamerman (2003), Vigilant and Williamson (2003) and Vigilant (2009).

41 Lifton (1974: 686).

42 Klass et al. (1996) and Neimeyer et al. (2006).

43 Lifton (1974: 685).

44 Ibid., 684.

45 Ibid., 686.

46 Curiously he continues by claiming: 'It is not only in Shinto belief, but in the European Romantic Movement and in the Anglo-Saxon cult of the great outdoors – indeed in every culture in one form or another' (1974: 686). While we would interrogate his claim of the *universal* pursuit of symbolic immortality through the natural pathway, we concur with his comparison to the Romantic Movement, for as discussed in Chapter 3, romantic values are certainly invested in the British practice of natural burial.

47 Boret (2011).

48 From an abstract of Boret's paper entitled 'When Life Crisis meets Environmental Crisis: Imagining Death and Ecological Immortality in Japanese Tree-Burial' presented at the European Association of Social Anthropologists (EASA) 2010 conference in Maynooth, Ireland; www.nomadit.co.uk/easa/easa2010/panels.php5?PanelID=590 [retrieved 09/05/10].

49 Smith (2005: 219).

50 Sheldrake (2001: 1). As argued by Rumble (2010).

51 Klass (1999, 2006) and Klass et al. (1996).

52 Walter (1996) and Valentine (2008).

53 Freud (1922) and Bowlby (1969).

54 Relph (1976: 38).

55 Ibid., 39.

56 Ibid., 147.

57 Abram (2001).

58 Ackroyd (2002).

59 For historical, comparative analysis of 'Sylvan patriotism' see Schama (1996: 172).

60 For comparative, historical detail on the culture of flowers in association with death and funerals refer to Goody (1994 [1993]: 283–320).

61 Tolia-Kelly (2007: 175).

62 Davies (1988).

63 Deakin (2008).

64 Jones and Cloke (2002: 230).

65 Macnaghten (2004: 232).

66 Ingold (2004: 204–5).

67 Macnaghten (2004: 232).

68 Davies (2005a).

69 Sehee's quote at 09:18 minutes and narrator's quote at 09:56 minutes in the video 'Green Burial – KQED QUEST', www.youtube.com/watch?v=gTzQ0GO elHk&feature=player_embedded [retrieved 24/04/10].

70 Bloch and Parry (1982).

71 Ibid., 15.

72 Beck (1995: 4).

73 Ibid., 36.

74 Ibid., 37, 40.

75 Ibid., 39.

76 Ibid., 37.

77 Warpole (2003a).

78 Beck (1995: 55).

79 Ibid., 48, 53; Veldman (1994).

80 Ibid., 53.

81 Rappaport (1999: 304).

82 Davies (2005a: 79–80).

83 Ibid., 87.

84 Ibid., 84, citing McGinn (1993).

85 Primavesi (2003: 123).

86 Osteen (2002b: 9–10).

87 Godelier (1999: 207).

88 Bloch (1998: 40–1).

89 Rival (1998: 27).

90 Ibid., 23.

Chapter 5

1 The use of electric and not gas cremators allowed Parsees to argue that the ritual purity of fire, an integral aspect of their tradition, was not impugned since flames as such did not touch the body (Schofield 2005: 428–9).

2 Jupp (2006).

3 Max Weber's notion of disenchantment is often aligned by others with secularization. Weber saw disenchantment as having existed in the West 'for millennia' (1991 [1919]: 139).

4 Rounded down approximate percentage population cremated: 1932 (1%), 1942 (5%), 1947 (10%), 1952 (19%), 1962 (38%), 1968 (51%), 1972 (57%) and 1982 (66%). From 1993 (70%) a relative plateau was established in the low 70% range. Davies and Mates (2005: 433–56).

5 In 1884 cremation declared not to be illegal in England and Wales. First cremation at Woking Crematorium, 1885.

6 See Davies (1996: 83–94).

7 Americans abbreviated 'cremated remains' to the neologism 'cremains'.

8 Davies and Guest (1999: 26–30).

9 In its *Alternative Service Book* of 1980 the Church of England offered its first real set of legal variations for funerals including the Burial of a Child since its 1662 *Book of Common Prayer*. An order for The Burial of Child was provided in the 1928 *Prayer Book* which was, itself, not granted final legal approval.

10 In 1990 some 25 per cent of British crematoria reported still using a form of clergy rota (Davies 1995: 24).

11 Davies (2011: 37–67).

12 Max Weber (1963 [1922]: 158–9) used '*habitus*' for a 'pattern of life'. It is more frequently identified as a key idea in Bourdieau (1977 [1972]: 72–87). It also possesses a long history in theology and spirituality, see Borella (1998 [1996]: 108).

13 Comte-Sponville (2008 [2006]: 49).

14 Some technical studies of 'the individual' challenge the dominance of western intellectualism in privileging an isolated entity, for example, Strathern (1990 [1988]).

15 See Davies (1997a: 78, 109, 166).

16 Meanwhile, some Islamic traditions maintain strong beliefs in judgment, hell and paradise; see Rustomji (2009).

17 Davies (1996: 21–2).

18 Wright (2003).

19 Scarre, G. (2007).

20 Cutting (2009: 356–7).

21 Anthropologist Victor Turner (1969: 52) considered the multivocal or polysemic nature of symbolism, where numerous meanings condense in a single symbol.

22 We should draw attention to the fact that this is not universal since some societies, for example Korea, use white to indicate death.

23 Gen. 3.19.

24 *Book of Common Prayer*, 'At the Burial of the Dead'.

25 Mt. 27.60, Mk 15.46, Lk. 23.53 and Jn 19.41–42.

26 Her comment raises a question. Is she implying that cemeteries are 'egoisti-
    cal'? And, if they are, is it because of marked graves?

27 Van Baaren (1989: 99).

28 Schutz (1964: 106–19). Cf. Eliade, 'nostalgia for paradise' (1968 [1960]:
    57–71).

29 Freud (1922: 201). See Clark (1982: 432–6).

30 See Davies (2002: 201), for the inalienable gift of the Eucharist occurring 'out
    of time'.

31 Davies (2005a: 83).

32 Davies and Mates (1995: 27–9).

33 Gen. 3.19 and 1 Cor. 15.36, respectively.

34 Gen. 1.31. The interplay of death and life are common in ancient mythology.
    See Eliade (1978 [1976]: 156–74) for Canaanite religion and the biblical crea-
    tion accounts.

35 Prince (1988: 98–118). Exemplifies eighteenth century English Romanticism
    of the landscape.

36 Latin *ex nihilo*, out of nothing, symbolizes ultimate divine being and the
    dependent nature of all else.

37 Gen. 2.7.

38 See Davies (1984: 32–6) for 'salvation' as a quality of plausibility.

39 Lev. 16.15–19 and Heb. 9.7–28.

40 Issues involved here concern the identification of the Last Supper with the
    Jewish Passover. See Davies (2008b: 149, 159–60).

41 Davies (1989 [1988]: 32–42).

42 See John Henry Newman's famous 1865 hymn 'Praise to the Holiest in
    the height', with its renowned lines, 'O loving wisdom of our God! When
    all was sin and shame, a second Adam to the fight and to the rescue
    came'.

43 Charles Wesley's 1742 hymn, 'O for a heart to praise my God' does echo this
    theme. 'My heart, Thou knowest, can never rest, Till Thou create my peace;
    Till, of my Eden repossessed, From self and sin I cease'.

44 Gen. 1.1–2.3.

45 Gen. 2.8–9, 3.22.

46 Rev. 22.2.

47 Other motifs depict God's people as a vineyard (Isa. 5.1–7), grafted stock
    (Rom. 11.16–21), and even Jesus as a vine (Jn 15.1–8).

48 Schweitzer ([1907] and 1919). Discussed in Davies (2008b: 67–72).

49 Lovelock (1995).

50 Typified by E. B. Tylor (1871) and his notion of 'animism'.

51 Gen. 15.5–6.

52 We are indebted to Systematic Theologian Prof. Risto Saarinen of Helsinki
    University for drawing our attention to this linguistic usage in a seminar

context. See also Saarinen (2010: 269–70). He derived the idea from John Newman (1996), A. E. Goldberg (1995) and John Lyons (1975).

53 Saarinen (2010: 271).

54 Similar to Hubert and Mauss's gift theory of sacrifice (1964 [1898]), which also cites Tylor's original gift-theory of sacrifice (2010 [1871]: 340–53).

55 Weber saw much civilized life and death as mutually meaningless (1993 [1919]: 139), while the death of soldiers was powerfully meaningful ([1915a] 1993: 335). See Jon Davies (1995) for the parallel of Christ's death and the death of soldiers in war.

56 Job 1.21. From a tale of family catastrophe and bereavement.

57 In the sense of a real ontologically on-going of the core of a person and not simply as memory held by others of that person.

58 Each of these innovative forms received what may have been their first joint publicity in a relatively detailed sketch in the 'Today' Programme of BBC Radio 4 on 31 August 2011.

59 The originator gives the etymology of 'promession' as the Italian *promessa* or promise.

60 See *How Promession Works*, http://www.promessa.org.uk/how-promession-works.php [retrieved 30 /06/10].

Bibliography

Abram, D. (2001), 'Reciprocity and the salmon water-borne reflections from the northwest coast.' *Alliance for Wild Ethics*. Retrieved 26/04/10, from www.wildethics.org/essays/reciprocity_and_the_salmon.html.

Ackroyd, P. (2002), *Albion: The Origins of the English Imagination*. London: Chatto & Windus.

Anonymous (2009), 'The rise of the green funeral.' *Ethical Living* (March/April), 12–14.

Ashwood, P. (2009), 'Embalming', in C. D. Bryant and D. L. Peck (eds), *Encyclopedia of Death and the Human Experience*. London: Sage, 1, 404–7.

Augé, M. (1995), *Non-Places: Introduction to an Anthropology of Supermodernity*. London: Verso.

Ayers, P. (2006), *Surgically Enhanced*. London: Hodder & Stoughton.

Baaren, T. P. van. (1989), 'Geographies of Death', in L. E. Sullivan (ed.), *Death, Afterlife, and the Soul*. London: Collier-Macmillan. 96–101.

Bachelor, P. (2004), *Sorrow and Solace, The Social World of the Cemetery*. New York: Baywood Publishing Company.

Bailey, T. (2010), 'When commerce meets care: emotion management in UK funeral directing.' *Mortality* 15(3), 205–22.

Baudrillard, J. (1993), *Symbolic Exchange and Death*. London: Sage.

Beck, U. (1995), *Ecological Politics in an Age of Risk*. Cambridge: Polity.

Becker, E. (1973), *The Denial of Death*. New York: Free Press.

Berberich, C. (2006), 'This green and pleasant land: cultural constructions of Englishness', in R. Burden and S. Kohl (eds), *Landscape and Englishness*. Amsterdam: Rodopi, 207–24.

Bloch, M. (1998), 'Why trees, too, are good to think with: towards an anthropology of the meaning of life', in L. Rival (ed.), *The Social Life of Trees: Anthropological Perspectives on Tree Symbolism*. Oxford: Berg, 39–55.

Bloch, M. and J. Parry (1982), 'Introduction: death and the regeneration of life', in M. Bloch and J. Parry (eds), *Death and the Regeneration of Life*. Cambridge: Cambridge University Press, 1–44.

Borella, J. (1998 [1996]), *The Sense of the Supernatural*, translated by G. J. Champoux. Edinburgh: T&T Clark.

Boret, S. (2011), *From Social to Ecological Immortality: Kinship, Identity and Death in Japanese Tree Burial*. Oxford: Oxford Brookes University (unpublished thesis).

Bourdieu, P. (1977 [1972]), *Outline of a Theory of Practice*. Cambridge: Cambridge University Press.

—(2004 [1979]), *Distinction: A Social Critique of the Judgement of Taste*. London: Routledge.

Bowlby, J. (1969), *Attachment (Attachment and Loss*, Vol. 1). New York: Basic Books.

Bradbury, M. (1999), *Representations of Death: A Social Psychological Perspective.* London: Routledge.

Chamberlain, C. (2005), 'Atmospheric emissions from cremators', in D. J. Davies and L. H. Mates (eds), *Encyclopedia of Cremation.* Aldershot: Ashgate, 147–8.

Clark, R. W. (1982), *Freud: The Man and the Cause.* London, New York: Granada.

Clayden, A. (2003), 'Woodland burial.' *Landscape Design* 322 (July/August), 22–5.

—(2004), 'Natural burial, British style.' *Landscape Architecture* (May), 68–75.

Clayden, A. and K. Dixon (2007), 'Woodland burial: memorial arboretum versus natural native woodland?' *Mortality* 12(3), 240–60.

Clayden, A., J. Hockey and M. Powell (2010a), 'Natural burial: the de-materialising of death?', in J. Hockey, C. Komaromy and K. Woodthorpe (eds), *The Matter of Death: Space, Place and Materiality.* Basingstoke, Hampshire: Palgrave Macmillan, 148–64.

Clayden, A., T. Green, J. Hockey and M. Powell (2010b), 'From cabbages to cadavers: natural burial down on the farm', in A. Maddrell and J. Sidaway (eds), *Deathscapes: Spaces for Death, Dying, Mourning and Remembrance.* Farnham, Surrey: Ashgate, 119–38.

Clegg, F. (1989), 'Cemeteries for the living.' *Landscape Design* 184, 15–17.

Comte-Sponville, A. (2007 [2006]), *The Book of Atheist Spirituality*, translated by Nancy Houston. London: Bantam Books.

—(2009 [2008]), *Atheist Spirituality*, translated by Nancy Houston. London: Bantam Books.

Connolly, J. and A. Prothero (2008), 'Green consumption: life-politics, risk, and contradictions.' *Journal of Consumer Culture* 8(1), 117–45.

Conradson, D. (2007), 'The experiential economy of stillness: places of retreat in contemporary Britain', in A. Williams (ed.), *Therapeutic Landscapes.* Aldershot: Ashgate, 33–48.

Constantine, S. (1981), 'Amateur gardening and popular recreation in the 19th and 20th centuries.' *Journal of Social History* 14(3), 387–406.

Cooper, N. (2000), 'Speaking and listening to nature: ethics within ecology.' *Biodiversity and Conservation* 9(8), 1009–27.

Cowling, C. (2009), 'All shades of green in the green shade.' *The Good Funeral Guide.* Retrieved 22/01/10, from www.goodfuneralguide.co.uk/2009/02/all-shades-of-green-in-green-shade.html.

—(2010), *The Good Funeral Guide.* London: Continuum.

Cresswell, T. (2004), *Place: A Short Introduction.* Oxford: Blackwell.

Cutting, A. (2009), 'Ashes in orbit: Celestis spaceflights and the invention of post-cremationist afterlives.' *Science as Culture* 18(3), 355–69.

Davies, D. J. (1984), *Meaning and Salvation in Religious Studies.* Leiden: Brill.

—(1988), 'The evocative symbolism of trees', in D. Cosgrove and S. Daniels (eds), *The Iconography of Landscape.* Cambridge: Cambridge University Press, 32–42.

—(1995), *British Crematoria in Public Profile.* Maidstone, Kent: Cremation Society of Great Britain.

—(1996), 'The social facts of death', in G. Howarth and P. C. Jupp (eds), *Contemporary Issues in the Sociology of Death, Dying and Disposal.* London: McMillan Press, 17–29.

—(1997a) *Death Ritual and Belief, The Rhetoric of Funerary Rites*, 1st edn. London: Cassell.

—(1997b), 'Contemporary belief in life after death', in P. C. Jupp and T. Rogers (eds), *Interpreting Death: Christian Theology and Pastoral Practice.* London: Cassell, 131–42.

—(2002a), *Anthropology and Theology*. Oxford: Berg.

—(2002b [1997a]), *Death, Ritual and Belief: The Rhetoric of Funerary Rites*. London: Continuum.

—(2005a), *A Brief History of Death*. Oxford: Blackwell.

—(2005b), 'Remains', in D. J. Davies and L. H. Mates (eds), *Encyclopedia of Cremation*. Aldershot: Ashgate, 57–60.

—(2005c), 'Non-place or allurement', in D. J. Davies and L. H. Mates (eds), *Encyclopedia of Cremation*. Aldershot: Ashgate, 145–6.

—(2006a), 'Changing values and repositioning cremation in society.' *Pharos International* 72(1), 15–16.

—(2006b), 'Forms of disposal', in K. Garces-Foley (ed.), *Death and Religion in a Changing World*. London: M. E. Sharpe, 228–45.

—(2008a), 'Cultural intensification: a theory for religion', in A. Day (ed.), *Religion and the Individual: Belief, Practice and Identity*. Aldershot: Ashgate, 7–18.

—(2008b), *The Theology of Death*. London: T&T Clark.

—(2011), *Emotion, Identity and Religion: Hope, Reciprocity and Otherness*. Oxford: Oxford University Press.

Davies, D. J. and M. Guest (1999), 'Disposal of cremated remains'. *Pharos* (Spring), 26–30.

Davies, D. J. and L. H. Mates (eds) (2005), *Encyclopedia of Cremation*. Aldershot: Ashgate.

Davies, D. J. and A. Shaw (1995) *Reusing Old Graves: A Report on Popular British Attitudes*. Crayford, Kent: Shaw and Sons.

Davies, D. J., C. Watkins and M. Winter (1991), *Church and Religion in Rural England*. Edinburgh: T&T Clark.

Davies, J. (1995), *The Christian Warrior in the Twentieth Century*. Lewiston, Queenston, Lampeter: Edwin Mellen Press.

Davis, F. (1979), *Yearning for Yesterday: A Sociology of Nostalgia*. New York: Free Press.

Deakin, R. (2008), *Wildwood: A Journey through Trees*. London: Penguin.

Dickens, P. (2004), *Society and Nature: Changing our Environment, Changing Ourselves*. Cambridge: Polity.

Durkheim, E. (1964 [1893]), *The Division of Labour in Society*. New York: The Free Press.

—(1971 [1915]), *The Elementary Forms of the Religious Life*. London: George Allen and Unwin Ltd.

Eliade, M. (1968 [1960]), *Myths, Dreams and Mysteries*. London: Collins.

—(1979 [1976]), *A History of Religious Ideas*, Vol. 1, translated by W. R. Trask. London: Collins.

—(1985), *A History of Religious Ideas: From Muhammad to the Age of Reforms*. Chicago, IL: University of Chicago Press, Vol. 3.

Francis, D., L. Kellaher and G. Neophytou (2005), *The Secret Cemetery*. Oxford: Berg.

Frazer, J. G. (1994 [1890]), *The Golden Bough*, R. Fraser. (ed.). London, New York: Oxford University Press.

Freud, S. (1922), *Beyond the Pleasure Principle*. London, Vienna: The International Psycho-analytical Press.

Gesler, W. (1993), 'Therapeutic landscapes: theory and a case study of Epidauros, Greece.' *Environment and Planning: Society and Space* 11(2), 171–89.

—(1996), 'Lourdes: healing in a place of pilgrimage.' *Health and Place* 2(2), 95–105.

—(1998), 'Bath's reputation as a healing place', in R. A. Kearns and W. M. Gesler (eds), *Putting Health into Place*. Syracuse: Syracuse University Press, 17–35.

—(2005), 'Therapeutic landscapes: an evolving theme.' *Health and Place* 11(4), 295–7.

Giddens, A. (1995 [1991]), *Modernity and Self Identity: Self and Society in the Late Modern Age*. Cambridge: Polity.

Godelier, M. (1999), *The Enigma of the Gift*. Chicago, IL: University of Chicago Press.

Goldberg, A. E. (1995), *Constructions: A Construction Grammar Approach to Argument Structure*. Chicago, IL: University of Chicago Press.

Goldschmidt, W. (1990), *The Human Career, the Self in the Symbolic World*. Oxford: Blackwell.

Goody, J. (1994 [1993]), *The Culture of Flowers*. Cambridge: Cambridge University Press.

Green, J. W. (2008), *Beyond the Good Death: The Anthropology of Modern Dying*. Philadelphia, PA: University of Pennsylvania Press.

Green, K. (2003). *Green Burials: Is there a Growing Demand?* Middlesex University (unpublished MA dissertation in resource management with a specialism in arboriculture).

Grimes, R. L. (2000), *Deeply into the Bone: Re-invention of Rites of Passage*. London: University of California Press.

Habgood, J. (2002), *The Concept of Nature*. London: Darton, Longman and Todd.

Hall, H. (2009), *Woodland Burial*. University of Durham (unpublished BA dissertation in theology and religion).

Harris, M. (2007), *Grave Matters: A Journey through the Modern Funeral Industry to a Natural Way of Burial*. New York: Scribner.

Hertz, R. (1960), *Death and the Right Hand*. Aberdeen: Cohen and West.

Hobsbawm, E. and T. Ranger (eds) (2005 [1983]), *The Invention of Tradition*. Cambridge: Cambridge University Press Canto.

Hockey, J., C. Komaromy and K. Woodthorpe (2010), *The Matter of Death, Space, Place and Materiality*. New York: Palgrave Macmillan.

Hofmeister, S. (2009), 'Natures running wild: a social-ecological perspective on wilderness.' *Nature and Culture* 4, 293–315.

Howarth, G. (2000), 'Dismantling the boundaries between life and death.' *Mortality: Promoting the Interdisciplinary Study of Death and Dying* 5(2), 127–38.

—(2007), *Death and Dying: A Sociological Introduction*. Cambridge: Polity.

Howes, D. (2005), 'Hyperesthesia, or, the sensual logic of late capitalism', in D. Howes (ed.), *Empire of the Senses: The Sensual Culture Reader*. Oxford: Berg, 281–303.

Hubert, H. and M. Mauss (1964 [1898]), *Sacrifice, its Nature and Function*. London: Cohen and West.

Illouz, E. (2009), 'Emotions, imagination and consumption: a new research agenda.' *Journal of Consumer Culture* 9(3), 377–413.

Ingold, T. (2000), *The Perception of the Environment: Essays on Livelihood, Dwelling and Skill*. London: Routledge.

Jackson, M. (2005), *Existential Anthropology: Events, Exigencies, and Effects*. New York, Oxford: Bergahn.

James, W. (1998), ' "One of Us": Marcel Mauss and "English" Anthropology', in W. James and N. J. Allen (eds), *Marcel Mauss: A Centenary Tribute*. Oxford: Bergahn, 3–26.

Jamieson, A. (23 January 2010), 'Owners pay to be buried with their pets.' Retrieved 22/07/10, from www.telegraph.co.uk/health/petshealth/7061716/Owners-pay-to-be-buried-with-their-pets.html.

Johnston, H. (Autumn/Winter 2004), 'The natural way burial movement.'CONNECTIONS: Scotland's Voice of Alternative Health Magazine. Retrieved 19/01/2009, from www.naturalwayburial.org.uk/USERIMAGES/If%20 you%20could%20be%2%20tree%20-%20Jan%2008.PDF.

Jones, L. (2000), The Hermeneutics of Sacred Architecture: Experience, Interpretation, Comparison. Vol. 1. Monumental Occasions: Reflections on the *Eventfulness of Religious Architecture*. Cambridge, MA: Harvard University Press.

Jones, O. (2005), 'An ecology of emotion, memory, self and landscape', in J. Davidson, L. Bondi and M. Smith (eds), *Emotional Geographies*. Aldershot: Ashgate, 205–18.

Jones, O. and P. Cloke (2002), *Tree Cultures: The Place of Trees and Trees in their Place*. Oxford: Berg.

Joyce, K. A. (2009), 'Green burials', in C. D. Bryant and D. L. Peck (eds), *Encyclopedia of Death and the Human Experience*. Thousand Oaks, CA: Sage, Vol. 1, 527–9.

Jupp, P. C. (1993), 'Cremation or burial? Contemporary choice in city and village', in Clark. D. (ed.), *The Sociology of Death: Theory, Culture, Practice*. Oxford: Blackwell, 169–97.

—(2006), *From Dust to Ashes, Cremation and the British Way of Death*. Basingstoke: Palgrave Macmillan.

Kamerman, J. (2003), 'The postself in social context', in C. D. Bryant (ed.), *The Handbook of Death and Dying: The Presence of Death*. Thousand Oaks, CA: Sage, Vol. 1, 302–6.

Karsenti, B. (1998), 'The Maussian shift: A second foundation for sociology in France?', in W. James and N. J. Allen (eds), *Marcel Mauss: A Centenary Tribute*. Oxford: Berghahn, 71–82.

Kearl, M. (2009), 'Social class and death', in C. D. Bryant and D. L. Peck (eds), *Encyclopedia of Death and the Human Experience*. Los Angeles, London: Sage, Vol. 2, 875–8.

King, E. (2009), 'The marketing of environmentally friendly funerals.' *Funeral Service Journal* 124(3), 86–90.

Klass, D. (1999), *The Spiritual Lives of Bereaved Parents*. Philadelphia, PA: Taylor and Francis.

—(2006), 'Continuing conversation about continuing bonds.' *Death Studies* 30, 843–58.

Klass, D., P. R. Silverman and S. L. Nickman (eds) (1996), *Continuing Bonds: New Understandings of Grief*. Washington, DC: Taylor and Francis.

Klaassens, M. and P. Groote (2010), Natural Burial Ground Bergerbos: An Alternative Place of Burial in the Netherlands. Proceedings of the Dying and Death in 18th–21st Centuries Europe: Refiguring Death Rites in Europe. International Conference. Supplement of Annales Universitatis Apulensis. Series Historica, Cluj Napoca, Romania, Accent.

Lifton, R. J. (1974), 'On Death and the continuity of life: a "new" paradigm.' *History of Childhood Quarterly* 1(4), 681–96.

—(1976), *The Life of the Self: Toward a New Psychology*. New York: Simon and Schuster.

Lovelock, J. (1995), *The Ages of Gaia: A Biography of Our Living Earth*. New York: Norton.

Lowenthal, D. (1985), *The Past is a Foreign Country*. Cambridge: Cambridge University Press.

Lyons, John (1975), *Introduction to Theoretical Linguistics*. Cambridge: Cambridge University Press.

Macnaghten, P. (2004), 'Trees', in S. Harrison, S. Pile and N. Thrift (eds), *Patterned Ground: Entanglements of Nature and Culture*. London: Reaktion, 232–4.

Mauss, M. (1974 [1954]), *The Gift: Forms and Functions of Exchange in Archaic Societies*. London: Routledge & Kegan Paul.

Mayer, F. S. et al. (2009), 'Why is nature beneficial? The role of connectedness to nature.' *Environment and Behavior* 41(5), 607–43.

McGinn, B. (1993), 'The letter and the spirit: spirituality as an academic discipline.' Christian Spirituality Bulletin 1(2), 2–9.

Miller, D. (2008), *The Comfort of Things*. Cambridge: Polity.

Milligan, C. (2007), 'Restoration or risk? Exploring the place of the common place', in A. Williams (ed.), *Therapeutic Landscapes*. Aldershot: Ashgate, 255–71.

Mims, C. (1999), *When We Die*. London: Robinson.

Mitchell, R. (2004), '$ells: body wastes, information, and commodification', in R. Mitchell and P. Thurtle (eds), *Data Made Flesh: Embodying Information*. London: Rouledge, 121–36.

Mitford, J. (1963), *The American Way of Death*. London: Hutchinson.

Morris, S. M. and C. Thomas (2005), 'Placing the dying body: emotional, situational and embodied factors in preferences for place of final care and death in cancer', in J. Davidson, L. Bondi and M. Smith. (eds), *Emotional Geographies*. Aldershot: Ashgate, 19–31.

Morrow, K. (2005), 'Pollution prevention and control act 1999 (UK)', in D. J. Davies and L. H. Mates (eds), *Encyclopedia of Cremation*. Aldershot: Ashgate, 343.

Needham, R. (1979), *Symbolic Classification*. Santa Monica, CA: The Goodyear Publishing Company.

Neimeyer, R. A., S. A. Baldwin and J. Gillies (2006), 'Continuing bonds and reconstructing meaning: mitigating complications in bereavement.' *Death Studies* 30, 715–38.

Newman, J. (1996), *Give: A Cognitive Linguistic Study*. Berlin. New York: Mouton de Gruyter.

Nisbet, E. K., J. M. Zelenski and S. A. Murphy (2009), 'The nature relatedness scale: linking individuals' connection with nature to environmental concern and behavior.' *Environment and Behavior* 41(5), 715–40.

Ortner, S. (1978), *The Sherpas through Their Rituals*. Cambridge: Cambridge University Press.

Osteen, M. (2002a), 'Gift or commodity?', in M. Osteen (ed.), *The Question of the Gift: Essays Across Disciplines*. London: Routledge, 229–47.

—(2002b), 'Introduction: questions of the gift', in M. Osteen (ed.), *The Question of the Gift: Essays across Disciplines*. London: Routledge, 1–41.

Owen Jones, P. (2008), 'The challenge of green burial', in P. C. Jupp (ed.), *Death Our Future: Christian Theology and Funeral Practice*. London: Epworth, 148–57.

Palmer, N. and M. Palmer (1997), *Sacred Britain: A Guide to Sacred Sites and Pilgrim Routes of England, Scotland and Wales*. London: Piatkus.

Park, C. (1994), *Sacred Worlds: An Introduction to Geography and Religion*. London: Routledge.

Parry, J. (1994), *Death in Banaras*. Cambridge: Cambridge University Press.

Parsons, B. (2010), The Pioneers of Preservation: the development of embalming in 20th century Britain. *Yorkshire Educational and Social Weekend* (unpublished paper, Scarborough 12–13 March 2010).

Pine II, B. J. and J. H. Gilmore (1998), 'Welcome to the experience economy.' *Harvard Business Review* 76(4), 97–105.

Porteous, J. D. (1996), *Environmental Aesthetics: Ideas, Politics and Planning*. London: Routledge.

Powell, M., J. Hockey, T. Green and C. Clayden (2011), ' "I bury boxes, not bodies": identity, emotionality and natural burial.' *ASA Online*. Retrieved 05/03/11, from www.theasa.org/publications/asaonline.shtml.

Prendergast, D., J. Hockey and L. Kellaher (2006), 'Blowing in the wind? Identity, materiality, and the destinations of human ashes.' *Journal of the Royal Anthropological Institute* 12(4), 881–98.

Prideaux, S. (2005), *Edvard Munch, Behind the Scream*. New Haven and London: Yale University Press.

Primavesi, A. (2003), *Gaia's Gift: Earth, Ourselves and God after Copernicus*. London: Routledge.

Prince, H. (1988), 'Art and Agrarian Change', in D. Cosgrove and S. Daniels (1988) *The Iconography of Landscape*. Cambridge: Cambridge University Press. 98–118.

Prothero, S. (2001), *Purified by Fire: A History of Cremation in America*. Berkeley, Los Angeles: University of California Press.

Qureshi, H. (7 October 2007), 'Woodland burials are not only eco-friendly: they're cheaper too.' Retrieved 22/01/10, from www.guardian.co.uk/money/2007/oct/07/ethicalmoney.ethicalliving.

Rappaport, R. A. (1999), *Ritual and Religion in the Making of Humanity*. Cambridge: Cambridge University Press.

Relph, E. (1976), *Place and Placelessness*. London: Pion.

Rival, L. (1998), 'Trees, from symbols of life and regeneration to political artefacts', in L. Rival (ed.), *The Social Life of Trees: Anthropological Perspectives on Tree Symbolism*. Oxford: Berg, 1–36.

Rugg, J. (2000), 'Defining the place of burial: what makes a cemetery a cemetery?' *Mortality* 5(3), 259–75.

Rumble, H. (2010), *'Giving Something Back': A Case Study of Woodland Burial and Human Experience at Barton Glebe*. Doctoral Thesis, Durham University. Available at Durham E-Theses Online at http://etheses.dur.ac.uk/679/.

Rustomji, N. (2009), *The Garden and the Fire: Heaven and Hell in Islamic Culture*. New York: Columbia University Press.

Saarinen, R. (2010), 'The language of giving in theology.' *Neue Zeitschrift fur Systematische Theologie* 52(3), 268–301.

Sanders, G. (2009), ' "Late" capital: amusement and contradiction in the contemporary funeral industry.' *Critical Sociology* 35(4), 447–70.

Scarre, G. (2007), *Death*. Stocksfield: Acumen.

Schama, S. (1996), *Landscape and Memory*. London: Fortana.

Schantz, M. S. (2008), Awaiting the Heavenly Country: The Civil War and America's Culture of Death. Ithaca: Cornell University Press.

Schofield, A. (2005), 'Zoroastrianism', in D. J. Davies and L. H. Mates (eds), *Encyclopedia of Cremation*. Aldershot, 428–9.

Schutz, A. (1971 [1945]), *Collected Papers*. Arvid Brodersen (ed.). The Hague: Nijhoff.

—(1971 [1964]) *Collected Papers Volume 11. Studies in Social Theory*. (ed.). A. Brodersen. The Hague: Martinus Nijhoff.

Schweitzer, A. (1907), 'Overcoming death', *Reverence for Life,* translated by R. H. Fuller (1974 [1966]). London: SPCK, 67–81.

—(1919), 'Reverence for life', *Reverence for Life*, translated by R. H. Fuller (1974 [1966]). London: SPCK, 108–17.

Sheldrake, P. (2001), *Spaces for the Sacred: Place, Memory and Identity*. London: SCM Press.

Shimazono, Y. (2008), 'Repaying and cherishing the gift of life: gift exchange and living-related kidney transplantation in the Philippines.' *Anthropology in Action* 15, 34–46.

Slater, E. (2007), 'Reconstructing "nature" as a picturesque theme park: the colonial case of Ireland.' *Early Popular Visual Culture* 5(3), 231–45.

Slater, E. and M. Peillon (2009), 'The suburban front garden: a socio-spatial analysis.' *Nature and Culture,* 4, 78–104.

Smith, M. (2005), 'On "being" moved by nature: geography, emotion and environmental ethics', in J. Davidson, L. Bondi and M. Smith (eds), *Emotional Geographies*. Aldershot: Ashgate, 219–30.

Speyer, J. (2006), 'An argument for environmentally friendly natural burial.' *Pharos International* 72(2), 6–8.

Stern, P. C. (2000), 'Toward a coherent theory of environmentally significant behaviour.' *Journal of Social Issues* 56(3), 407–24.

Strathern, M. (1990 [1988]), *The Gender of the Gift*. Berkeley and Los Angeles: University of California Press.

Sykes, K. (2005), *Arguing with Anthropology: An Introduction to Critical Theories of the Gift*. London: Routledge.

Tarlow, S. (1999), *Bereavement and Commemoration: An Archaeology of Mortality*. Oxford: Blackwell.

—(2000), 'Landscapes of memory: the nineteenth-century garden cemetery.' *European Journal of Archaeology* 3(2), 217–39.

Thomas, S. (2011), *Earth to Earth: Natural Burial and the Church of England* (film). Durham: Durham University Centre for Death and Life Studies

Thompson, J. W. (2002), 'A natural death.' *Landscape Architecture*, 74–9 and 134–7.

Titmuss, R. M. (1973 [1970]), *The Gift Relationship: From Human Blood to Social Policy*. Middlesex, England: Penguin.

Tolia-Kelly, D. P. (2007), 'Organic cosmopolitanism: challenging cultures of the non-native at the Burnley millennium arboretum.' *Garden History: Cultural and Historical* Geographies of the Arboretum 35(Suppl. 2), 172–84.

Tremlett, P. F. (2007), 'Death-scapes in Taipei and Manila: a postmodern necrography.' *Taiwan in Comparative Perspective* 1 (November), 23–36.

Turner, V. (1967), *The Forest of Symbols: Aspects of Ndembu Ritual*. Ithaca, NY: Cornell University Press.

—(1969), *The Ritual Process*. London: Routledge and Kegan Paul.

Tylor, E. B. (2010 [1871]), *Primitive Culture*. Cambridge: Cambridge University Press.

Valentine, C. (2008), *Bereavement Narratives, Continuing Bonds in the Twenty-First Century*. London: Routledge.

Vandendorpe, F. (2000), 'Funerals in Belgium: the hidden complexity of contemporary practices.' *Mortality* 5(1), 18–33.

Van Gennep, A. (1960), *The Rites of Passage*. Chicago, IL: University of Chicago Press.

Veldman, M. (1994), *Fantasy, the Bomb, and the Greening of Britain: Romantic Protest, 1945–1980*. Cambridge: Cambridge University Press.

Vigilant, L. G. (2009), 'Symbolic immortality', in C. D. Bryant and D. L. Peck (eds), *The Encyclopedia of Death and the Human Experience*. Thousand Oaks, CA: Sage, Vol. 2, 924–7.

Vigilant, L. G. and J. B. Williamson (2003), 'Symbolic immortality and social theory: the relevance of an underutilized concept', in C. D. Bryant (ed.), *The Handbook of Death and Dying: The Presence of Death*. Thousand Oaks: Sage, Vol. 1, 173–82.

Walter, T. (1996), 'A new model of grief: bereavement and biography.' *Mortality* 1(1), 7–26.

Walter, T. and C. Gittings (2010), 'What will the neighbours say? Reactions to field and garden burial', in J. Hockey, C. Komaromy and K. Woodthorpe (eds), *The Matter of Death: Space, Place and Materiality*. Basingstoke, Hampshire: Palgrave Macmillan, 165–77.

Watkins, N., F. Cole, and S. Wiedemann (2010), 'The war memorial as healing environment: the psychological effect of the Vietnam veterans memorial on Vietnam War combat veterans' posttraumatic stress disorder symptoms.' *Environment and Behavior* 42(3), 351–75.

Weber, M. (1930 [1904–5]), *The Protestant Ethic and the Spirit of Capitalism*. London: Allen & Unwin.

—(1963 [1922]), *The Sociology of Religion*, translated by E. Fischoff with introduction by T. Parsons. London: Methuen.

—(1991 [1915]), 'Religious rejections of the world and their directions', *From Max Weber: Essays in Sociology*, translated, edited and with an introduction by H. H. Gerth and C. Wright Mills, with a new preface by Bryan S. Turner. London: Routledge, 323–59.

—(1991 [1919]), 'Science as a vocation', *From Max Weber: Essays in Sociology*, translated, edited and with an introduction by H. H. Gerth and C. Wright Mills, with a new preface by Bryan S. Turner. London: Routledge, 129–56.

Weller, S. (1999), 'An amber light for green wood burial schemes.' *Association of Burial Authorities (ABA)* (Summer), 3–4.

West, K. (2005), 'Ecology', in D. J. Davies and L. H. Mates (eds), *Encyclopedia of Cremation*. Aldershot: Ashgate, 172–4.

—(2008), 'How green is my funeral?' *Funeral Service Journal* 123(1), 104–8.

—(2010), *A Guide to Natural Burial*. London: Sweet and Maxwell.

Williams, A. (2007), 'Introduction: The continuing maturation of the therapeutic landscape concept', in A. Williams (ed.), *Therapeutic Landscapes*. Aldershot: Ashgate, 1–12.

Williams, R. (1974), *The Country and the City*. New York: Oxford University Press.

Woodburn, J. (1982), 'Social dimensions of death in four African hunting and gathering Societies', in M. Bloch and J. Parry (eds), *Death and the Regeneration of Life*. Cambridge: Cambridge University Press, 187–210.

Worpole, K. (2003a), 'Where the dead live.' *Prospect Magazine* (April). Retrieved 20/11/07, from www.prospectmagazine.co.uk/ArticleView. asp?P_Article¼11894.

—(2003b), *Last Landscapes: The Architecture of the Cemetery in the West.* London: Reaktion.

Wright, T. (2003), *The Resurrection of the Son of God.* London: SPCK.

Zukin, S. (1991), *Landscapes of Power: From Detroit to Disney World.* Berkeley: University of California Press.

Index